# ASK
## YOUR
## GUIDES

# ALSO BY SONIA CHOQUETTE

## Books/Oracle Cards

*The Answer Is Simple . . .
Love Yourself, Live Your Spirit!*

*The Answer Is Simple Oracle Cards*

*Ask Your Guides Oracle Cards*

*Diary of a Psychic:
Shattering the Myths*

*The Divine Energy Oracle*

*The Fool's Wisdom Oracle Cards*

*Grace, Guidance, and Gifts: Sacred
Blessings to Light Your Way*

*The Intuitive Spark:
Bringing Intuition Home to Your
Child, Your Family, and You*

*Soul Lessons and Soul Purpose:
A Channeled Guide to
Why You Are Here*

*The Time Has Come . . .
to Accept Your Intuitive Gifts!*

*Traveling at the Speed of Love*

*Trust Your Vibes at Work,
and Let Them Work for You*

*Trust Your Vibes Oracle Cards*

*Trust Your Vibes: Secret Tools
for Six-Sensory Living*

*Tune In: Let Your Intuition Guide
You to Fulfillment and Flow*

*Vitamins for the Soul: Daily Doses of
Wisdom for Personal Empowerment*

*Waking Up in Paris: Overcoming
Darkness in the City of Light*

*Walking Home: A Pilgrimage
from Humbled to Healed*

*Your 3 Best Super Powers: Meditation,
Imagination & Intuition*

## CD Programs

*Attunement to Higher Vibrational
Living,* with Mark Stanton Welch
(4-CD set)

*How to Trust Your Vibes at Work,
and Let Them Work for You*
(4-CD set)

*Meditations for Receiving
Divine Guidance, Support,
and Healing* (2-CD set)

*The Power of Your Spirit:
A Guide to Joyful Living* (4-CD set)

*Trust Your Vibes: Secret Tools for Six-
Sensory Living* (6-CD set)

All of the above are available at your local
bookstore, or may be ordered by visiting:

Hay House USA: www.hayhouse.com®
Hay House Australia: www.hayhouse.com.au
Hay House UK: www.hayhouse.co.uk
Hay House India: www.hayhouse.co.in

# ASK YOUR GUIDES

Calling in Your Divine Support System
for Help with Everything in Life

## SONIA CHOQUETTE

**HAY HOUSE, INC.**
Carlsbad, California • New York City
London • Sydney • New Delhi

Originally published as *Ask Your Guides* 978-1-4019-0787-7.

**Library of Congress Cataloging-in-Publication Data**

Names: Choquette, Sonia, author.
Title: Ask your guides : calling in your divine support system for help
    with everything in life / Sonia Choquette.
Description: Revised edition, 2nd edition. | Carlsbad, California : Hay
    House, Inc., 2021.
Identifiers: LCCN 2020044123 | ISBN 9781401961381 (trade paperback) | ISBN
    9781401961398 (ebook) | ISBN 9781401961404 (Audiobook)
Subjects: LCSH: Guides (Spiritualism) | Guardian angels.
Classification: LCC BF1275.G85 C48 2021 | DDC 133.9—dc23
LC record available at https://lccn.loc.gov/2020044123

Tradepaper ISBN: 978-1-4019-6138-1
E-book ISBN: 978-1-4019-6139-8
Audiobook ISBN: 978-1-4019-6140-4

15  14  13  12  11  10  9  8

1st printing, April 2006
2nd edition, January 2021

Printed in the United States of America

*To my mother, Sonia Polixenia Apostu Choquette,
who taught me about my loving spirit guides and angels,
allowing me to live more freely, fully, fearlessly,
and with confidence throughout my life.*

*To my beautiful daughters, Sonia and Sabrina Choquette-Tully,
who have been the best earth angels, guides, and friends I could
have ever asked for. I am blessed beyond measure
by your presence and love in my life.*

*And to my beautiful angels and guides,
without whose support I would never have had
such a blessed and glorious life journey thus far.*

# CONTENTS

# PREFACE

## Angels to the Rescue

In January of 2015, I moved to Paris with my daughter, Sabrina. It was a traumatic and exciting time. I had just gone through a painful divorce, and Sabrina, too, had just abruptly ended a long-term relationship. Intuitively guided to move on with our lives in this radical way, we sold our things, packed our bags, and were off to Paris just six short weeks after getting the inner guidance to go.

Needing to quickly get settled meant finding a suitable apartment for us to rent. We immediately invoked the ministry of "broken hearts angels" to help us with our search, and never thought for one second that they wouldn't.

And they did, more than once. The first time, the angels led us to an Airbnb in a colorful, bohemian neighborhood near Sacré-Cœur that was too entertaining and unpredictable for us to be able to dwell on the past. This home helped jump-start our emotional healing. We stayed there for three months. During that time, we got a realistic sense of what it meant to live in Paris and decided that we felt ready to dive in deeper and sign a long-term apartment lease.

Calling again on the ministry of "apartment-finding angels," we were serendipitously shown a gorgeous apartment in the 7th arrondissement, the quintessential Parisian neighborhood of our dreams. Complete with high ceilings, three big bedrooms, fireplaces in every room, a renovated kitchen (in and of itself a miracle in the City of Lights), two bathrooms, and floor-to-ceiling French doors, allowing light to stream in from morning until night, it was perfect.

This new apartment promised to be an oasis of beauty and calm after the cute but cramped apartment we had been living in at Sacré-Cœur. But it was, unfortunately, way, way too expensive for our budget. Wondering why the ministry of angels had brought us to one so lovely yet unaffordable, I suddenly got the distinct sensation that it only *appeared* to be too expensive for us and felt guided to ask for a significant discount on the rent.

As I sipped a coffee at a nearby café, the ministry of angels nudged me to offer what I *could* afford and see if the landlord accepted it. When I mentioned this to the agent representing the landlord, she immediately shot it down, saying that making a lower offer wasn't done in Paris. Since I had nothing to lose, I insisted she at least try, and after a lot of persuasion on my part, she reluctantly agreed.

As two insufferably long weeks went by, both Sabrina and I became more stressed by the day as our present apartment lease was quickly coming to an end and we had no other place to go. Finally, one afternoon, only four days before the end of our lease, we received word from the agent that the landlord had surprisingly agreed to our terms and was willing to rent at the price we had proposed. We were ecstatic!

Grateful beyond belief upon hearing this good news, I knew in my heart this was due to the ministry of angels and immediately lit a stick of incense in gratitude, thanking them for giving us this generous gift of a beautiful home.

The very afternoon that we signed the new lease (with only 48 hours remaining on our old one) we packed up and were on our way to our gorgeous apartment. That is how the ministry of angels works. They save us, help us, gift us, offer us solutions, open doors that appear closed or locked, and bring us what feel like miracles time and time again. I frankly don't know how anyone can, or would want to, live without calling on these loving divine beings for their help.

# INTRODUCTION

# What We Can Expect

I grew up in a home filled with spirit guides of every sort. I came upon the awareness of my spirit companionship gradually, being first introduced to my guides when I was very young by my mother, who talked to the guides all the time. She was the first to let me know that I was never alone in the world and that I had guides who were assigned to watch over me.

She conferred regularly with her own guides, and often it was they, not she, who made decisions in our home. She referred to them as "my spirits" because that's what they were—spiritual beings without physical bodies. She consulted her spirits on all manner of things, from where to park the car to what to serve company for dinner, and she had special spirits for all types of assignments. There were shopping spirits to help my mother find the bargains that were a necessity for a family with seven children living on my father's retail-salesman's salary. There were sewing spirits to help her find fabric and make patterns, and healing spirits to help when we kids got the mumps. There were family picnic spirits to help find the perfect mountain spot for our Sunday outing; sales spirits to help improve my dad's business; and painting spirits, whom my mom called on when she indulged in one of her favorite pastimes—oil painting. And then there were the Romanian and French spirits of deceased relatives just passing through.

Our spirit guides had a place at the table and were part of *every* conversation. They were consulted on matters large and small, and when we were in doubt, they were often allowed the final word. Because of all the spirits, ours was a crowded home, filled with energy, opinions, and ideas, but mostly filled with love and a deep-seated security that stemmed from knowing we were never alone.

My own guides helped me through childhood illnesses, family squabbles, and school problems; they were with me every step of the way, gracing my days with miracles beyond my wildest imagination. From my earliest memory, I knew that I had my guides' loving support, I felt protected by their watchful eyes, was assisted by their practical solutions, and was surprised by their bountiful gifts.

Beyond our family doors, talk of the spirit world took place in my Catholic school on the west side of Denver. There we were introduced to angels and saints—one for every day of the year—as well as a personal saint who shared some version of our own name. What's more, we had Mother Mary, Jesus, and the biggest spirit of all, the Holy Spirit.

As kids we went to mass every morning, lit candles to get our spirit guides' attention, and had heartfelt conversations imploring them to intercede for us on all matters, including helping with tests, getting a good seat in the lunchroom, and, of course, winning our volleyball and basketball games.

As far as I was concerned, the spirit guides listened—I *did* do well on tests, have unusual luck in the lunchroom, and win an awful lot of volleyball games. And why shouldn't I have? I not only prayed to the spirit helpers and guides for assistance, I absolutely believed that they responded, and I felt their help and their presence. I assumed everyone did—at least until the third grade when my best friend, Susie, complained about being unable to spend the night at my house because her mom said no. When I suggested that she ask her guides to help change her mother's mind, she said she didn't know what I was talking about. When I explained it to her, she said I was weird.

Feeling defensive, I asked her why she went to mass and prayed every morning if there weren't spirit guides to help her. She said she went because the nuns made us go, not because there were spirits.

Frustrated, I insisted that there *were* spirits and told her if she was very calm and half closed her eyes, not shutting them entirely, she could even see them. "They don't always look like people," I said. "Sometimes they look like sparklers dancing in the air. Sometimes they look like a burst of white light, like the flash of a camera. Sometimes you don't see them at all, but you feel them, as though the air is a little thicker in certain places, or cooler and breezy, and sometimes you just feel them in your heart, but they're there."

Susie rolled her eyes, whistled, and called me a weirdo again, so of course I didn't tell her about my favorite guide, Rose, who lived above my closet and looked like St. Thérèse, or about Joseph the Essene, who walked behind me at school. Nor did I tell her about the guide I'd seen standing in the corner of her bedroom during a sleepover—the one who looked like a weathered, very old Native American woman wrapped in a rough, red-and-white blanket and who smiled at us when we were in bed. Goodness knows, if she thought me weird just for mentioning guides, who knows what she'd say if I told her more! Not wanting to risk my already-tenuous social position at school, I laughed off her comments and suggested that we spend the night at her house instead of mine.

From then on, I began to realize that the rich world of spirit from which I drew such comfort was virtually unknown to most people. It made me sad that the communication I enjoyed with my guides was absent for most others. While I wasn't exactly sure how other people had become so disconnected from the spirit world, I was absolutely sure that they weren't better off for it.

As an adult, I've come to believe that our disconnection from the spirit world is a Western disease. Industrialization and intellectualism have snatched our center of awareness from our hearts—the place where we meet and commune with spirit—and planted it squarely in our heads, where our egos reign over us with threats of isolation and annihilation. The good news is that whatever the reason for the separation, we can always reconnect our inner awareness back to our hearts if we want to. With a little effort and cooperation from us, our spirit guides will gladly show us the way.

## WHAT DO YOU EXPECT?

To begin, it's important to understand exactly what you can expect when you make contact with your spirit guides. You see, there are many, many levels of guides, nonphysical entities, and energies in the spirit world, each vibrating at its own unique frequency, much like multiple radio stations simultaneously sending out distinct signals. Not only does each guide have its own frequency, but each person on this planet also has their own particular vibration.

Those of us who live in our hearts have a *high* vibration (or "good vibes"), which is not too distant from the spiritual frequencies of those in the nonphysical plane. This makes connection with spirit guides easier. Those of us who have forgotten that we are spiritual beings and identify only with our minds and bodies have a lower vibration that is further away from the frequency range of spirit guides, so the connection is much more difficult to establish. This is why some people are more aware of guides than others.

> *With a little effort and cooperation from us,*
> *our spirit guides will gladly show us the way.*

If you think about it, everything in the Universe is spirit, vibrating at different frequencies. We all know, for example, that atomic particles vibrate at particular frequencies, just as light waves do. Ocean waves have frequencies—there's even the rhythm of our heartbeats. Because everything is a sea of vibration in motion, it's only natural that we, as spiritual beings, are able to connect with other spirit frequencies. If we recognize *ourselves* as spirit, we can more easily recognize the inhabitants of the nonphysical world as well.

The spirit world is as populated as ours—myriad different guides work at various frequencies all the time. Consequently, there are many kinds of guidance with which we can connect: guides who once lived in the physical world; family members who have crossed to the Other Side; guides you've shared past lives with; guides who come as spiritual teachers to oversee your path; healers who can assist in your physical and emotional care; helpers who make day-to-day living easier; nature spirits and elementals that connect you with the earth; animal spirits to guide your path; even joy guides to keep your own spirits high when life becomes too heavy and hard. There are angels, saints, devas, masters, and God. There are even guides—or wannabe guides—who are not on a high level at all, but who are just troublemakers that must be watched. (I'll write more about them later.)

Sadly, I've also come to realize that what is second nature to me—being aware of and working with my guides—is unfamiliar to many, if not most, people around me. It's so unfortunate that I've witnessed others, unconscious of the spirit plane and disconnected from their guides, struggle in fear and desperation, feeling lonely and abandoned as they fight through life with no awareness of the loving spiritual support that's available to them at all times.

Because I've been so blessed by my guides' support and have realized it from childhood, I've made it my life's mission to help others become aware of their own guides. Just as *I've* been helped, I want everyone to know that they can be helped, too. I'm not special in receiving guidance—no one is. We're all Divine children of the Universe, and each of us has a spiritual support system committed to making our life's journey easier and more successful, from the moment we're born to the moment we leave our physical bodies and return to spirit. Not being aware of this fact handicaps us.

The Universe is designed to care for and guide all its creatures: birds have radar, bats have sonar, and we have guides. When we awaken our sixth sense and learn how to connect with our angelic guides, our lives naturally fall into a pattern of ease and flow during which we grow our souls, fulfill our life's purpose, and make our time on Earth endlessly entertaining.

This book will provide simple guidelines to help you connect with your spirit guides so that you can enjoy all of the abundance, support, and delight you're entitled to.

We're all "trust-fund babies" of the Benevolent Mother and Father God, and it's our birthright to expect a charmed and blessed life. The key to receiving such gifts, however, is to accept that we can't succeed on our own. We must open our hearts and minds to the loving support that's available to all of us. By embarking on this journey, you'll soon be experiencing support, success, and blessings beyond your wildest imagination.

# THE PURPOSE
# OF THIS BOOK

My intention in writing this book is to introduce you to your spiritual support system, the many loving celestial helpers available to help you succeed in all ways on your soul's journey through life. I hope that by passing on this knowledge I, too, can help you to live with far more ease, grace, and confidence than you would living under the limitations of fearful ego perceptions alone.

In these pages, I will share who your guides are, where they come from, and how they benefit you. I will also offer numerous ways in which you may easily communicate with your guides, as well as how you can recognize the delightful, creative, yet *subtle* ways in which your angels and spirit guides endlessly strive to get your attention in service to your success.

I'll introduce this fantastic spiritual network gradually, until it begins to feel more and more natural for you to experience divine guidance in your life. I'll also show you how to raise your vibration to match the higher frequency of the spirit world, making a connection with this elevated plane easier to achieve.

I will describe the various types of guides in depth, explain their characteristics and reasons for working with you, and share stories and anecdotes about how these divine light beings have helped me or others. I will also help you develop trust in the guidance you receive instead of questioning, doubting, or ignoring it altogether. In this way, you will be able not only to fully avail yourself of your spirit guides at all times, but also to know how to confidently call upon your guides as the need arises.

You will receive effective practices and tools to strengthen your direct connection with your guides. Knowing the Universe has your back as it does, you will begin to relax and experience the magical, charmed life the Universe wants for you.

## HOW THE BOOK IS SET UP

This book is grouped into six sections, or themes, starting with the basic tools for becoming sensitive to the world of spirit. Once you master those, you'll learn to prepare your body to tune in to subtle energy, and then you'll gradually be introduced to higher and more subtle realms of spirit assistance.

Consider this as a course or training, much like a music appreciation class. At first, you'll learn the notes of the realm of spirit, then the melodies of spirit guidance, and finally, the composition and orchestration of six-sensory, Divinely guided, creative living. By allowing yourself to be Divinely guided, you enter the flow of life and begin to experience the magic of this beautiful Universe.

Approach this book at your own pace, and work with your guides one small step at a time. Read each chapter several times if you wish, and then practice the suggested exercise for a couple of days and see what happens. Each chapter builds upon the last, gently creating a solid foundation for recognizing spirit guidance and helping you to quickly and comfortably trust your guides and ask for their help—no matter what challenges you're facing. Think of this book as a tour of the spirit world with me as your experienced tour guide.

I encourage you to journal your progress in a designated notebook as you work through this book. It will serve as evidence that your guides are with you and will be important in building your confidence, trust, and ability to recognize guidance as it shows up.

If you aren't one to write, you can also use the voice recorder on your smartphone to record your experiences and do the exercises in the book. This works just as well, if not better in some ways, as your voice is your greatest witness that guides are here.

In truth, we all experience many guided moments all day long, day after day, but have the tendency to forget them, tune them out, or doubt their validity. Recording these fleeting insights makes it impossible to ignore them and will soon confirm that what you sense is valid guidance and worth paying attention to.

I've also included several links in the book to guided and channeled meditation journeys, taken from my live workshops and classes, which you can access at hayhouse.com and soniachoquette.net. These meditations transmit a powerful frequency that will open your intuitive receptors quickly. Stream them and listen daily if possible, either in the morning just after you wake up, or in the evening when going to sleep. These meditations are profoundly healing and will establish a strong connection between you and your guides. Many of my students have said these meditations have been life changing. I hope they will be for you as well.

Because I've worked with guides my entire life (and have taught others how to connect with theirs for more than 45 years), I'm deeply familiar with and at ease in the spirit world. I want you to feel the same. When you open yourself to working with your spirit guides, you change the rules that govern your life, and everything becomes easier.

Through the suggested practices in these pages, you'll begin to directly experience the loving support that the Universe has for you. Even though we all have the *potential* to be guided, wanting guidance isn't enough. Just as watching an exercise video won't give you abs of steel, neither will just *knowing* about your guides or *wanting* to be guided fully open the door. Unless you actively invite your guides to help you every day and consciously make the space in your heart and mind to sense and accept their help, you're going to miss the reliable inner guidance they offer.

It may feel odd to be so focused on the subtle realms at first, but if you stick with it, it will soon feel natural and you'll enjoy the experience of your guides—after all, guides are fun and have a great sense of humor. Don't hesitate to ask them for all the assistance you need, since their purpose is to help you.

Pay attention to all clues that enter your awareness, and don't wait for the spiritual equivalent of Elvis to appear while dismissing all the rest. Spirit guidance is subtle and, therefore, easy to miss. It's up to you to raise your awareness enough to recognize Divine help as it's offered. If you make it your intention to connect with your various guides, you'll soon have the evidence that they're on the job, by noticing the way your life takes on a magical quality.

Trusting the guidance you receive in the moment rather than doubting or hesitating to accept what you feel will be your greatest challenge, mostly because we are so used to feeling alone and struggling through problems in the dark. Working with your guides eases the struggle but you will have to adjust your attitude to allow for this. As spiritual beings, we are unconditionally loved and supported by our Creator. We are never alone, nor do we ever face more than we can handle without first being given all we need to succeed. We are here to rise above earthly struggles and live a Divine life of grace and flow. We intuitively know, in our hearts, and all the way down to our very cells, that this is our purpose. The way is straightforward—be open to help, get out of your head, move into your heart, start listening to the loving support that your guides and the spirit world offer, and act on it. They're delighted to serve and support you . . . so let them.

> *As spiritual beings, we are unconditionally*
> *loved and supported by our Creator.*

# PART I

# WELCOME TO THE WORLD OF SPIRIT

# CHAPTER 1

# Recognize Your Spirit First

Before you can connect with your spirit guides, you must first become aware of your *own* beautiful spirit. Seeing and experiencing yourself in this way may be unfamiliar, but it's the truth of who you are—who we all are—and the foundation of living a blessed spirit-guided life.

While growing up, my mother always referred to my siblings and me as "spirits," and we did the same with her. When I'd ask her for guidance, for example, before she would answer, she'd ask, "What does your spirit want?" or "What does your spirit say about this?" sending me inward first to find the answer. In that way, she made it clear from the start that the real authority in my life was my spirit, and that my spirit was what I needed to consult first and foremost on all matters in my life.

Learning from such an early state of my life that we are all in possession of our own individual spirits made it natural to connect and converse with other spirits who were there to support me, both on this and other planes, whenever I needed help. I grew up unquestioningly viewing myself and others in this way, but the power of that truth was never made more evident than when my eldest daughter, Sonia, was born.

I remember how totally calm and serene, even Buddha-like, she was when she came into the world. At first, she was immobile and slightly blue, but then, with a powerful surge, she took her first breath, and with tremendous energy, her entire being suddenly burst alive. Her color became bright pink, and she let out a wail to let the world know she'd arrived. Right there, before my eyes, I witnessed her spirit entering her body and beginning her human journey with that single breath. Ever since, I can't look at another human being for long, myself included, without remembering on the deepest level that we all had a similar entrance. Recognizing that the breath that gives us life is our spirit helps us appreciate *and respect* the formidable divine force that is *in us all.*

Although we all share the same eternal breath of life, our spirits express that force differently in each one of us, like flowers that are similar yet unique at the same time. Each spirit has its own individual and special character, a specific vibration that's totally distinct from our personality (which serves as a defensive shield around our spirit), and it's essential to know the difference. The best way to understand the force and power of your own spirit is to start recognizing what makes you *personally* come alive.

## YOUR TURN

Describe your spirit, the eternal, energetic divine life force that manifests as uniquely *you.* Is your spirit gentle, passionate, commanding, tentative, creative, shy, or playful? Intense? Reserved? Observant? Silly? Thoughtful? Kind? Dynamic? Clever? Grounded? Disruptive?

Say the words out loud and note how it makes you feel to hear them. *Verbally* acknowledging your spirit, as opposed to just thinking about it, helps you view yourself as an embodied spirit and not just see yourself through the lens of your limited and fearful ego, which is where most humans experience life. Any embarrassment, awkwardness, or discomfort you may feel hearing the words spoken out loud is the work of your ego, trying to dissuade you from pursuing a connection with your spirit. Recognize it and move on. Seeing yourself as spirit takes you out of the fishbowl perspective of the ego and reveals more of the truth of who you are, a divine eternal being on a creative human journey. And the more you see yourself as spirit, the more you see the spirit in all things, including guides.

Describe your spirit here:

My spirit is _____.

## FEED YOUR SPIRIT

Recognize what *nourishes and strengthens* your spirit. These are the interests, activities, involvements, and creative efforts that uplift you, give you strength, bring you joy, and energize you at your core. They are things that leave you feeling fulfilled, satisfied, creatively engaged, enthusiastic, and joyful. What delights you, consumes your attention, and brings out the best, most creative, inspired feeling in you? These insights reflect the nature of your unique spirit and let you know who you really are.

For example, I'm inspired by classical music, incense-smelling perfumes, and the scent of pine trees in the mountains. My bohemian spirit loves to travel and seek adventure: Egyptian bazaars, street performers, rickshaw rides through New Delhi, scooters in Thailand. My spirit also comes alive with storytelling, introducing others to the spirit world, and collaborating on creative projects. These things fill my soul with joy, entertain me to the core, and leave me feeling engaged, fulfilled, and on fire—in other words, me at my best. I am a traveler, teacher, dancer, storyteller, adventurer, connector spirit. That is me.

My friend Marion's spirit is nothing like my own. She is a healer, investigator, wanderer, communicator, inquiring spirit. She loves science, psychology, mothering others, alternative healing, teaching, qigong, and lectures and workshops on the latest spiritual breakthroughs. She comes alive on a long hike along the Napali coast, golfing, skiing down a mountain at medium speed, in organic markets and health food stores, or when sitting among strangers at conferences, getting to know them, one by one, in deep conversations. Her spirit is more extroverted and grounded than mine.

Although Marion and I have very different characteristics of spirit, as do we all, we share the same essential breath of life. By recognizing the unique spirit in ourselves, we change the channel of our perception from looking solely at the physical, exterior world, to incorporating a deeper, more spiritually aware inner world into our line of sight.

## What feeds your spirit?

My spirit is fed by _____.

## Who is your spirit?

I am a _____ spirit.

## NAME YOUR SPIRIT

Once I realized that my spirit was distinct from my ego-based personality, and was much wiser and more profound, intuitive, creative, fearless, truthful, and accurately informed than my ego was, I decided to give my spirit her own name, Bright Light. I chose the name because I experienced my spirit as a bright light who cleared up the confusion and shed the light of higher truth on all matters in my life.

Once I named my spirit, I easily tapped into this divine part of myself by simply asking Bright Light to guide me whenever I needed insight. Calling her name made checking in with my spirit easy, instantly changing the channel of my attention from my ego to that of my Higher Self, the part of all of us that is spirit.

When offering classes on intuition and connecting with spirit guides, I invite my students to name their spirits as well. They all take to the idea immediately and come up with names for their spirits just as quickly as I did. I believe we all know deep down there is more to us than meets the eye, more than our families and our society have shaped us to be, more than our fearful egos have allowed us to be. No one, in all my years of teaching classes on spirit guides, has been unable to recognize and name their spirit the moment they were asked to. And once a person does name their spirit, they immediately take a deep breath and smile, feeling a long-yearned-for relief in identifying this deep, authentic part of themselves.

My students have come up with creative names like Clarity, Dr. Know, Cloud, Sister Blue, Divinity, and Red Fox. One client recently came up with the super-silly name "Figgy." There is no rhyme or reason to the names my students pick, except for one: all the names seem to perfectly "fit" the energy of the student's spirit, and other students in these classes quickly agree that the chosen name feels "right."

Naming your spirit is the most natural, practical way to quickly communicate with your Divine Self. Just as you instantly respond when hearing your name, your spirit responds equally fast when hearing its name, too.

## YOUR TURN

Take a moment right now to name your spirit. Trust yourself. It's fun and entertaining, and the beginning of the best relationship you will ever have. Sense if the name that pops up *feels* right by saying it out loud. Does it feel authentic? Does it resonate? Does it make you instantly burst into a Cheshire cat–like grin and light up your face and eyes? If yes, your spirit has just come out of hiding and into the light of day.

Don't worry about getting the name "right" on the first try, either. Like naming a baby, you may need to try out a few names before you discover the best one. If your spirit name isn't instantly clear, sound out a few names until one *feels* right for you. Never fear; it will come.

Sometimes your ego tries to block your spirit name because it is controlling and senses that it is about to be dethroned. If so, it will momentarily cause you to come up blank, or fake you out by suggesting "spiritual" names like Swami Know-It-All or something equally pretentious. Don't be fooled. That is *not* your spirit name.

You will know if your ego is giving you the wrong name because it won't make you light up or smile like a true spirit name will. Just laugh this off and keep exploring. Your spirit name *will* reveal itself if you keep asking. Just don't *think* about it. Ask your spirit directly by placing your hand over your heart and saying, out loud, "What is your name?" Answer quickly. Go with your first instinct rather than trying to figure it out. Let your spirit surprise you with the name.

If you still feel blocked, ask your spirit its name "for now." In other words, give yourself full permission to change your spirit name whenever you want. You don't ever have to be stuck with a name. It's your spirit, and so you have full authority to name and rename it anytime you want.

This relieves the pressure of getting the name "right" for the perfectionists among us. Some people do change their spirit name at some point, although most people don't. But it doesn't matter. As long as your spirit has a name, and it feels like *your* spirit and not your ego faking you out, it works. After all, as Shakespeare said, "A rose by any other name would smell as sweet."

## What about you?

My spirit's name is _____ for now.

## EXPRESS YOUR SPIRIT

Naming your spirit is a great beginning, but only the first step toward living at the highest, most authentic spiritual level. You have to *express* your spirit to be fully available to the spirit world.

For example, if yours is an artist's spirit, you need to create art. If you've been told art has no value and making art is a waste of time, your spirit is silenced and languishes, losing its expression. If yours is an investigative spirit, it needs deep, exploratory conversation, a chance to delve beneath the surface of things and discover what is hidden. If you are told to always be "polite," keep things on the surface, and not "stir the pot" with your probing questions, your spirit will be frustrated and unhappy because it is not allowed to freely be itself.

As children, our spirits spontaneously express themselves all the time. Sadly, we eventually become controlled by others and by social conventions, and our spirits shut down, feeling silenced and ignored. Even though we are not children anymore, we are still free to express our spirits fully today. We are in charge now, and we can call our spirits forward. We do this by the choices we make.

YOUR TURN

Do you know what expresses your spirit? Write in your spirit journal all the answers you can think of. Make a list and start doing those things now. Just as you would want to know what a new best friend loves, or what makes your new romantic partner thrive, knowing what expresses your spirit is the key to your deepest and most lasting happiness.

For example, my spirit fully expresses when I dance. I lose myself in the music and elevate to another dimension. My spirit also expresses itself when I write, and lately when I make videos, which is a new discovery. When I am doing any of those things, I lose all sense of time because I am having so much fun.

What about you?

My spirit best expresses when I _____ .

## HONOR YOUR SPIRIT

Years ago, I did a spiritual reading for a woman named Valerie, who suffered from severe depression, fatigue, and a growing lethargy and disinterest in everything in her life. Consequently, she was unable to get through a single day without collapsing from exhaustion halfway through it, feeling miserable and dead inside.

> *Guides do not tell us what to do and expect us to blindly follow it. Guides only suggest what will support our spirit and lead us back into alignment with our true nature. Then they leave it up to us to listen or not, honoring our free will.*

Not knowing what mysterious illness or mental condition was causing such a loss of vitality, she visited every doctor, healer, and psychic for answers. She was tested for everything from hypothyroidism to Lyme disease to mold to metal poisoning to Epstein–Barr virus to bipolar disorder to depression, with nothing but inconclusive or negative results and no concrete answers.

Feeling desperate, she called me. I immediately identified her problem: She had a severe case of what I call starvation of the spirit. Her guides showed me that she was an artist, a musician, and contemplative at heart, a spirit who loved music, nature, and peace. Her spirit needed solitude, the company of animals, intimacy with family, and a place to garden and write.

Valerie had all of this growing up in the small Wisconsin town where she was born, and where she had been very healthy and content for the first part of her life. Then she married her high-school sweetheart, an adventurous spirit who worked as a freelance airline mechanic on private aircraft and ambitiously applied for new jobs in different cities every few months. Since marrying, Valerie had moved with her husband six times in five years, mostly to larger towns where they shared small apartments, mostly with noisy, insensitive strangers, because her husband didn't want the long-term commitment of a lease. His spirit loved adventure and sought the change and excitement of new jobs and locations as often as he could find them, but this left her spirit shell-shocked and suffering.

Because of her loyalty to her husband, Valerie lost connection with her own spirit, and her energy gave out. Her guides suggested that she get back to the quiet, natural life she needed and stop subjecting herself to these abrupt and sudden shocks in order to revive her spirit and heal her body.

"Does this mean I should divorce my husband?" Valerie asked. "Not necessarily," I replied. "All your guides are suggesting is that you become more aware of what your spirit needs and honor this if you want to feel better. Find a creative solution that works for both of you."

Guides do not tell us what to do and expect us to blindly follow it. Guides only suggest what will support our spirit and lead us back into alignment with our true nature. Then they leave it up to us to listen or not, honoring our free will.

> *Spirit never commands us to follow a particular path or puts us in a situation where the answer is all-or-nothing or black-or-white.*

Choosing to listen, Valerie moved back to the quiet, natural surroundings of her hometown, where her spirit thrived. She took a job in a small Waldorf school teaching art, spent time with her family of origin and dear old friends, started a community garden, and soon began to feel much better.

She and her husband didn't divorce, however—instead, he worked 10-day stretches in whatever city he was living in at the time, then came back to Wisconsin for his four or five days off in between shifts to spend time with her. The new arrangement worked well for both of their spirits. Spirit guidance will always open doors to workable solutions in all areas of life. We just need to believe there are solutions and be open to finding them.

Spirit never commands us to follow a particular path or puts us in a situation where the answer is all-or-nothing or black-or-white. We have free will and can do what we choose to do. Only the ego backs us into a corner and gives us the false impression that we are victims of circumstance and without choice. Spirit is creative and shows us many loving insightful ways to make our lives work. That is one of the benefits of consulting your spirit over your ego. Its options are far more creative and livable. When you clearly identify what your spirit needs you have a far greater chance of discovering what the best choice is for you.

To be happiest, my spirit needs a passport; good coffee; fascinating, walkable cosmopolitan cities; friends with whom I can have deep, authentic conversations as well as lots of silly fun; time for shopping; students to teach; lots of alone time; music; dance; and plenty of sleep.

## What about you?

My spirit needs _____.

## LOVE YOUR SPIRIT

When asked, many of my clients and students realize that they've never thought about their spirit let alone consider what nurtures it. Instead, they've just dutifully pushed ahead through life as they have been taught to do and hoped things would get better one day. Many, sadly, feel more like they're *enduring* life rather than *living* it, and have lost touch with their spirit altogether.

In our puritanical culture, we are taught from childhood on to put others first, make work the primary focus of our lives, and to consider any personal interest or care "selfish." It's easy to understand how this type of spirit-deadening disconnection occurs. Unless we change this toxic belief, make time for ourselves, and stop ignoring our spirit, many of us will continue to feel unfulfilled, uninspired, bored, restless, drained, and fatigued. These are all signs that it's time to reconnect to spirit.

## My spirit loves

- Free time
- Deep conversations
- Funny TV shows
- Detective novels
- Travel with my daughters
- Time to walk for hours alone
- Journaling

## What about you? What does your spirit love?

- _____
- _____
- _____
- _____
- _____
- _____

## SIMPLE WAYS TO CONNECT WITH AND EXPRESS YOUR SPIRIT

- Journal
- Learn new things
- Meditate
- Cook
- Spend time alone
- Speak kindly of yourself

- Laugh at your mistakes
- Forgive yourself
- Take long walks
- Surround yourself with beauty
- Garden
- Get regular bodywork
- Take calming baths

## CREATIVE WAYS TO EXPRESS YOUR SPIRIT

- Paint
- Make films
- Write
- Start a blog
- Travel
- Dance like mad
- Create or play music
- Volunteer
- Go to Burning Man
- Ski in the backcountry
- Take a road trip
- Start your own business
- Take a sabbatical

## Try This

Either writing here or in a journal, or recording your responses on your smartphone voice recorder, answer the following questions:

When do you feel most alive? _____

What leaves you feeling energized and fulfilled? _____

What leaves you feeling centered, relaxed, at ease, and peaceful? _____

What makes you laugh, leaves you feeling lighthearted and weightless in your skin? _____

These answers reveal what nourishes and expresses your spirit. They eventually open the door to connecting with the world of spirit guides.

## RELAX

If you want to meet your guides, do something that relaxes you, that takes your mind off of the outer world and gives you a mental break. It might be a creative task like sewing, which my mom does when she wants to get away from it all. I have a client who finds the most relaxing thing is to iron her freshly laundered clothes. As she steams out the wrinkles in her clothing, her worries seem to disappear as well.

Conrad Hilton used to go into his study, turn off the lights, sit quietly in the dark, and wait for guidance on his projects. Carl Jung, famous for his work on the collective unconscious, often spoke of his spirit guide, Philomen, whom he convened with while taking long walks in nature.

Making regular time to quiet, calm, and relax your mind opens the door to the spirit world. You don't have to just sit and stare out the window during these times (although that works well). You can also do such relaxing things as folding laundry, jogging, playing a musical instrument, chopping vegetables, working in the garden, or simply stretching. Anything that takes your mind off your daily concerns gives you more access to your inner guidance.

This is *valuable time* spent, so don't let anything interfere. Society pressures us to believe that focusing on things other than being productive is a waste of energy and an indulgence. This outwardly focused value system cuts us off from our inner world and our true selves, leaving us feeling out of integrity and adrift. Create your own value system, one that puts connecting inward and listening to your inner guidance at the *top* of your priority list, as it is the source of your greatest inspiration and meaningful insight.

I relax and talk to my guides when listening to meditation music on headphones, cleaning my house, folding laundry, and writing.

What about you? When do you relax
and talk to your guides?

Below is a link to a channeled guided 40-minute meditation to help you connect with your beautiful spirit. Sit quietly or lie down without interruption and listen with headphones to this meditation, ideally first thing in the morning, or whenever you want to feel the grace, love, and support of your authentic and Divine Self.

Visit https://www.hayhouse.com/downloads and enter the Product ID **1381** and Download Code **resources**. You can also visit http://www.soniachoquette.net.

Now that you've tuned in to your spirit, let's move on and focus on how to tune in to the spirit world around you.

# CHAPTER 2

# Entering the Wide
# World of Spirit

Once you reconnect with *your* own spirit, the next step in connecting with your guides is to become aware of the spirit in others. After all, modern science confirms that everything in the Universe is composed of pure consciousness vibrating at various frequencies. Material things only *appear* to be solid, but this is only an illusion; in fact, their energy and matter are in constant motion. Spirit is the moving force behind everything. The more aware of this we are, the more in tune with its guidance we become.

Years ago, when I first began apprenticing in the psychic and healing arts, my teacher, Charlie Goodman, told me that physical appearances are the least accurate representations of reality and I should never solely rely on them for insight. Instead, I should look *beyond* the surface of everything, to search more deeply and clairvoyantly for what is hidden in people and in situations. This insight guided me to pull back the veil between the physical and nonphysical worlds and connect with the unseen world of spirit.

Spirit energy vibrates at a higher frequency than the physical world, so you can't see it with your physical eyes. But it *can easily be felt* and experienced in your heart and with your "inner eyes." Particular areas of the body are highly receptive and sensitive to vibrations of spirit, including your gut, the back of your arms and neck, and the throat area, all places that register this elevated frequency. Spirit energy will become more and more apparent to you the more you pay attention to these areas of your body.

## Try This

To successfully sense the spirit energy of those around you, begin by closing your eyes and let your attention shift from your head to your heart. The easiest way to do this is to inhale slowly. Then open your jaw wide and exhale with a long, loud sigh. At the end of this exhalation, notice how your awareness has re-centered directly in your heart, the perfect place in which to sense subtle spirit energy. You will also notice that doing this calms and quiets your chatty mind, a kind of instant meditation.

> *To successfully sense the spirit energy of those around you, begin by closing your eyes and let your attention shift from your head to your heart.*

Next, focus on someone else, paying attention to the sensation in your heart as you *tune in to* their unique vibration. To do this begin by placing a hand on your heart as you bring that person to mind. Take a deep breath and feel their energy in your heart space. Describe out loud how that person's energy affects you. Think of this as if you are listening to a person's heart song, rhythm, or music. Our heart senses and feels these rhythms and vibrations quite well, just like we do when hearing a piece of music. Once you have an experience of listening with your heart you will no longer need to place your hand there. You can simply shift your attention to your heart with your intention. We naturally reflect our heart's intuitive perception when saying, for example, "She has such a 'sweet vibe,'" or "he has such 'intense vibes,'" and so on. We are feeling the energy of their spirit.

Quickly describe, out loud, what you sense about another person's spirit. Trust your spontaneity and let your heart speak freely. Don't edit yourself—that's just your ego trying to prevent you from making a genuine heart connection. You'll find that what flows will be surprisingly accurate.

For example, I experience my daughter Sonia's spirit as gentle, sensitive, proud, and quietly stubborn. Her spirit is patient, calm, and a bit fixed. She is naturally grounded, open-hearted, and generous. Her spirit is reliable, committed, creative, and laid back, although it can become ferocious if circumstances dictate that someone or something she loves is threatened. In that case, she steps in without fear to protect and stop the threat. Being familiar with her spirit is like being familiar with a beloved song. I instantly recognize her unique vibration wherever I go.

I was once browsing in a department store when I felt my daughter nearby—even though I knew she was spending the weekend with a girlfriend and had no plans, to my knowledge, to be at the mall. My sense of her was so strong that I turned around to see if she was behind me. Not finding her there, I continued to shop until five minutes later, when I heard her voice. I turned, and there she was! Her girlfriend's mother had brought them to the mall to see a movie, and they'd decided to walk through the department store to pass the time until the show started. She wasn't surprised to see me at all. Just as I'd sensed her presence, she, too, had sensed my spirit and it had signaled to her that I was nearby as well. We both laughed and hugged upon seeing each other, saying, "I *knew* you were here! I felt it."

My student Harriet shared that it never occurred to her to think of herself as spirit. Yet the idea intrigued her as it promised to bring more color and excitement to her otherwise unexciting life.

At the time, Harriet was 67 years old, had been single for more than 30 years (thanks to a bad marriage), and was working part-time as a secretary for an unpleasant and boring insurance broker. She felt stressed and bored to tears by both her job and her dull existence and desperately wanted to make changes that would bring more excitement and satisfaction to her life.

Instead of focusing solely on changing her *outer* world, I suggested she start by noticing the spirit in all people, herself included, as a way to change and enliven her *inner* world, including her unflattering perception of her life.

In describing her spirit, the words that popped out reminded her that she was naturally social and loved being with people, talking, laughing, and communing with others, all of which she had long ago abandoned. Buoyed by that awakening, she next began focusing on the spirit of others. The first was her neighbor who lived in her condo building and whom she had encountered in passing for years, but quite honestly had ignored until now.

Curious, she tuned in to his spirit and sensed his warmth, open-heartedness, and sense of fun, which instantly uplifted her own spirit. "It made me wonder how he experienced my spirit. Maybe I felt like a real drag to him. Not wanting that, I perked up and smiled whenever I saw him, which was also new for me."

Harriet's appreciation of her neighbor's positive spirit gave her a push to make conversation. After several pleasant exchanges— including one in which she indicated what a delightful spirit he had—her neighbor spontaneously invited her to join the bridge club that met in the rec room of their condo building twice a month. There she met several other neighbors. After a few weeks, she confided to the group her unhappiness at her job. Hearing this, a dentist who was present said he needed a new receptionist to run his large downtown office and asked if she'd be interested. "Can you believe it?" Harriet later told me. "He actually said, 'I like your spirit, Harriet. Goodness knows we can use your positive energy around the place.' It was surreal. And of course, I accepted on the spot."

Surely her guides had a hand in this careful orchestration. That is how it works.

### Did You Know That . . .

The best part of witnessing the spirit in all things is that it makes your dull world come alive. Seeing the world through the eyes of spirit, you begin to see hidden connections, opportunities, and even support right before your eyes. Once your mind and heart open to spirit, it's only another small shift to directly connect with your spirit guides as well.

## PETS AND PLANTS

Another practice is to notice the spirit of your pets. Can you feel and identify the spirit of your dog, cat, or even your fish, for instance? I know that the spirit of my now deceased poodle, Miss T, was very sensitive, humorous, elegant, and quite proud. She was rather unhappy whenever she looked scraggly and needed a hair-cut, and her spirit was delighted and quite satisfied when she left the groomer after a fresh shampoo and trim. On the other hand, my neighbor's dog, Emily, had a far less particular spirit than Miss T—in fact, she couldn't care less about grooming, was quite adven-turous, and ready to run and play at any moment. Her spirit was silly, curious, and far more confident and social than Miss T's was.

I've never encountered a person who couldn't describe their pet's spirit—much better in fact, than that of many of the people in their lives. Perhaps it's because our pets love us so uncondition-ally that our hearts fully open to their spirit naturally.

Next, stretch your awareness even further to sense the spirit in your houseplants and garden flora. You may think it's crazy but it's not. They, too, are living energies. Can you notice a dif-ference, for example, between the spirit of a healthy plant and one that's dying? Or that of an orchid versus a lily, or a potted plant as opposed to one that grows freely? You can if you try. Your ego mind may think this is silly, but in fact, becoming *clairvoyant* means developing a clear and accurate view of the true nature of all things, not just of people and animals.

With a little practice, you will soon be sensing and feeling the many subtle planes of energy around you as easily as you register the physical plane.

## YOUR TURN

Start noticing the spirit in everyone and everything around you as a matter of habit. Describe spirits in simple terms such as "light," "heavy," "quick," "steady," "bright," or "dull." Don't worry about getting it "right." Let your imagination take over and don't censor your impressions. The key is to bypass your brain and let your *feelings* express directly. Trust me. This is more natural than it may feel at first. You are aware of more than you think you are.

My mother's spirit is _____.

My neighbor's spirit is _____.

My boss's spirit is _____.

My child's spirit is _____.

My best friend's spirit is _____.

Below is a link to a channeled guided 30-minute meditative journey to introduce you to the spirit world. Sit quietly or lie down without interruption and listen with headphones to this meditation, either first thing in the morning, or when falling asleep.

Visit https://www.hayhouse.com/downloads and enter the Product ID **1381** and Download Code **resources**. You can also visit http://www.soniachoquette.net.

Now that you've been introduced to the world of spirit, let's move on to meet your first divine helpers: your angels.

# PART II

# ANGELS:

## The First
of Your Divine
Companions

# CHAPTER 3

# Angels: Our Perpetual Divine Support System

The very first group of Divine helpers sent by God to support us through life are angels. The word *angel* means "messenger," so the primary purpose of these celestial beings is to help us communicate with God and God with us. They keep us safe, protected, and feeling reassured as we journey through life.

Angels are celestial beings who manifest in human form when necessary. Angels help us learn to love ourselves and others, accept life as it comes, have compassion for all people, summon our courage, find forgiveness, and increase our inner strength and faith as we encounter life's challenges. They have five primary missions in total.

The first is to console us when we meet with disappointment, injury, or distressing situations that make no sense from our vantage point, leaving us feeling abandoned, confused, rejected, unworthy, or diminished. Angels console our hearts when we encounter these painful moments and are unable to see a bigger picture or through the fog of these unwanted upsets. They offer solace that humans may not have the ability to provide.

Angels surround you, for example, when you don't get the job you were sure was yours after the third promising interview. They show up when your life partner cheats on you and then denies it. They are with you when you are being bullied in school or when your childcare falls through and you have no backup. They help you get through blindsiding moments such as these and back on solid footing.

The second mission of angels (and especially your guardian angel, who I cover in the next chapter) is to offer protection and keep you out of harm's way as you make your way through life. Their protection comes in many forms. In addition to keeping you physically as safe as possible, your angels also help you protect your emotional self. They help you find the confidence to establish better emotional boundaries and the strength to say "No" to people and situations that don't respect or honor you or threaten you in some way. Angels may also protectively nudge you to change your plans or go in a different direction to avoid danger. Angels help us restore our self-esteem and love ourselves.

They are with you when you stand up to the narcissistic partner or overly demanding parent or friend who disrespects you, leaving you feeling angered and frustrated. They are the ones giving you the idea to join a support group when lost in codependency, unable to make healthy, self-loving choices.

The third mission of angels is to comfort you when in grief or suffering the dark night of the soul. The human experience can bring unspeakable, unexpected, unbearable pain, especially when faced with random acts of violence or tragic accidents. Angels comfort us in such times and help us find our way through our grief by soothing our souls and reminding us that in spirit there is no real separation from our loved ones, even in death.

> *Angels help us restore our self-esteem and love ourselves.*

Years ago, a long-standing client from Newtown, Connecticut, called to ask me if I would come and talk to the parents of the victims of the Sandy Hook Elementary School shooting, and possibly offer them some spiritual consolation. Knowing there was nothing I could say to ease their grief, I prayed to the angels to guide me in providing whatever good I could offer. Then I agreed to go. When I arrived, I was overwhelmed by the dense cloud of shell-shocked grief and sorrow encapsulating the surviving parents, friends, and family members of the victims assembled in that room. Thankfully, I also sensed the presence of a thousand angels. Instead of trying to make spiritual sense of what had just occurred, I invited them instead to share stories of their children, reassuring them that their loved ones were with the angels in heaven and that more angels were among us as well. What began as a tearful and intensely angry conversation gave way to people sharing signs they had received since the tragedy, assuring them that their lost one was with the angels.

One young mother said she woke up on a recent morning hearing a beautiful classical song coming from her iPhone for no reason. She was both startled and moved to tears by the music. She instantly knew in her heart that it was a love song sent to her by her daughter. Another devastated mom shared how she looked out her kitchen window and spotted a single white swan in the pond behind her home, even though it was the middle of January when normally no swans were around. She, too, knew that it was a message from an angel telling her that her son was at peace. Another woman, the aunt of one of the children killed, open her palm and revealed three feathers she had just found on the doorstep of the house we were in. This was clearly a sign from the angels letting us all know of their presence during this dark hour.

It took months and months for me to recalibrate my energy after experiencing this sorrowful afternoon, so I cannot imagine how painful it must have been for the loved ones of those murdered to get on with their lives. I was grateful for my own angels for guiding me to remain available to these people for conversation, guidance, or just to talk or vent their rage in the future and for as long as they needed or wanted. Several people accepted my offer and we spoke for months thereafter. I know I couldn't have been of any genuine service or support to these suffering souls if not for the help of the angels.

The fourth mission of angels is to help us overcome self-destructive patterns of behavior, such as drug and alcohol addiction. They show up when we hit rock bottom, when we are ready to give up on life or have lost all sense of our personal value and worth. Angels help us break free of these delusional demons and chase the darkness away, restoring our inner light and connection to God. They give us the strength to overcome our self-defeating behaviors and evolve into better versions of ourselves than we are presently expressing.

A recent client named George shared with me the story of his descent into hell after he started taking meth. "One day I was a young reckless guy setting up my life, having fun, although admittedly being more than a bit careless with drugs and alcohol. I thought I had it all under control. Then I tried meth. The next thing I knew, in a matter of seven months, I was a shell of my former self, hopelessly addicted to this poison and destroying my life to feed my addiction. I lost my job, my girlfriend, my home, and my dignity. I became a thief to afford my habit and was arrested for breaking into my ex-girlfriend's parents' home to get stuff to pawn for money."

George was sentenced to five years in prison. Just days after he arrived, he had a dream that an angel showed up in his cell and sat with him all night. "Its presence was profoundly loving and nonjudgmental, but clear. It told me I had to clean up and devote myself to service in the world. It was so real that I knew this was more than a dream. It was a visitation. I felt such love and compassion from this angel that from that moment on, I had a complete change of heart and direction. It was a miracle really, considering how low I had sunk and what shame and despair I was feeling. Before the angel showed up, all I wanted to do was die. Now I had a burning desire to fully recover and do something good in the world."

George served three years of his five-year sentence and then was released. During his time in prison, he began studying psychology and decided to become an addiction counselor. He also started writing and is now working on a book to help discourage others from falling into the same dark hole that he so quickly did. Thanks to the angel visitation, George found his way back to a life of meaning and grace. He assured me that this would never have happened on his own.

A final mission of angels is to help us find the patience to weather the storms of life. They escort us through passages of pain that overwhelm and frighten us or leave us feeling despair. In 2016, there was a massive exodus from Syria to Europe at the height of the Syrian civil war, and hundreds of thousands of refugees walked across Europe trying to get away from the death and destruction that had decimated their country. Watching reports about these people on the news, I also intuitively saw hundreds of angels walking with them, keeping them from total despair and giving them the strength to get through this unspeakably horrendous experience. Their journey seemed endless and fraught with almost as much danger as they had left behind, but angels gave them the patience and fortitude to carry on until they found new ground and safety. The patience and determination these migrants had to build a life in a world where they were so often clearly reminded that they were not wanted was awe-inspiring. Many are still camped outside my door here in Paris and living on the streets with their children. So many seem broken beyond repair, but I always see or sense an angel in the vicinity, especially if they have young children sitting on their laps in the cold. They are waiting for something better, and it's their patience with this untenable situation that keeps them alive. They are my daily teachers. Their angels are their daily saviors.

### Did You Know That . . .

- Angels are a significant force in every faith tradition, and are probably one of the few things that all world religions agree on.

- Christians have seven major archangels, while the Islamic religion acknowledges four.

- In the Jewish mystical tradition, Metatron is the highest angel of all; in Islam, he is known as Mitatrush.

- Angels are mentioned almost 300 times in the Bible.

To connect with your angels, give your logical brain a rest, accept their presence, and realize that no one needs to believe that you've had a connection except for you.

However, since angels *are* the most universally accepted of our spirit helpers, you can usually bring up the subject to just about anyone and be confident that most will be receptive. In fact, the more people are involved in the conversation, the higher the chances that at least a few will admit to having had an experience with their personal angel (even at the risk of being dismissed as crazy!).

Zillions of angel sightings have been reported; in fact, *you've probably* had a personal angel encounter yourself, even if you're wary of calling it that. Ask yourself if you've ever experienced a "near-miss" incident or by some strange intuition been spared some sort of trauma. Recall how it unfolded and how it left you feeling. You can rest assured that, no matter how subtle the experience, it was an angel on duty, helping you out.

## INTERACTING WITH YOUR ANGELS

Once you've taken the leap of faith, accepted the presence of angels in your life, and acknowledged their support by being gracious and appreciative, you can explore other effective ways to connect with them.

- When you wake up in the morning, thank your angels for watching over you in the night.

- As you prepare breakfast, ask your angels to pave the way for easy travel and positive flow in your day ahead.

- Throughout the day, ask your angels to stand at your office door and block negativity, screen your phone calls, or ride next to you on airplanes, on trains, and in your car.

- If you're facing difficult appointments, ask your angels to connect with the spirits of those you're meeting with to establish a positive connection.

Don't forget to thank your angels for all their hard work at the end of each day. Light sticks of sweet-smelling incense and make an offering to them in appreciation for their help. You can also ring little chimes and bells, both to call them and to thank them for help.

Another way to summon your angels is by playing or singing uplifting and beautiful melodies in your home, your car, or even your office for them to enjoy. Angels love music!

## Pray

The best way to connect with your angels (or any Divine helpers, for that matter) is to pray to God to send angels to help you. Prayer is the angel hotline to heaven. Pick up "the phone" without a moment's hesitation and call on them for all the help you need.

Regard your prayers as commissions to be delivered to the Divine Mother, Father, and Holy Spirit, and pray that your angels take them where they need to go—then trust them, because they know what they're doing.

Pray every day. Pray for help in every matter. Pray both when you are afraid and when you are celebrating. If you continuously pray, you will be continuously helped. Praying is simply talking to God or to the Universe regularly and asking for love and support as you journey through life. And because you are loved unconditionally and treasured by God and the Universe as a Divine Child, your prayers will always be answered, even if not precisely how you expect them to be.

Angels serve you but work for God. They help you because God wants you to be helped. That is why you pray to God. God is the boss. God hears your prayers and sends angels in response. Lots and lots of them.

And don't forget to celebrate your successes and victories with your angels, since they're your most intimate champions and probably helped quite a bit with achieving those successes. No one cheers us on more enthusiastically than our angels. We need to be sure to share the gold!

## Show Gratitude toward Your Angels

Train yourself to notice your good fortune and be grateful to your angels for their help. Angels appreciate being appreciated. It lets them know you are aware of their loving support. The more appreciative you are of their presence, the more blessings you will receive.

## My List of Blessings for Today

I'm grateful that . . .

- I was able to sleep well.
- My computer fixed itself after I rebooted it.
- My mom is in good health.
- I have two beautiful grown daughters, and the friendship and fun they bring to my life.
- I no longer own a car.
- I have such creative friends in Paris.
- I have strength and resilience.

## YOUR TURN

I'm grateful that . . .

- _____
- _____
- _____
- _____

Now that you've learned about angels in general, let's move on to particular types of angels and how they help you, beginning with your personal guardian angel.

# CHAPTER 4

# Guardian Angels: Your Personal Bodyguards

Once you awaken to the perpetual support of angels, you will naturally begin to view the Universe as a more beautiful, nurturing, positive place, one in which everything and everyone is connected, looked after, and loved—and that includes you!

The very first Divine angel to connect with you is your personal guardian angel. Guardian angels are very significant to human beings because they're the only spirit guides who are intimately connected to us from the beginning of our lives to our very last breath. They watch over, guide, and nurture us, keeping our minds, bodies, and souls safe until we're ready to return to spirit, and then they personally walk us back to heaven.

There are various theories about when our guardian angels first connect with us. Some people believe that it's at conception, others at birth, while still others think that it's when we first laugh.

I can't speak for all guardian angels, but I *can* say that in my work as an intuitive guide and teacher, they've always shown up to announce the news of a baby, so *I* feel that they first connect with us at conception (and often make their second appearance nine months later!).

I distinctly remember that when my daughter Sonia was born, I was so overwhelmed that I just held her to my heart and didn't even look to see whether she was a boy or a girl. Then, suddenly, I heard an unfamiliar voice ask, "Well? Boy or girl?" When I looked up, I saw a beautiful face with the most brilliant light around it directly above me, smiling at us with such warmth and excitement that it instantly calmed me.

Looking at the baby for the answer, I exclaimed, "It's a girl!" only to glance back up to see that the light was gone. Believing that incredible face belonged to one of the nurses, I scanned the room to find her. However, at that very second, my daughter let out a cry and, exhausted, exhilarated, and overcome with emotion for my new baby, I lost all thought of the nurse. Later that day, after I regained a little composure, I recounted the experience to my doctor and asked who the nurse was and where she'd gone.

"Oh yes, I liked her, too," she replied. "I've never seen her before, though, so she must be new." The next day, when the doctor checked in just before I was ready to go home, she said, "By the way, I asked around and no one has any information on that nurse you asked about. It's so strange."

With that, a tingle swooped up my spine to the top of my head and worked its way back down, and I swear that right then, my newborn daughter smiled. I knew at that moment that her guardian angel was with us. With a burst of confidence, ready to embark on the new adventure of motherhood, I turned to her father and said, "Let's go home."

## GUARDIAN ANGELS: YOUR PERPETUAL PROTECTORS

Your personal guardian angel is the spiritual equivalent of a bodyguard, constantly protecting and sheltering you from all manner of harm.

Last year, my friend Ellen, who lives alone in Northern California, went to bed at 9 P.M., aware of distant fires in the area, but confident that she was safe for the night. At 2 A.M., she felt as if someone was literally shaking her awake and urging her to get up. Once awake, she thought it was a dream. But then she smelled fire and knew that was why she had woken up so abruptly. She barely had time to grab her Pekingese dog and her purse and run to the car.

On the road Ellen met firefighters driving through the neighborhood in a cloud of dense smoke, sirens blaring, yelling through a bullhorn for everyone to wake up and evacuate. "Apparently the winds kicked up and the fires quickly moved our way. It was chaos, with people running and cars almost piling on top of one another as they poured into the one small road out," she shared. "I was frightened for my life for the next hour as I snaked my way out of danger, and it wasn't until several hours later, once I was settled into my son's house fifty miles away, that I suddenly realized I didn't just wake up from the smell of smoke. I was shaken awake by a strong force. I immediately knew it was my guardian angel who woke me up. If that hadn't happened, I wonder if I would have made it out before the area became engulfed in flames. I'm glad I don't have that answer."

Another client, Mark, said he was on his way to work early one morning, when out of the blue he felt he had to pull over to the side of the highway and check his tires. Since he lived in the country and the exits were few and far between, he tried to dismiss the feeling at first, thinking this was crazy and he would check them later. "But the feeling was so strong, I just had to listen to it," he said. "I took the next exit and pulled into a gas station. I checked the tires and they were fine. But suddenly I experienced a tremendous pain in my chest that wouldn't ease up. It took my breath away and I knew I was in trouble. I walked to the cashier and told him what was happening. He called the paramedics, and ten minutes later an ambulance arrived. Long story short, I was having a heart attack. Because I pulled over, I was able to get immediate help and avert a disaster, maybe even death. I shudder to think about it. I knew it was my guardian angel that told me to do that."

> *Your personal guardian angel is the spiritual equivalent of a bodyguard, constantly protecting and sheltering you from all manner of harm.*

Visiting Los Angeles with her husband, my client Debbie ordered a crib for her three-month-old daughter and put it in the front room of their two-room hotel suite. That night a severe earthquake rocked the city and everything in the room fell, including plaster, overhead light fixtures, and mirrors. Panicked, the parents scrambled out of bed and raced to their baby's crib. Chunks of the ceiling littered their path and the chandelier that was directly above the crib had fallen and lay shattered on the floor, but the crib was untouched and the baby slept soundly through the upheaval. The only thing on or near the baby was a small white feather. Debbie and her husband grabbed their daughter and sobbed with gratitude for her guardian angel's protection.

## YOUR GUARDIAN ANGEL SHOWS UP IN MANY WAYS

Another fact about guardian angels is that they're the only spirit helpers with the power to materialize, and they often do so as they work to keep you nurtured and safe. They may show up to save your life, to protect you from heartbreak and despair, or just to make life's more difficult challenges possible to cope with. Although you only have one guardian angel, they can reveal themselves in any number of costumes, at any age, and in all shapes and appearances. You see, contrary to popular belief, guardian angels don't necessarily appear with silver flowing robes and glowing hair—sometimes they look like homeless people or rock stars.

Years ago, a client named Kate, who worked at the Pentagon, reported a run-in with her guardian angel. On 9/11, despite the fact that she was running late for work, Kate dashed in for her daily Starbucks fix and in her rush out the door collided head-on with a handsome young man who was walking in, spilling her coffee all over him. Horrified, Kate was apologetic as she tried to wipe it up. The man was an incredibly good sport and said three times, "Don't worry. I made you do this so that you'd slow down." That mishap made her even later for work, and because of it, she was saved from the horror that had unfolded on that tragic morning.

Kate returned to Starbucks the next day and asked the guy who helped them clean up if the man she'd run into was a regular customer. When he said that he'd never seen the man before, she immediately intuitively sensed in her heart that he was an angel who had saved her life.

In addition to performing lifesaving intercepts, our guardian angels also work with our spirits and our Higher Selves throughout our lives to keep our spirits up, especially when we become mired in self-doubt and lose our confidence. For instance, when my client Lisa was dumped by her boyfriend of three years for her best friend, she was shattered by the betrayal and couldn't seem to get past it. While waiting in line at the post office before work one day, she struck up a conversation with an extremely well-dressed older gentleman who told her what a beautiful person she was, and what a lovely partner she would make someone someday. Hitting a nerve of self-doubt, she rolled her eyes and replied, "Given the way things have been going lately, I'm not so sure." Smiling at her on the way out the door, he winked and said, "Believe me. Your true love is on his way." Feeling uplifted, Lisa looked around for the gentleman once outside to say thank you for the words of encouragement, but he was nowhere in sight. Walking to her car, she realized that he may very well have been her guardian angel, placed in line just for her.

If you want to quickly feel your guardian angel's presence, count your blessings out loud each day. Soon you will begin to realize just how near your guardian angel is by how many beautiful things happen day after day.

Both of my daughters had a string of guardian angel encounters when they were young. When Sabrina was around three, she became very ill with a fever. During a particularly difficult night, she told me that her guardian angel brought in many baby angels for a parade to cheer her up. I sat on her bed with her while they danced around her room and listened to her squeal with delight as she grabbed my arm and asked, "Do you see the baby angels?

Do you see them?" Sick with worry for her at the time, I, unfortunately, did not, but when I saw her joy, a wave of lightness swept through me. Although I didn't actually witness the angels, I certainly felt them, and with that I knew that Sabrina would recover that night, which she did.

Sabrina was 11 years old when, once again, her guardian angel intervened to bring a little joy to an otherwise miserable situation. During winter break, I gave her permission to go on her first unsupervised trip to the mall with her friends to have dinner and see a movie. Feeling rather adult and very excited about her new freedom, she loaded up her Christmas purse with all of the gift cards she'd received as presents and the $20 we gave her and set out. Despite my warnings to pay attention and keep an eye on her purse, she became so engrossed in the movie that she left it on her seat. The minute she hit the lobby, she remembered and dashed back to retrieve it, but it was gone. And to make matters worse, her friends laughed at her instead of empathizing.

When I arrived minutes later to pick Sabrina up at our prearranged time, I found her inconsolable, ashamed about her error, and grieving over the loss of what amounted to her entire Christmas stash. Torn between sympathy for her predicament and irritation at her carelessness, I started walking my sobbing daughter to the car.

Suddenly, a young girl who was the mirror image of Sabrina darted out of a group of kids and ran over to her. Looking straight at us, she said, "Excuse me," and pulled Sabrina aside, asking, "Are you okay? I know that you lost your wallet in the movie and that you feel bad, but don't worry. Just be okay with it. You'll be fine. You aren't stupid—it was just your lesson." Then she hugged her and ran back to her friends.

It was such a surprise, and the girl was so sweet and kind, that Sabrina instantly overcame her grief. She told me that she wanted to thank her new friend, but the girl had disappeared. Sabrina walked around for a few minutes, then came back, shrugging.

"She was an angel," she said matter-of-factly. "She told me that I'll get over it, so I guess I will." From that instant, I never heard another word from Sabrina about the loss.

Was the girl a guardian angel? Considering how kids that age usually act, I'd definitely say yes.

Very often, your guardian angel will appear when you most need them, but you won't realize who they were until after the fact, when they leave such reassuring energy with you that you can't believe you didn't identify their presence. My client Grace, for instance, had just lost her mother to cancer and her husband to divorce when she received news that her best friend had died in a freak accident.

Overwhelmed with grief, she took her seat on a flight to attend her friend's funeral. As she was settling in for the trip, a very old, fragile, sweet-looking woman was transported down the aisle in a special aircraft wheelchair to take the seat next to her. They began to talk, and Grace poured her heart out to this stranger, who listened, made her laugh, and reassured her that the best of life was yet to come.

All the while, the older woman clasped a small prayer book in her hands and reminded Grace that all she needed to do was to keep asking God for help. By the time the two-hour flight had ended, Grace was feeling so much better that it finally occurred to her to ask the woman her name, to which she replied, "Dolores Good."

As Dolores was escorted off the plane in her wheelchair, Grace saw that she'd forgotten her prayer book, so she rushed to the front of the aircraft to return it. When she asked the flight attendant at the door where Dolores had gone, she couldn't tell her, so she raced through the terminal to look. Yet Grace had no luck—it was as though Dolores had vanished into thin air! Going back to the flight deck, my client asked if they had any information about a Dolores Good. The agent pulled up the passenger register and, looking quite perplexed, said that there was no one on the flight roster with that name; in fact, no one was listed for seat 17D at all. When Grace insisted that Dolores was the passenger who had gotten off the plane in a wheelchair, the agent informed her that the request to assist her off the plane had come from another terminal, so he couldn't look it up.

Frustrated, Grace looked closely at the prayer book to discover that it was titled *The Lord Is Good*. She laughed as she made the connection between Dolores Good and "the Lord is good," realizing immediately that Dolores was her guardian angel.

### Did You Know That . . .

- Guardian angels are the only spirit beings that can appear in human form.

- They have never been human.

- They can show up from the moment of your conception and stay with you for the duration of your life.

- They guide, protect, and nurture you—body, mind, and spirit.

- They are with you at the moment of your death.

While I've had many guardian angel experiences during my life, it was not until I was in my thirties and in great psychic and physical distress that my guardian angel paid me a visit in human form. I'd retreated to Hawaii in the dead of winter to recuperate from a long and exhausting bout of sleep deprivation after the birth of my two-in-a-row babies, a never-ending house renovation, and overwhelming obligations. (This is a story I recounted in my first book, *The Psychic Pathway*, but it bears retelling here.)

For the first several days after I arrived in Oahu, all I did was sleep, but on the third day, I roused myself and went down to the beach, where I sat quietly near the water reflecting on my life. Although I had two beautiful daughters, I struggled with my husband. I wasn't happy. Our lives were stretched too thin, we were over our heads in debt, and all Patrick and I did was fight. Having very little outside support at the time, both my husband and I were overwhelmed with responsibility. It was painfully clear to me that all of the joy had drained away from our lives and we were merely surviving from day to day.

As I sat on the beach, far away from it all, I prayed for a change, something to get my life back on track. The following day, I strolled along the beach for an hour or so, then spontaneously turned and wandered toward the city to explore. I entered a metaphysical bookstore with the feeling that I'd been led there. A single woman was working behind the counter as I began to browse, and I found myself feeling grateful that she seemed preoccupied so that I could wander around without interruption. After a few minutes, a beautiful Jamaican-accented man walked from the back room directly toward me. He was about 6′2″, dressed all in white, and had a gorgeous smile and a twinkling laugh. The minute he saw me, he said, "Hello, I have been waiting for you."

"Me?" I asked, surprised.

"Yes," he answered as he motioned me over to a bin of spiritual posters. "Look here," he said, pulling out a poster of a female angel collapsed on the beach. "This is you."

"Very perceptive," I laughed. "I *do* feel like that right now."

"Now look here," he continued. "This is what you must do." He pulled out another poster, this time of a male angel embracing the female angel and flying toward heaven.

I suddenly felt a sad twinge of pain, realizing how far apart Patrick and I had drifted. Neither of us had any time to ourselves, let alone the opportunity to enjoy each other or our daughters.

"Connect with your partner and remember to dance," the man said, smiling as he swayed to the back room. Before he disappeared behind the curtain, he turned around one last time and said, "I will be back."

I stood there holding the two posters, puzzling over what he'd just said, when the woman behind the counter asked me if I needed help.

"No, thank you," I answered. "The gentleman in the back room has helped me quite a bit already."

She frowned. "Gentleman? What gentleman?"

"The one who just walked into the back room," I answered.

Shaking her head at me as though I were nuts, she said, "There's no one else working here." After ducking into the back room to check for herself, she emerged (still shaking her head) and reaffirmed, "There's no one there."

Confused, I looked down at the angel posters. Then I remembered the man's shimmering, all-white outfit, and I knew in that instant that *he* was an angel . . . *my* angel. He had stepped into my life out of nowhere to bring me the message to relax, simplify my life, enjoy Patrick and the girls, and *trust* that everything would be all right—reassurance I desperately needed to hear just then. Because he said he'd be back, I knew in my heart that my family and I would be helped. I was finally able to smile and then laugh out loud as a comforting feeling swept over me.

"Never mind," I said to the woman as I slowly walked outside, shocked at what had just happened. I was so grateful that this being had shown up like a flash of light to brighten my dreary life that day and show me the way forward. From that moment on, I've called my guardian angel "Flash."

Have you met your guardian angel? What happened? Write it down here.

_____

_____

_____

_____

## TALK TO YOUR GUARDIAN ANGEL

### Try This

Practice saying this simple child's prayer every night before you go to sleep so that you can begin to feel the presence of your guardian angel by your side immediately:

*Angel of God, guardian dear, to whom God's love commits me here, Ever this day, be at my side, to light, to guard, to rule and guide.*

### Things to ask of your guardian angel

- Protect me
- Keep me safe
- Reassure me
- Calm me down
- Walk with me
- Comfort me
- Travel with me
- Give me confidence
- Keep me on my path
- Surround me with positive energy

Now that you've learned about guardian angels, let's move on and discover the archangels and how they serve our lives.

# CHAPTER 5

# The Archangels

In addition to working with your personal guardian angel, you can also receive tremendous energetic support from the archangels, who are considered God's most important messengers and motivators in the celestial hierarchy. You can invoke them for added help at any time, and because these angelic forces are so powerful, calling on them is the equivalent of asking the best quarterbacks in the Universe to step in and help you win the game of life.

Early in my Catholic upbringing, I was introduced to seven archangels: Michael, Gabriel, Raphael, Uriel, Raguel, Chamuel, and Remiel. Eventually, I discovered other archangels, such as Metatron, the king of the archangels, who oversees all angel activity on all planes and acts as the gatekeeper to the higher dimensions of spirit, and Sandalphon, who oversees the inner earth and is the gatekeeper to the realm of the spirits of the natural world. You may notice that most archangels' names end in "el." It's no coincidence, since "el" means "shining being" in Hebrew, which is what archangels are.

Each archangel oversees a particular domain, so you can invoke specific archangels to help you with specific needs. Allow me to briefly introduce each archangel to you:

- **Michael,** Archangel of the South, standing behind you and vibrating to the color electric blue, is the archangel of fire. Call on him to protect you, watch your back, and move you to take action when your life lacks vitality, excitement, and passion. When you are ready to face your fears and try something new, maybe even intimidating, such as switching your career or traveling somewhere alone for the first time, call on Michael to guide and watch over you as you venture forward.

- **Gabriel**, Archangel of the West, walks on your left side, vibrating to the color diamond white, like early-morning sun rays glistening on a lake. Considered the second archangel in command, he is the archangel of water. He oversees and cleanses your emotions. He calms your doubts, boosts your confidence, and washes away anger and resentment. He is especially helpful to those who are wrestling with anxiety, stuck in disappointments of the past, and failing to move on.

- **Raphael**, Archangel of the East, standing to your right, vibrating to the color neon green, is the archangel of air. Not only does he clear and refresh your thoughts and beliefs, he's also the perfect archangel to summon for boosting your creativity. In charge of healing, Raphael clears your body, mind, and spirit of limitations brought about by limited thinking. Invoke Raphael before any creative project to bring in fresh perspective and focus, and to help create work that's inspired and meaningful.

- **Uriel**, Archangel of the North, walking in front of you, vibrating to the color ruby red, oversees your security on the earth plane and clears the path to abundance. He watches over all your material concerns, from your physical home to your personal possessions, such as your car, computer, bank account, purse, or backpack. Uriel is a multitasker. He grounds your journey through life, so you feel secure and anchored. He sends warnings when necessary to direct you away from harm and oversees your material security.

- **Raguel,** Archangel Above, vibrating to the color turquoise, is the archangel standing above you. He brings harmony, order, and justice. He calms others so they behave and keep the peace. When my children were young and we had to travel long distances on airplanes, I invoked Raguel to help ensure that *my* little angels behaved. It must have worked because we took many cross-country and European flights and my daughters somehow intuitively knew (without threats from me) that they had to behave . . . or else! In fact, we were often complimented on their exemplary behavior, which the girls loved to hear.

- **Chamuel,** Archangel Below, underneath your feet and vibrating to the color light pink, is the archangel of love and healer of relationships. Call on him to keep your heart open and loving, kind and noncompetitive, forgiving and generous. Chamuel sweetens your soul, increases compassion, aids in forgiveness, and lightens your heart.

- Finally, **Remiel,** Archangel Escort to Heaven, vibrating to the color light green, is the archangel of hope. He's a powerful entity whom I've invoked quite a bit as an intuitive guide when working with hospice patients, since his assignment is to greet us at death's door and escort us to heaven. There have been many times when I've held the hands of the dying until I could feel Remiel's presence. When he shows up, the vibrations of fear, stress, and drama that come with our transition from the earth to heaven give way to absolute peace and calm. This is the moment when our guardian angel guides us into Remiel's loving embrace, and in that instant, everyone present knows and feels that the soul is safe again.

In addition to these seven archangels, there are two more mighty archangels to call upon for extra protection and connection to the guided world.

- The first is **Metatron**, vibrating to the color gold, like the sun. He is the king of the archangels and master of the Divine masculine forces of the Universe. He serves as the gatekeeper to the higher planes. He vibrates to the frequency of unconditional love, and it is his job to oversee the spirit realm, including all angels and spirit guides and light beings in the Universe. Metatron is archangel to the higher planes and therefore stands above you, along with Raguel.

- The second is **Sandalphon**, archangel of the Divine feminine inner world, vibrating to the colors violet and silver. This archangel acts as the gatekeeper to the inner world of the earth and of our soul. She keeps us aware of our soul's path and purpose. She also connects us with nature, including spirit animals and the fairies. Sandalphon is the guardian of the inner planes and therefore stands below you, along with Chamuel.

Archangels, like your personal guardian angel, support the fulfillment of your soul purpose. They move you to take risks and to explore and share your gifts, whether they be painting, dancing, cooking, gardening, writing, healing, teaching, or leading others.

Archangels oversee your creative purpose and expression, because your creativity is the expression of your soul's purpose. Without having a creative outlet, your soul's expression and purpose can get cut off. Thankfully, the archangels are here to help to restore your connection with your creativity if that happens.

For example, when I was eight years old, my third-grade music teacher made me sit out during the Christmas choir presentation, claiming loudly, in front of the entire class, that I didn't have a musical note in my body. I outwardly laughed the incident off, but inside I was wounded and humiliated beyond belief. After that horrible experience, no one could ever again pry another note out of me. Because I loved music passionately, I felt as though I'd undergone a severe psychic amputation.

One day, about 20 years ago, I was given a holy card with Uriel's picture on it, citing him as the archangel of music. Knowing that recovering my singing spirit would require some significant healing "mojo," I asked Uriel to help free my voice. After that, ever so cautiously, I took a chance and (alone, of course) began to hum.

When you invoke the archangels, you get results, so I wasn't surprised that shortly after calling on Uriel, I serendipitously met a musician named Mark Welch, who offered to travel and work with me. I knew Uriel sent Mark, because he was so encouraging and grounded that I felt safe singing with him. Before I knew it, I was singing at every workshop presentation and book signing in which we appeared, all around the world! Was I on key? Well, no, not in the beginning, but eventually—with Uriel's (and Mark's) help—my singing improved. It didn't matter though. I wasn't performing. I was singing to express my own soul's joy, and through this, *I* got better. That's all that mattered.

Together Mark and I wrote, and recorded, many soul-healing songs and meditations based on my books, which have helped thousands of people, including *Attunement to Higher Vibrational Living*, a channeled 4-CD guided meditation set recorded in Kauai and published by Hay House. Thank you for bringing back my music, Uriel!

My mother lost 95 percent of her hearing from injuries she sustained in World War II at the age of twelve, and she often lamented how she wished that she could still hear and enjoy music. When I told her about Uriel, she became excited, saying "I'm going to ask Uriel to help me hear music again." Shortly after doing so, she had an incredible healing experience: she said that all night long, she dreamed she was serenaded by the most exquisite celestial music that she'd ever heard. She couldn't describe how lovely it was, but judging by the glow on her face, it was apparent that she'd been deeply touched.

What was even more exciting, however, was that the music continued night after night. Mom listened and danced to the same heavenly music so often that we began to joke that she'd better hurry to bed so she wouldn't miss her concert. She'd laughingly answer, "I wouldn't dream of it."

Invoke the archangels to help you express your soul artfully, creatively, and freely. Then get ready, because big shifts will come soon after.

### Did You Know That . . .

- Archangels are God's most important messengers.

- They are the power-booster packs of your spiritual support team.

- They oversee the awakening and expression of your artistic talents.

- They are powerful, friendly, and loving, and don't have egos like human beings.

- They love to be called upon because to serve you is to serve God.

- They can be invoked through chanting their names slowly, like a song.

I often suggest that clients ask the archangels to help them be more creative and find their purpose. Some have reported after the fact that the results far exceeded their wildest expectations. For instance, Anne taught emotionally and cognitively challenged students in a public high school, and although she was devoted to her mission, there were so many students that needed more help than she could provide in her class that Anne was stretched to her limits. I suggested that she invoke Raguel to help ease the stress.

"How on earth do I do that?" she asked.

"You don't," I said. "Raguel isn't *on Earth*—he's in heaven—and he brings potent calming energy to any stressful situation and shifts it for the better, so try."

Anne called on Raguel all weekend long and "downloaded" her frustrations, asking that he help calm the kids in her classroom so that she could teach instead of referee for a change.

The following Monday, the principal told her their school had been targeted for some new classroom strategies since the ones in place were failing. The first change the school board decided to implement was to cut her group of 29 kids into three smaller groups. She couldn't believe her eyes when, five minutes later, 20 of her most challenging students were transferred to other teachers, leaving her to work with the remaining 9, making her job far more manageable by comparison.

"Was it Raguel?" she asked me, incredulous that her prayer had just been answered.

"Anne, this is the Chicago public school system we're talking about," I reminded her, as we both laughed. "Wouldn't you say that what happened *had* to have been orchestrated by someone with supernatural clout?"


## HOW TO INVOKE THE ARCHANGELS

I was taught that invoking archangels is best done in a particular way. Of course, prayer is always the very best way to engage with any Divine entity, but a specific method to get archangels' attention is by singing or chanting their names, syllable by syllable, in a songlike manner, like this:

*[breathe]* Mi-cha-el *[breathe and rest]*
*[breathe]* Ga-bri-el *[breathe and rest]*
*[breathe]* Ra-phae-el *[breathe and rest]*

*[breathe]* U-ri-el *[breathe and rest]*
*[breathe]* Ra-gu-el *[breathe and rest]*
*[breathe]* Cha-mu-el *[breathe and rest]*
*[breathe]* Re-mi-el *[breathe and rest]*

Breathe and chant each archangel's name repeatedly until you sense their presence. Don't hurry—just be patient. They will respond. You'll know they're with you because their vibration swooshes over you, giving you a chill or a rush.

If you have a specific request for *one* of the archangels, you can sing to that angel directly, chanting its name several times. Then ask for assistance.

Regardless of whether you want to invoke an individual archangel or the whole group of archangels, be sure that they know you mean business. Remember that God helps those who help themselves, so unless you're ready to make changes, not even the archangels can assist you. Their help is there when you are ready to grow, but making the change is up to you.

Archangels are the power-booster battery pack of your spiritual support team. They alone can catapult you forward, but only when you're ready to do so.

This reminds me of my client Heather, who wanted to tap into her creative writing ability and talked incessantly about writing a book "one day." As she broached the topic for the 164th time, I asked her why she hadn't started. She confided that while this was indeed her heart's desire, she couldn't seem to find the time or motivation to begin, although she'd written her book many times in her mind.

Since I'd been in Heather's "woulda, coulda, shoulda" writing shoes myself, I shared my secret of invoking Raphael to move me to action whenever I got stuck. Intrigued, she asked me to show her how, so I taught her to "chant him in" and asked her to let me know what happened.

Three months later, when I ran into her, I asked about her book progress. Heather rolled her eyes in response and said, "You can't imagine! Ever since I took your advice and chanted in Raphael to help me, I haven't missed a day of writing. Something greater than me gets me into my chair and won't let me go until I've written for at least an hour. I can't do another thing until I'm done. I'm actually birthing a book!"

"Yep, that's Raphael," I said. "Ask, but be sure that you mean it!"

That's the beauty of connecting with the archangels—they compel you to act and prevent you from wasting time. Unlike your guardian angel, who protects you and runs interference, archangels are the quarterbacks of your spiritual guidance team—they clear the way.

> *That's the beauty of connecting with the archangels—*
> *they compel you to act and prevent you from wasting time.*

## CREATING YOUR PROTECTIVE CUBE OF SPACE

My spiritual teacher, Charlie Goodman (whom I write about in my books *Diary of A Psychic* and *The Psychic Pathway*), taught me to perform the following daily ritual, surrounding myself in all six directions: above, below, front, back, left, and right, with archangels to protect and keep me safe and on my soul's path as I moved through each day.

I have done this ritual every single day since, not missing a day. Repeating this practice all these years has created an invincible energetic field of loving protection around me, which gives me the confidence to travel the world freely, knowing I am thoroughly protected and have absolutely nothing to fear. I want to share it now with you.

## Your Cube of Space Ritual

Look around the room, then breathe in deeply and slowly. Placing your tongue on the roof of your mouth to calm your thinking, now exhale fully, intentionally releasing all energy you are holding on to in your physical, emotional, and mental body, as if emptying the trash. Repeat this cleansing breath three times.

Next, take in another deep breath and then exhale with a loud sigh, as if going down a slide and ending at the base of your heart, the seat of your soul.

Next, chant in **Raphael**, *Ra-pha-el,* archangel of air and the mental plane, envisioning his color, electric green, as he responds to your call. Ask him to stand to your right and sweep through your energy field, right to left, front to back, and above and below, in all six directions, clearing you of all unwanted mental energy and leaving you entirely lucid as you begin your day.

Next, chant in **Michael**, *Mi-cha-el,* archangel of fire, envisioning his energy vibrating to the color electric blue. Ask him to watch your back and sweep in all six directions surrounding you, removing all threat of any disturbance or unwanted intrusion, and leaving you safe and secure this day.

Next, chant in **Gabriel,** *Ga-bri-el,* archangel of water and the emotional plane, vibrating to his color, brilliant white. Ask him to stand to your left and sweep through your energy, left to right, above and below, front to back, in all six directions, clearing you of all unwanted emotional energy and leaving you at peace.

Next, chant in **Uriel**, *U-ri-el,* archangel of the earth plane, vibrating to his color, ruby red. Ask him to stand in front of you and sweep through your energy, front to back, right to left, above and below, in all six directions, clearing any obstructions, bringing you blessings and abundance as you move through the day.

Next, chant in **Raguel,** *Ra-gu-el,* archangel above of harmony and justice, and vibrating to the color turquoise. Ask him to stand above you and sweep through your energy in all six directions, front to back, right to left, above and below, clearing the way and assuring calm, harmonious flow and order at the highest level throughout this day.

Next, chant in **Chamuel,** *Cha-mu-el,* archangel below of forgiveness, and vibrating to the color soft pink. Ask him to stand beneath you and sweep through your energy in all six directions, front to back, right to left, above and below, filling your heart with love, sweetness, generosity, compassion, and patience as you move through this day.

Next, chant in **Remiel,** *Re-mi-el,* archangel within of divine vision, intuition, and hope, vibrating to the color light spring green. Ask him to stand beside you this day and sweep through your energy from the inside out, in all six directions, front to back, right to left, above and below, activating your intuition, elevating your perceptions, shedding light and guidance on your path as you peacefully move throughout this day.

Next, chant in **Metatron,** *Me-ta-tron,* king of the archangels, higher in the hierarchy of angels than Raguel, vibrating to the color deep gold. Ask him to stand above Raguel above you and sweep through your energy in all six directions, clearing the way and helping you fulfill your purpose at the highest level this day. Let this intention include any known project or responsibility you may face as well as the unexpected.

Finally, chant in **Sandalphon,** *San-dal-phon,* archangel of the inner earth and Divine feminine, higher in hierarchy than Chamuel, vibrating to the colors violet and silver. Ask her to stand below you, supporting Chamuel and sweep through your energy, in all six directions, grounding you on your soul path and invoking the Earth spirits to support you throughout this day.

Then end with "So it is" and confidently begin your day.

Once I do this ritual, surrounded by my "archies" (as I lovingly call them) in all six directions, I venture into the world with confidence and energy to face anything life brings.

I invoke the archangels to accompany me onstage, when I work with private clients, when I travel, and when I write. I ask them to stand in the four corners of my home, and in every corner and above and below every hotel or place I stay when I travel. I ask the archangels to surround me at every moment of my life—and so should you.

Below is a link to my powerful 30-minute Cube of Space Morning Archangel Invocation. Sit quietly or lie down, and without interruption listen with headphones to this meditation in order to surround yourself with their loving protection, support, and guidance as you enter each day.

Visit https://www.hayhouse.com/downloads and enter the Product ID **1381** and Download Code **resources**. You can also visit http://www.soniachoquette.net.

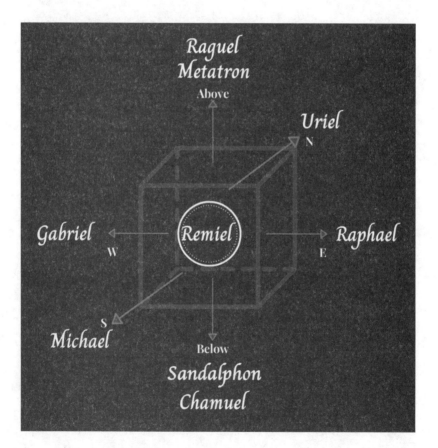

## Things to ask of the archangels

- Clear my mind
- Clear limiting beliefs
- Cut cords to the past
- Remove negative intrusions
- Watch my back
- Surround me with love
- Clear my emotions
- Release stuck patterns
- Let go of what isn't helping me
- Ground me
- Bring more prosperity
- Elevate my creativity
- Inspire me
- Increase my intuition
- Help me forgive and let go
- Activate my gifts
- Make me aware of my purpose
- Help me live in the moment

Now that you've learned how to connect with the archangels, let's move on and discover the ministry of angels.

# CHAPTER 6

# The Ministry of Angels

As a Divine Child of God, you are precious and loved, and therefore given an infinite number of angels to help you live a peaceful, prosperous, purposeful, and protected life.

Your angelic support system is composed of not only your personal guardian angel and power-packed archangels, but also what's known as the ministry of angels, who are available for specific assistance and support in virtually every area of your life.

Working with the ministry of angels makes life so much easier since they are "the bringers of goodness." They take great joy in bearing gifts, ushering surprises, delighting your senses, and easing your way. There are infinite departments in the angel ministry, such as parking, computers, shopping, sewing, traveling, office, healing, and so forth—where there's a need, there is a ministry of angels to serve. The ministry is available 24/7 and will mobilize into action immediately when called upon. The only stipulation is that your needs are benign and aren't harmful to anyone else. Beyond that, you are encouraged to fully engage and enjoy their blessings.

> *Working with the ministry of angels makes life so much easier since they are "the bringers of goodness."*

## THE MINISTRY AT WORK

I regularly call on the support of the ministry of "travel angels" because, due to my work teaching around the world, I travel over 100,000 miles a year. Being such a road warrior causes lots of physical wear and tear, not to mention emotional stress, and would be way too challenging to manage if I didn't have the support of the ministry of angels to rely on. They continuously work on my behalf to secure wonderful airplane seats; quiet, bright hotel rooms; delicious, healthy restaurants; patient, kind gate agents; excellent, safe taxi drivers; and kind people on the road. In other words, all the things that make travel a joy.

Just last month, they saved me again. This time, I was on my way from Paris to London via the Eurostar, a high-speed train that runs daily between the two cities.

Usually, taking the train to London from Paris is easy-peasy, and I never give it a second thought. As I was scheduled to teach a class in London in the late afternoon, I booked the first train of the day, allowing me more than three hours to drop off my bags at the hotel and have lunch before I had to get where I was going.

The company that had invited me to speak booked a premium class seat, which I very much appreciated. After stowing my bags, I settled in for a comfortable ride, firing up my computer, plugging in my phone charger, and putting on my headphones to listen to music. One minute later, an Italian family of three, including a toddler, descended upon me, the father asking if I would mind changing my seat with his, as their seats were not together, and because the two seats next to me were unoccupied it would allow them to sit next to one another. Of course, I agreed (even though his seat was in the next car).

Repacking and moving to a different seat, I began to settle in once more. Only to my dismay, the outlets at this new seat didn't work when I plugged in my computer. Because I had work to do and needed an outlet, I had to move *again*. Ugh!

The third time, I ended up seated next to a well-dressed older gentleman, who was extremely gracious when I asked if he minded if I sat next to him. We chatted for a few minutes, then both returned to our own worlds, me into my computer and he into his newspaper.

The train soon departed and off we went. That is, until an hour into the trip, when the train unexpectedly came to a screeching halt. Two minutes later, an announcement came over the loudspeaker.

The conductor informed us that the train had encountered a mechanical problem and had to be taken out of service immediately. We were told to gather our belongings, get off the train at the next stop, and wait there until we could board subsequent trains from Paris, as available seats allowed.

"Oh no," I groaned out loud to the gentleman next to me, "this is a nightmare. I'm going to miss my speaking engagement."

The gentleman remained serene and nonreactive upon hearing this announcement, then calmly summoned the porter who serviced our car. He quietly said to him, "I am a surgeon scheduled for surgery this afternoon. My assistant," he said, glancing at me, "and I must absolutely be on the next train. It's a matter of grave importance."

Understanding the doctor's urgency, the porter said, "Of course, monsieur doctor. I'll arrange this immediately." After he left, the doctor winked at me. "Stick with me. We will be on our way in no time."

And, sure enough, we were. As promised, the porter spirited us off the train, through the sea of hundreds of disgruntled and confused passengers on the platform, and into a private area designated for employees only. We were told to wait there until he returned, which would be soon. Fifteen minutes later, the train behind us pulled into the station. The porter immediately stepped into our waiting room and escorted us through the crowd to the front of the train and instructed us to quickly take any seat.

Not only did we painlessly get a seat on this new train but got first-class seats! Looking at the doctor, I said, "You are an earth angel! Thank you so much for helping me."

Smiling, he said, "That is not the first time I've been called this." I believed him.

Settling in, I instantly knew the ministry of travel angels were on the job, making sure I got to where I needed to go on time. I arrived in London and went on with my day as planned.

### Did You Know That . . .

- The ministry of angels are your foot soldiers.

- They are the deliverers of goodness.

- They attend to all of your needs.

- They serve you to please the Creator.

- They have a powerful, swift, laser-like vibration.

My mother taught me to work with the ministry by saying, "Put your angels on it and expect good things," whenever I needed help. Then she'd pause and say, "I expect to hear about those good things when you come home."

To this day, I call on my angels to help with whatever challenge is at hand. It's such a part of my life that I wouldn't dream of attempting to accomplish anything without their help—to do so would be like hitchhiking in the dark after being offered a first-class ride.

## YOUR TURN

Calling on the ministry of angels is simple—just open your heart and say, "Help." It is best to start with a short prayer, as with starting any undertaking, such as, "Ministry of angels, oversee all that I do and make it easy, magical, and filled with gifts. Thank you." Feel their presence as they swoop in to help. Better yet, give them the freedom to work on your behalf at all times by asking them to stay on permanent assignment. Just remember to thank them when you notice their good works bearing fruit in your life.

## Things to ask of the ministry of angels

- Help me get along with my neighbors
- Help me complete my project
- Help me accomplish my goal
- Lead me to the best people for my immediate need
- Make travel easy and safe
- Help communications go well
- Lead me toward open doors
- Help when I'm afraid
- Help me conceive a baby
- Help me attract love
- Help me through a divorce
- Help me find a job

Now that you've learned how to connect with the ministry of angels, let's move on and learn about the SOS angels.

# CHAPTER 7

# SOS Angels

When you run into big trouble and need super-powerful angels to help quickly, call in the SOS angels. They are the emergency workers of the angelic forces, on call and always ready to help. They will never let you down.

This past summer, my daughter Sabrina and her husband, Ahmed, a Ph.D. candidate, ran into an unexpected glitch with their visas. It looked like they were going to lose their right to stay in the U.K. in just eight short hours. Needless to say, it was highly anxiety-provoking, and no matter who they turned to for help, they were told there was simply no solution. It seemed that the university staff were the only ones who could help them. Unfortunately, it was summer, and most of the staff was on vacation. Sabrina and Ahmed had no option but to leave by midnight.

This was when Sabrina knew it was time to bring out the big guns: the SOS angels. It was scary to blindly put her trust in them, in the face of such a dire situation, but she knew her request would be answered.

True to their reputation, and just hours before the visa renewal deadline, the SOS angels did come through. Out of the blue, Sabrina was spontaneously inspired to turn on her computer and contact an immigration lawyer she randomly found online. In the moment this felt like a desperate move (it was), but to her relief, this particular lawyer (unlike the 10 previous lawyers she and Ahmed had already spoken with) immediately thought of a little-known loophole that could get their visas extended until the university staff returned and could sort things out for them. It was a miracle.

The lawyer patiently stayed on the phone with Sabrina and her husband for two hours, guiding them through the entire process of correctly filling out the tricky online application and sending it in, with only *minutes* to spare before they ran out of time. Once the visa extension application was submitted, they had the legal right to stay. The crisis was averted. Talk about an SOS angel save!

The key to working with SOS angels is to have absolute faith that they will help, and try your best to keep calm and grounded while they wield their magic. Breathe. Meditate. Expect help. Don't dwell on the problem. Get quiet and listen for inner instructions. They will come, and you will be helped. Guaranteed.

---

*The key to working with SOS angels is to have absolute faith that they will help, and try your best to keep calm and grounded while they wield their magic.*

---

SOS angels are never far away. Just when you think you have been abandoned and there is no hope in sight, they show up. My client Mathew was born with failing kidneys, and by the time he was 41 it was clear that he needed a kidney transplant if he hoped to live a full life.

The search for a donor had begun at home years earlier, and so he knew that his long-estranged brother was the match he needed. Even though they hadn't spoken in years, Mathew was optimistic when he picked up the phone and called to ask. His brother was unmoved and said, "No, I don't want to," and hung up on him. It felt like a kick in the gut for Mathew to be turned away so coldly.

When he called me, time was ticking, and Mathew was afraid. His health was deteriorating, and there was no donor in sight. I told Mathew to call upon his SOS angels and ask for their help. He had never heard of such angels but didn't question me for a moment. I told him I would do the same and we prayed for help together.

Two days later, Mathew called me. Another donor appeared out of nowhere and agreed to help him, no strings attached. "It's a miracle, Sonia. I don't know this guy at all, or how he heard that I needed a kidney. The doctor's office just called to tell me," he said in amazement. "The doctor had no more information than I do on where the donor came from. I can't explain how this happened, but I'm just grateful it did. We are beginning the process of preparing today, and hopefully in a month I'll be as good as new."

After the transplant Mathew found out that his younger sister had been looking for years and years to find a donor for Mathew, anticipating that their brother would not agree. She was the one who had located a donor.

The transplant was a success, and Mathew has a new lease on life. "I'm a believer," he said when we last spoke. "It was the SOS angels that brought my transplant about. I didn't ask questions. I just said thank you. They saved my life."

**Have you had an SOS angel experience?**
**Share it here:**

_____

_____

_____

_____

**Do you know anyone else who has had an SOS angel experience?**
**Share it here:**

_____

_____

_____

_____

## Things to ask of an SOS angel

- Help me with this emergency
- Help me pay this bill
- Help me survive this accident
- Help me get through this lawsuit
- Help me get the loan I need
- Help me through this surgery
- Help my loved one through their crisis
- Help me stay grounded through this loss

Now that you've learned how to connect with the SOS Angels, let's move on to learning how to integrate angels into your daily life.

# CHAPTER 8

# Calling All Angels

Call to mind each one of the different types of angels, then pause to feel the subtle energy of that particular angelic frequency. Sense with your heart and imagination, not your intellect. Notice the peace and calm that washes over you as you tune in to each angelic vibration and enjoy the intricate and beautiful collection of energies surrounding you on a nonphysical level.

Call on all your angels all the time. Become sensitive to their presence. Close your eyes right now and sense your guardian angel standing nearby. Are they on your left? Right? Across the room or just behind you? (Most of the time, I sense my angel, Flash, at my right side; however, when I'm doing personal readings, he's between me and my client).

Next, focus on the archangels and notice how much more intense from regular angels their vibration is. Can you sense their loving but powerful strength? Are they all around? In one area of the room over another? Trust what you feel and say so. Then, sense the subtle differences between the individual archangels. For example, Michael has an intense, warrior-like energy, while Gabriel's energy is peaceful and calming. Again, trust your feelings, and don't let your ego interfere by suggesting that this is all nonsense and that you are making it up. You are sensing your angels with the help of your imagination, since spirit connects with you through your imagination. Nevertheless, it's still a real perception—it's just different from the kind of energy you are used to acknowledging.

Now imagine the vibration of the ministry of angels. Notice the subtle differences between a guardian angel, an archangel, and the ministry of angels. These "intuitive sit-ups" I'm suggesting get you into the habit of noticing angels with various levels of vibration. With practice, your perception of the angelic realm will soon become as clear as identifying different textures, scents, or sounds. You are just awakening a part of your awareness that has been asleep.

## Be Grateful

To remain connected to your angels, regularly and automatically thank them, preferably out loud, for all the behind-the-scenes help and support they offer you. Name as many things as you can think of that you are grateful for in your life. It is so tempting to ignore these wonderful aspects of your life and focus on disappointments and lack; however, this habit of negativity blocks your ability to connect with angels and receive their help.

I know that being grateful might be challenging when nothing feels as though it is going well. But if you are too negative, you tune your angels out. When I say negative, I am not talking about the occasional down mood we feel when life gets tough. I am referring to having a chronically negative outlook. Regularly acknowledging your blessings will break the cycle of negativity and is essential if you want to connect with your angels.

Even better, thank your angels in advance for the good things yet to come your way. Like a child expecting presents at Christmas, fully expect the angels will take care of your future, no matter what, because they will. Have absolute confidence in your angels and place your well-being fully in their care, expecting only the best outcomes in every area. You won't be disappointed if you do.

> *Have absolute confidence in your angels and place your well-being*
> *fully in their care, expecting only the best outcomes in every area.*

## YOUR TURN

For the next several days or weeks, focus on feeling your angelic forces and get accustomed to their loving and supportive nonstop presence. Practice noticing these energies several times each day until you feel as though you've "clicked" into them.

One at a time, as though practicing scales on a piano, identify the vibration of each of the following:

- Your spirit
- The spirits of those around you
- Your guardian angel
- The archangels
- The ministry of angels
- SOS angels

Now that you have become comfortably familiar with angels and how they help you, we'll move to the next spiritual level of support and direction—your spirit guides.

# PART III

# PREPARING
# TO MEET YOUR
# SPIRIT GUIDES

# CHAPTER 9

# Frequently Asked Questions about Your Spirit Guides

In addition to your angels, you have an infinite number of divine helpers on the Other Side known as "spirit guides." These guides are as varied as the people in your life and serve all kinds of short- and long-term purposes. If you imagine that your angels are your heavenly bodyguards and foot soldiers, then your spirit guides are your volunteer corps—reserves who are ready, willing, and able to serve as needed for specific assignments when called upon.

Several questions inevitably arise when it comes to the subject of spirit guides, and the answers can be very specific, depending upon the particular guides in question. This chapter will serve as your crash course in spirit guides, answering the most-asked questions and laying a foundation for the more detailed explanations that will unfold as you're introduced to the different types of spirit guides in the next section of the book.

To begin with, here are the four most commonly asked questions regarding spirit guides:

## 1. What's the difference between angels and spirit guides?

There are several essential differences between angels and spirit guides that include everything from their experience (or lack thereof) in human form, to their purpose, the level of involvement they can have in our lives, and the way that they communicate with us.

For example, while angels have never had an earthbound experience, most spirit guides have had at least one, so they understand firsthand the particular trials and challenges that we face as humans. Consequently, they're available to us when we need them to encourage and assist us, and to teach us how to grow our soul and master our creativity in human form.

The key words here are "when we need them." Unlike angels, who are on a Divine assignment from God to serve us around the clock from the beginning to the end of our lives, and to influence us every day (whether we're aware of them or not), spirit guides, although available, can't serve or direct us without our permission. They can (and do) often succeed in catching our attention and getting us to ask for their help, but they must respect that it's our life and they can't enter it without an invitation.

Finally, angels have a much higher vibration than guides, since they're so close to God, and they're easy to connect to. They protect, inspire, energize, empower, and help us, but they don't necessarily offer direct advice or instruction, which is what our spirit guides do.

## 2. Who are your spirit guides?

Since most spirit guides are beings who've lived at least some part of their existence on Earth, it's not surprising that they've come back to serve us. In fact, guides often connect with us because they have had similar challenges in their earthly lives and want to offer guidance based on their own history to ease our way. Others show up to help us with specific projects or tasks because in their past lives they were experienced, even masters, in the area we're working on at any given time, so they can teach us something.

Spirit guides may be family members who've crossed over but elect to stay connected with us from the spirit plane, offering comfort, direction, and help until we meet them on the Other

Side. Similarly, some guides may have shared a personal relationship or did spiritual work with us in this or past lives, and they want to continue working with us in this life, too, in order to contribute to the continuing enrichment of our soul's experience, as well as their own.

Spiritual teacher guides are some of our most influential guides—they help us learn our soul lessons. At times these guides work individually with us. Other times they show up as teaching councils or as groups of wise elders and master teachers all working with us at once.

Scouts and runner guides are spirits who've lived very close to the earth in past incarnations, such as Native Americans or Aboriginal Peoples. They help us find things of all sorts. They also help us reconnect with nature, including getting out of our heads and reconnecting with our bodies, which are part of the natural world. They help us become more grounded and present, which helps us find what we are looking for.

Light beings from other parts of the Universe (who, consequently, have not had earthly lives) assist in elevating our consciousness as a species. There are many light beings presently working with us to end some of the worst human challenges we face in these times, including climate change, nationalism, and the pervasive unconscious tendency to view others as different and therefore inferior or dangerous. Light beings are working to help clear these false perceptions and replace them with the ability to see the truth: we are all one, connected in spirit, here to learn to love ourselves and others unconditionally. Many of these elevated light beings come from other solar systems. This is why we are hearing of so many more UFO sightings. These light beings are showing up more and more to help us turn our planet around and back to health before it is too late.

Healer guides assist in keeping us healthy in body, mind, and soul. We have both individual healer guides as well as healing teams, groups of guides who work to balance our thoughts, relieve our emotions of stale and toxic stagnation, open our hearts and forgive the past, as well as better care for our physical bodies.

Then there are inner world spirit guides, who help us recover any soul loss experienced as a result of emotional trauma along the way. We even have animal spirit guides who accompany, guide, and lead us on our soul journey through this life.

While we have access to all of these loving spirit helpers, the most valuable guide any of us has is our own Divine Higher Self. All the other angels and guides are here to assist in leading us to this awareness above all.

## 3. Where do spirit guides come from?

Spirit guides come from many different realms and energy fields. There are guides who were once human and now help from the spirit realm, guides assisting from higher dimensions, guides from the natural world, and also many guides now entering the field from other galaxies and solar systems—some of which have never had physical bodies—who are connecting with us to help restore the planet to balance and peace.

## 4. How many spirit guides do we have?

Charlie Goodman taught me that people generally have at least 33 guides (excluding their angels) working with us at any given time, but we have an infinite number of guides to call upon whenever we need help. The more we grow our consciousness and raise our vibration, the higher the number of guides working with us will be, all assisting us in accomplishing our life purpose and achieving our personal life and soul goals.

For example, I first began working with just two guides when I was a very young child, one whom I called Dot because I experienced her as a bright blue dot of light in my mind's eye (I believe she is my Higher Self), and another named Rose, whom I mentioned earlier in the book. Rose is my primary soul companion, and I've discovered that she and I have shared past lives.

Around the age of 12, I connected with another guide named Joseph, with whom I also shared a past life as an Essene. He comes and goes, but he's always nearby to help me when I need him in deep spiritual growth matters, and funnily enough, with travel. I believe this is because the travel he helps me with is usually related to my teaching commitments around the world.

As I got older and my soul continued to evolve, I became aware of several new spirit guides, this time spirit teachers. The first three were French bishops associated with the Rosicrucians, a secret mystery school formed in the Middle Ages. They were my teachers in several shared past lives spanning the time between the Middle Ages and the early 1800s.

Two additional teachers, feminine spirit guides that appeared in my early twenties, are from another galaxy. I call them the "Pleiadean Sisters." I feel that I've had no past-life connection with them. They have simply come to assist me as I teach people to understand their life's purpose and keep their hearts open, in spite of past pain.

Eventually, I attracted the support of another group of guides who call themselves the "Emissaries of the Third Ray, Second Octave of Love." These guides appear as blue beings, and both teach and heal. They have come to teach me and others how to raise our vibrations. This group of guides doesn't work with individuals. They generally prefer to speak *through* me to my classes. They also send healing transmissions through me to help shift the students in my classes to a higher, more heart-centered, less intellectual focus.

These transmissions are the equivalent of what happens when you attach a jumper cable between one car with a dead battery and another with a full charge to transmit enough juice to get the dead battery to turn over and get going again. Many people's heart chakras are "dead batteries" due to pain, trauma, heartbreak, disappointment, addiction, and suffering, so they shut down. The Emissaries transmit enough higher vibration through me to open their hearts once again.

## GUIDES COME AND GO

While you generally accumulate more guides as you progress through life, the cast of characters changes depending on where you are in your soul journey. Over the years, I've had many guides—mainly teachers and healers—who've appeared for a time and then left to allow new entities to take their place as my life challenges shifted and evolved. This happens all the time—it's like a revolving door!

We all attract and change guides over time. It's much like changing teachers as we move up from one grade level to another in school. Life is our greatest school, and the Universe provides the appropriate teachers and teaching assistants we need to succeed at each level we are in by way of our different spirit guides.

The guides love us. They are here to serve. And they want us to succeed in every way. They show up to help us grow in every endeavor we choose to involve ourselves in. When their work is done, they move on.

For example, my friend Peter is an actor and writer. Early in his writing career, he attracted the support of a spirit guide named Walter, who showed up to help him write comedy.

Peter first sensed Walter's presence while working in his study late one evening. Stuck and feeling uninspired, he said out loud, "Come on. I need help!" Suddenly, out of the blue, Peter started writing some funny one-liners for the play he was working on at the time.

Surprised, and laughing at what he had just spontaneously written, Peter asked, "Where is this coming from?" A second later, he sensed a voice in his heart saying, "Good evening, Peter. I'm Walter. Happy to help."

Walter had a wild sense of humor, and with his help, the play started to come together. From that point onward, Peter asked Walter for help every time he sat down to work on the play, and he got it. Shortly after finishing the script, Peter no longer felt Walter's presence. Apparently, Walter's work was done, so he moved on.

A few years later, Peter began working on presenting a TED Talk. A new guide showed up to help him, a vaudevillian actor from the 1920s named Lenny. Every time Peter practiced his talk, he felt Lenny by his side, like a speaking coach, offering tips on timing and body language, and even what he was saying. As before, once Peter's TED Talk was over, Lenny was on his way.

My friend Lee had many helpful spirit guides help her get through her rigorous Ph.D. program in religious studies in Denver. Her primary spirit guide was named Leo. He helped her research altar practices over the ages, directing Lee's attention to obscure books, articles, websites, and other resources that proved invaluable to her work.

She also felt the presence and support of a guide named Dr. Chen, an ancient Chinese Buddhist philosopher who showed up when Lee started researching ancient Buddhist temple practices. She also attracted a sweet Mexican child guide named Manu, who appeared one day when Lee was researching Día de Muertos (the Day of the Dead). Manu was a happy little guide who kept Lee's spirits up when her Ph.D. work was nearly crushing her. Shortly after Lee presented her dissertation and was granted her doctorate, all three of these guides slipped away.

I have a client named Gloria who took up painting recently, a long-held interest that she finally decided to make time for once her children were out of the house. She enrolled in a local painting class. On the first day of class, Gloria was asked to start painting so that the instructor could gauge her level of skill. Terrified of embarrassing herself, Gloria quietly prayed for help. Within moments she felt a warm presence standing to her left side and the name "Alexander" popped into her head. She didn't hear him—she *felt* him reassuring her the entire time she worked. Soon her fear of embarrassment lifted and she became lost in the process. She completely forgot about impressing the instructor and loved every minute of her class. Alexander's warm and reassuring energy took away her fear and gave her the confidence she needed to carry on.

Gloria is still painting and still senses Alexander with her. She also told me of another spirit guide named Cyrus who showed up to help with her self-esteem. Cyrus must be a joy guide or a healer or both, as he helps Gloria to not be so hard on herself, something she has struggled with her entire life as a perfectionist. Since Cyrus showed up, Gloria has found it easier to openly laugh at her mistakes and move on. "It's a miracle," she said, "because I have been so critical of myself all my life and felt so ashamed all the time. Now I don't. I'm better!"

My older sister Cuky works with many guides who were family members she was very close to as a child growing up in Denver, especially Grandma and Grandpa Choquette and our great-aunt Emma Bernard, all of whom keep her spirit light, loving, and laughing.

As a healer herself, Cuky has also attracted some excellent healing guides, including several ancient Hawaiian and Polynesian healers and warriors with whom she's shared past lives. These entities appear in her healing room, where she consults with clients, and she channels them through her body as she works to clear past psychic debris and free her clients' spirits of toxic emotional baggage.

### Did You Know That . . .

- Guides can be helpers, healers, teachers, runners, past-life connections, family members, extraterrestrial beings from other galaxies, and even animals.

- You have the right to ask only for the highest guides, and when you do, you're under no obligation to listen to any guidance that doesn't feel right or good to you.

- The more open you are to your guides and their help, the better your life will be.

- The only function of guides is to offer their support to you.

Keep in mind that some spirit guides are better than others, so it's essential to ask to work only with the best ones possible. Whether in a body or not, we're all on a journey toward higher consciousness, and we, therefore, need to remember that just because someone has crossed over into spirit and wants to serve as a guide doesn't necessarily mean that he or she is instantly enlightened.

> *When connecting with your guides, be clear about your intentions and remember that your life is your responsibility, not to be turned over to any guide to run for you.*

This reminds me of my client Amy's mother, Maria, who crossed over into spirit and was serving Amy as a guide. Although Amy was thrilled beyond belief to once again feel connected to her mother, she soon realized that Maria was nearly as cautious and fearful as a spirit as she'd been when she was alive. Every time Amy wanted to take a trip or do something adventurous or indulgent, she asked her mother for guidance and would instantly feel her replying, "Be careful!" or "My, that's expensive!" instead of, "Go for it. Enjoy!"

"I fought with her fears throughout my entire life," Amy told me, exasperated. "Now I feel that she'll bug me into infinity!"

Laughing, but sympathetic, I replied, "Why don't you simply stop asking for your mother's guidance and just ask for her love? Body or spirit, she's still the mother that you know and love— and if you're going to ask her opinion, don't be surprised when you get it!"

When connecting with your guides, be clear about your intentions and remember that your life is your responsibility, not to be turned over to any guide to run for you.

You can tell if a guide is from an elevated vibration (and is worth listening to) because they don't interfere or tell you what to do even when you want them to do precisely that. High spiritual guides understand that they're not there to run your life in any way (nor should you let them), and that you're here on the earthly plane attending "spiritual school" to learn to claim your Divine creative power.

Guides are like coaches on a sports team, or teachers in a classroom. They'll do all they can to help you, but they won't play the game or do your homework *for* you. They share what they know, make suggestions, draw your attention to things you've missed, and point you toward success, but they will never take over and run your life for you.

YOUR TURN

Getting to know your guides and learning to work with them will add magic to your life and will help relieve your stress. They want to assist you whenever they can and are simply waiting for you to invite them to get involved.

The best way to begin connecting with your spirit guides is to spend some time thinking about the areas of your life in which they can best be of service. Take an inventory of your life and figure out which areas are working and which aren't. Make a mental or written list of what you'd like to experience that you aren't experiencing now. Where are you most interested in gaining spiritual guidance? What endeavors or disciplines would you most like assistance exploring? The more specific, the better. Once you've decided where you'd like spiritual support, we'll discuss the steps that are necessary to connect with the guides who can help you accomplish your goals.

Your guides can help you with

- Soul gro wth
- Clearing karma
- Supporting your soul purpose

- Connecting you with loving and supportive relationships
- Love life
- Bringing in prosperity
- Solving problems
- Keeping you healthy
- Emergencies
- Business decisions
- Real estate
- Releasing the past
- Work

## Make a list of the top five things you'd like your guides to help you with now

- _____
- _____
- _____
- _____
- _____

Below is link to a channeled 40-minute deep meditative journey for invoking new guides and releasing past ones. Use this meditation when you feel ready to grow, change directions in life, start a new path, embark on a new project, or simply feel intuitively called to summon new support from your ever-ready divine crew.

Visit https://www.hayhouse.com/downloads and enter the Product ID **1381** and Download Code **resources**. You can also visit http://www.soniachoquette.net.

Now that you've been primed in working with spirit guides, let's move on and learn how to call in your guides for help directly.

# CHAPTER 10

# Getting Ready to Meet Your Spirit Guides

Now that you know you have access to a variety of beautiful spirit guides, it is time to connect with them directly. Following is your step-by-step guide for doing so.

## STEP #1: BE OPEN TO GUIDANCE

This first step may seem like an obvious one: be open to receiving guidance. It's so obvious, in fact, that whenever I ask my clients and students if they are open to guidance, most act as if I'm crazy and insist that, of course, they're totally open—why else would they be talking to me or reading books like this? While you may *feel* you're open, I've observed in my experience as an intuitive guide and teacher that it may not be quite that simple.

Over the year, I've passed along countless advice from guides to clients that would clearly ease their way, only to watch more than a few totally ignore or reject the guidance that was offered. I've also watched clients take copious notes during their readings only to leave their notebooks behind . . . and *never come back for them later!*

I've had clients talk nonstop through an entire session, hardly leaving space or opportunity to receive any guidance whatsoever, preferring just to hear themselves speak. Now, there's nothing wrong with that—but it's something quite different from being open to guidance.

I've even been guilty of ignoring spiritual guidance myself—such as the time when I asked my guides about a very talented new friend whom I really enjoyed and wanted to work with. The guides cautioned me, sending the distinct vibe that it wasn't a good idea to work together, saying she was someone who would want to take all the credit for herself. I didn't want to hear it, so I ignored my guides' input. I also ignored the advice of my sisters, my friends, and even my kids, all of whom said that working with this woman would end up being a problem. I was stubborn to a fault and didn't listen to anyone. I was so unavailable to anything other than my own opinion that I tuned everyone out. In the end, they were right. It was disaster. Guides may offer help, but we ultimately learn the way we choose to learn. This was a lesson I needed to learn the hard way.

So, as you can see, it can be extremely challenging to be open to guidance and support once we've set our sights on certain things. In our single-mindedness, we may not even realize we are blocking support.

When I was a child, clients came to see my mother for intuitive readings in our dining room on Saturday afternoons. During those sessions, I often heard my mom first ask, "Do you really want guidance today, or do you just want me to agree with you?" before their reading began. They would laugh, but it was a good question.

Observing people intimately for as long as I have, I actually believe the honest answer to this question for most people would be, "I want you to agree with me," which unfortunately the guides can't and won't do. They can reassure you, support you, direct you, and offer solutions, but they will never lie to you or mislead you. That is, of course, if they are spirit guides of the highest vibration, which is the only kind of guide we are interested in attracting or working with.

So, before asking your guides for help, check in with yourself to see if you are open to receiving input other than what you want to hear. We humans can be fixed and stubborn creatures who get so attached to our perceptions and beliefs that we automatically tune out the rest. Unless we are open to hearing, sensing, or being shown something new and perhaps uncomfortable, very little of the tremendous support available from our guides will get through to us.

Asking your guides for input is really no different than asking for advice from anyone else. Unless you are honestly open to receiving help, no matter how good it is, it will go in one ear and out the other and do you no good at all. Eventually your guide will tire of being tuned out and move on.

Our guides are here to offer support and assistance but will never intrude. They are not authorities to follow and submit to. They are loving friends in the spirit realm who respect and honor your authority over your life and just want to be of assistance when you *do* want guidance. It is up to you when that is.


## STEP #2: BE QUIET AND LISTEN

Spirit guidance comes in wisps and glimmers of energy that gently bring our attention to something we are missing as we move through each day. These alerts are so subtle in most cases that it's easy to miss them altogether unless you pay attention to your feelings, notice the signs, and make space in your consciousness when they do appear. If you are rushing about, preoccupied, always talking or overthinking, you will drown out guidance. This means it is best to slow down, pause, and quiet your thoughts regularly, so you are available to more than your noisy, reactive brain.

The best way to hear guidance is to be quiet for at least a few minutes every day. I recommend adopting a meditation practice. There are many ways to do this, and even apps on your phone available to help you get started. The easiest way to meditate is to simply follow your breath, like this:

Breathe in for four counts.
Hold for four counts
Exhale for four counts.
Hold for four counts.

Repeat 10 times.

This calms the mind and helps you become quiet inside. Even a few relaxing breaths re-centers you in your heart and helps you listen to how you *feel* instead of what you *think*.

Meditating every day is like sitting with a beloved and trusted friend. Your friend (your Higher Self, God, the Universe, your guides, and angels) knows you very well and already understands your problems. You don't have to explain, defend, or say a thing to clue them in on what's happening with you. They are with you all the time. They know better than you already. And they want to bring relief, insight, understanding, direction, solution, and healing—and will, if you *listen*. And you do this by sitting quietly and focusing on your breath.

Here are a few more simple things you can do to train yourself to listen deeply so that you may better receive spirit guidance.

## Try This

### DEEP LISTENING

To deepen your ability to listen to the spirit realm, close your eyes and listen to a favorite piece of calming, classical music without interruption. Choose a piece that speaks to your heart and try to pick out the various instruments in the composition. As you lose yourself in the music, don't be surprised if sudden guidance and insight tumble into your mind. This is what Einstein did to get guidance. It worked for him and can work for you, too.

## Try This

### EMPTY THE GARBAGE

This is one of my favorite tools for tuning in to spirit guidance.

Sit quietly and look around you.

Notice one or two physical things right before your eyes. Take your time and do more than a drive-by glance. Breathe deeply, slowly, and really focus on these things one at a time. Sense their weight, color, depth. With your eyes, wonder how they would feel if you were to touch them. Would the object feel smooth? Rough? Bumpy? Imagine if you were to try and pick up this object. How heavy would it feel? Would it be warm to the touch or cold? Is each item soft or hard?

Continue to breathe slowly and deeply as you do this. Once you complete this outer exploration, shift your attention to your inner world. Again, notice how you *feel* inside. Without engaging in *why* you feel the way you do, simply sense the feelings themselves. Do you feel anxious? Is your energy heavy? Agitated? Restless? Or is it calm and relaxed? Do you feel tense? Open? Defensive? Available? At ease?

Avoid judging how you feel. It doesn't matter. It is only energy. Just observe how the energy you are holding on to *feels* as you hold on to it.

Once you take this pulse of your inner world, inhale again, slowly. Then, exhale as if you are blowing out many candles until there is no more air to expel, and with that, imagine emptying yourself of all this energy in your body, as if emptying the trash.

When your exhalation is complete and all the air is out, again inhale *slowly*. Once you can no longer take more breath in, hold it for a quick three seconds, and then exhale fully with a deep, loud, relaxing sigh.

Then breathe normally and smile.

You will notice that your mind is quiet and completely calm now and allows you to listen without distraction. Continue to breathe in this relaxed state of inner peace, with eyes either open or closed, and turn your attention to your heart. Don't look for words. Listen for feeling. Be patient and don't force a thing. You may not feel a thing. If this is true, enjoy the peace.

You may not sense guidance immediately, but like clearing a room of old junk and clutter, you are creating space inside your being to eventually receive guidance throughout the day as it comes. This daily three-minute effort trains you to switch into a listening state of mind and be more available to spirit guidance when it does appear.

---

*You may not sense guidance immediately, but like clearing a room of old junk and clutter, you are creating space inside your being to eventually receive guidance throughout the day as it comes.*

---

## Try This

### CHANGE THE CHANNEL

One of my favorite tools is "changing the channel." To do so, simply say: *My head says [fill in the blank] in response to your question or concern.* Then pause and follow with: *My heart and inner guide says [fill in the blank] in response to the same question or concern.* This exercise changes the channel of your awareness from your mental chatter to inner guidance.

For example

I am wondering if I should start my own restaurant business.

*My head says . . . "It is risky to do this!"*
*My head says . . . "You have no guarantee it will work."*
*My head says . . . "How will I know I will survive?"*

*My heart says . . . "You love cooking and others love what you create!"*
*My heart says . . . "Trust your calling. You've been considering this for years for a reason."*
*My heart says . . . "Go for it! You are ready. Others will help and it will make you happy."*

Notice how your head leaves you feeling stressed and fearful. Then notice how what your heart says leaves you feeling open and relaxed. Your heart is the gateway to the truth inside you. The more you ask your heart for guidance, the better the decisions you make will be.

Your head (or in other words, your ego) is trying to protect you, but instead often just boxes you into a life you don't want. Your heart (or in other words, your spirit) opens the door to a new and more authentic, creative, guided experience. It does present a risk to your ego, but it brings with it the gift and promise of the ability to manifest a more authentic meaningful life.

## STEP #3: SINCERELY ASK FOR HELP

As I've already stated earlier, another powerful way to receive guidance is to ask for it, often and always. You can ask in any way that you like, since any ask is a personal conversation with God, the Universe, and all of God's helpers. The more you ask for help, the less you control, and the more you allow divine energy in to help you. The more you ask, the higher and higher your own frequency becomes, as well, making it easier to connect to your guides.

When you listen to your ego, it's like being tuned in to an AM radio broadcast. When you ask for guidance and listen to your heart and spirit, your receptive bandwidth significantly increases, allowing you to receive a much higher transmission, as if logging on to the Internet with its infinite channels of guidance, as opposed to mental "talk radio."

The more you ask, the more expansive your receptive bandwidth becomes, until you become a satellite, receiving divine guidance all the time as you gracefully flow through life.

When asking for help, you bare your heart and soul to your Creator, who lovingly listens and brings relief. Do remember to thank God and the Universe for all of the blessings in your life as well. Prayers of gratitude raise your frequency most because they open your heart and focus on the love and support you have in your life.

One of my favorite ways to ask for help is with this prayer:

> *Creator of the Universe and all forms and expressions that support the goodness of life, thank you for [fill in the blank] that You have blessed me with today. Guide me this day to use my talents at the highest level for the greatest good for all concerned. Amen.*

## STEP #4: LET THE SPIRIT MOVE YOU

Being movable means being open and receptive to acting on the guidance you receive, when you receive it, and not resisting what you are urged to do. Surprising as it may seem, being active and physically moving your body every day helps with this, whether it be by walking, running, swimming, biking, skateboarding, dancing, Hula-Hooping, skiing, surfing, or climbing, especially outdoors. Such physical activity helps you be available when the sprit guides move you to do something quickly with no time to think it over. This type of guided impulse might include being nudged to take a sudden turn off the road you are on because your guides want you to avoid an unknown traffic jam ahead. By acting on this impulse, you make it to work on time. If you had resisted it, you would have been late.

There's another reason why being physically flexible and active is quite helpful—even *essential*—to spiritual connection. Our minds tend to become easily fixed and selective, and quickly block things out that do not align with our established point of view. Our spirit, on the other hand, is fluid and introduces more into our awareness than our intellect can tune in to or does accept. The more we move our bodies, the more responsive to spirit we become, and the more open to new information we become, thus, we are more guidable as well.

I can't tell you the number of times my guides have given me a slight nudge here or there, inviting me to make a sudden or unexpected move that ultimately spared me trouble and kept me in the flow. If I weren't both mentally and physically agile and open to acting on guided impulses, I might have ignored and thus lost out on these opportunities presented.

## Family Vacation

Many summers ago, my family of four, along with two friends, were on our way from Chicago to Paris for our annual two-week summer vacation. The airport was packed as it was the height of summer travel, and excitement and a fair amount of stress were in the air. At the gate, I stood watching the previous passengers deplane when suddenly, out of nowhere, I had an overwhelming urge to switch to another flight. Recognizing this as assistance from my spirit guides, I didn't hesitate to question the feeling and did as I was guided to do.

I immediately stepped out of line and, without saying a word to anyone, approached the agent's desk and said, "Hi. I know this is an unusual request, but would you mind checking to see if I can exchange my family's tickets on this flight for another flight?"

The agent looked at me as if I was crazy, having just handed me the six boarding passes only moments earlier. "What do you mean? I just gave you seats on this flight and it will be boarding in a few minutes."

"I know," I responded, not knowing exactly why I was asking, but certain that the guidance I had received was for a good reason. "But still, I'd like us to go on another flight, please."

Shaking her head and dismissing me outright, she said, "Absolutely not. You have seats on this flight. That's all there is to it. Now please step aside as I have to prepare to board."

"I understand," I replied. "But since I am a premier passenger, I have the right to ask. I know this is highly unusual, but would you please humor me and check anyway?" Then I smiled again and stood firm.

Understandably stressed because the inbound passengers had now almost entirely deplaned and she would soon have other things to do, she made it perfectly clear that she didn't want to look. "It's the middle of July," she argued. "Every single seat to Paris in all of North America is fully booked. There are no alternatives. It's this flight or nothing."

Unmoved by her refusal to accommodate me, I persisted. "Would you mind looking anyway, and I'll stand here and pray?" I asked, thinking the whole time, *She must think I'm insane, and I don't blame her.* Still, knowing from experience that what I felt was not to be ignored, I stood in the fire of my request.

Seeing that I wasn't going to give up until she checked for alternative flights, she relented. She started pounding on her computer keys to let me know what she thought of my ridiculous request and half-heartedly checked for other flights.

"The later flight to Paris from here is fully booked," she said definitively. "I know that already. So I'm not even going to look." Banging on a few more computer keys and staring at the screen in silence for 10 seconds, she continued, not once looking at me. "As I thought, the flight through Newark is full. So are the flights through Montreal and Atlanta." She slammed a few more keys, continuing to stare at the screen in silence as I stood and prayed.

Shaking her head in exasperation that I was insisting that she do this, and now of all times, she looked for another few seconds at the screen, then said triumphantly, "No. There are no flights anywhere to accommodate you today. Changing your tickets at this point is *not* possible. And highly unnecessary," she added, raising her eyebrows to let me know this was a complete waste of time.

By now, my family, still in line, was watching, not knowing what I was up to, but used to my unexpected departure from routine at times.

I smiled at the agent to try and relieve her annoyance but stood firm in my request. I knew from a lifetime of experience that I was being guided and made the choice to trust my vibes.

She was about to tell me to board this flight or go home, clearly having lost all patience with me as she now had to prepare to board, when the captain of the plane emerged from the jetway. He approached her and whispered into her ear loudly enough for me to hear, "I'm sorry to tell you this, but this aircraft is experiencing a mechanical problem and is being taken out of service. It isn't going anywhere. We have to cancel the flight."

Shocked when she heard this, her eyes popped wide open, and she stared incredulously at me. "How did you know?" She gasped, not sure what to think.

I shrugged and said, "I was guided by my angel to ask for another flight, so I did."

"Unbelievable!" she muttered, shaking her head in amazement and confusion. Now hammering energetically on the computer keys in rapid-fire, she stopped after fifteen seconds, stared at the computer screen to confirm what she was seeing, then pushed the print button. "I don't know who you are or how you knew this flight was not going tonight, but I *am* impressed. I found six seats on the 9 P.M. flight after all. It's a miracle, but you called it. Now take these boarding passes and get out of here because in just a moment, complete chaos is going to break out when these two hundred other passengers learn this flight is canceled. Now go!"

I grabbed the boarding passes she handed me without looking at them, thanking her profusely. Then I signaled my family and friends to follow me. Not missing a beat, they stepped out of line and ran behind. Fifty feet away from the gate, as she announced the flight cancellation to the crowd, I turned and said, "I got us seats on the 9 P.M. flight. My guides told me to ask for them ten minutes ago, so I did. Thank God I got the memo before the flight was canceled, or we wouldn't be going tonight at all!" As I started handing out the new passes, I saw there were five coach seats in my hand and one in first class.

"Thank you, angels. Thank you, guides!"

## STEP #5: FORGIVE, DON'T JUDGE

The last, and frankly, most important way to prepare to receive guidance is to forgive. Nothing scrambles psychic circuits and disconnects you from high frequencies faster and more often than holding a grudge. These negative energies not only disconnect you from guidance, but they also disconnect you from your spirit, from others, and from the beautiful world.

I know that this is a tall order, but if you think it through, you'll see that forgiving is far less work than condemning and holding on tightly to your negative feelings. All humans are manifestations of one Divine spirit vibrating at different levels of consciousness and frequencies at one time. Like cells in a body, we're all on this planet together. When one cell attacks another in the body, we call that cancer. Similarly, when we attack one another (or ourselves) through condemnation and judgment, it's equally toxic to our entire being, body, mind, and soul.

The benefit of forgiveness is that it allows your awareness to remain available to seeing, sensing, feeling, and noticing the things that matter most, such as your spirit, your angels, and your guides. The easiest way to release grudges is to state your intention every day to stop judging.

Affirm: *I forgive myself for judging and resenting. I release myself from all of my judgments and resentments, as well as from all negative perceptions. With my breath, I share my spirit with all and return to peace and balance. So be it.*

My client Serena held a strong grudge against her older sister Beth, for failing to back her in an argument with a mutual friend. She felt that Beth had taken the friend's side and hadn't considered Serena's point of view *at all.*

Feeling betrayed by them both, Serena decided to cut them out of her life for good. Coming from a tight-knit Irish family with seven siblings altogether, her decision did not go unnoticed, and soon her other siblings got involved. They asked Serena why she wasn't talking to Beth, forming opinions of their own, and adding to the drama. Before Serena knew it, the *entire family* was involved and weighing in on her decision. Stubborn and righteous, Serena didn't care that her resentment had caused such family dissention. Ironically, she stuck to her principles that family should back family, no matter what, and her grudge remained in place.

As the years passed, Serena's stance affected every holiday and family get-together and celebration. To avoid running into Beth, Serena had to pick and choose carefully which family events to attend and which to avoid, creating further hurt and more grudges that involved other family members who now felt slighted.

Serena, in the meantime, spurred on by the hurt that she was suffering over her sister's actions, began to look inward and develop her spiritual side. This eventually brought her to my books and a workshop on working with guides.

On the second night of the four-day workshop, Serena had a dream in which she was speaking with her guide (appearing as a tall door-to-door encyclopedia salesman) who suggested she forgive her sister tomorrow and not waste time. The dream was so clear and direct it surprised her a little. She woke up with a lingering sense of urgency about the message and felt she needed to listen.

Before class began on the third day, Serena sent her sister an e-mail saying she forgave her for not defending her all those years ago and wished her well. Serena was not prepared to fully welcome

Beth back into her life, but she did want to reopen the doors to her heart, which had been slammed shut all those years ago.

Serena received no response to that e-mail. However, on the evening of the third day, Serena did receive a call from the friend who had provoked the fight in the first place, apologizing for the pain she had caused. She went on to say that she had recently suffered a mini stroke, which scared her to death, and so wanted to clear her conscience of this lasting estrangement now that she felt her life was so vulnerable.

Serena was surprised and accepted her apology. Then she, too, apologized. She thanked her friend for the call and wished her well on her journey to recovery. Hanging up the phone, Serena felt as if a vise grip had just been taken off her heart. She was now free to once again fully breathe.

Our class ended on the fourth day and Serena went home, excited and inspired. She felt as if she had a new lease on life now that she wasn't spending so much energy resenting her sister and friend. She was ready for something new and wonderful to take its place.

Another week passed by and sadly, her friend suffered another health crisis, this time a fatal stroke. Serena was shocked, as her friend was only 58 years old. While this was very sad news, Serena was glad to know that she had forgiven the grudge she had carried toward her all these years. This turn of events reminded Serena that life is easily taken for granted and any one of us can go at any time. With that in mind, Serena called Beth and made peace. It now felt as if an elephant of heavy energy was being taken off her chest and she could breathe again. The two sisters attended the mutual friend's funeral together, more appreciative of one another and the fact that they were more alive and well than either had been in the years since their fight began. It was time to heal the grudges among the rest of their siblings.

Now that you've learned ways to directly contact your spirit guides, let's move on and learn how your guides communicate with *you*.

CHAPTER 11

# Making Initial Contact
# with Your Guides

Once you begin asking for help from your guides, they, in turn, begin to make subtle yet direct contact with you, approaching you very gently at first, to let you know they hear your request and are willing to help. No request goes unanswered, yet until you become more familiar with their unique vibrations, you may wonder if anyone is there, or if your mind is playing tricks on you. Even if you do sense their presence, in the early stages of working with guides you may be tempted to dismiss what you sense because you aren't sure it's guidance. To get around this, openly express whatever you feel your guidance is telling you the moment you feel it, real or not.

For example, if you suddenly feel a guide suggesting you apply for the new position at work, say so out loud instead of dismissing it. You are not obliged to follow this guidance, but once you say it out loud, it will be difficult to ignore. If it is true guidance, the feeling will become stronger, not weaker, and hopefully you will then listen. Once you state it, you can't ignore or dismiss it the way you can if you keep it bottled in your brain.

Also, beware of having unrealistic expectations of what receiving guidance should look like. Don't expect a Hollywood-like apparition, complete with a space suit, to beam down to you in the night. This is nonsense and rarely happens. I say "rarely" because there are times when a guide will manifest in a more intense way, but this is not common. The guides are generally too gentle for that kind of entry.

If anything, most people are surprised by how understated spirit guides can be. So, if you're waiting for a booming voice or an apparition of Merlin to appear at the foot of your bed, you'll most definitely be disappointed.

Contact with spirit guides is experienced on a deep, inner level, not as some external entity coming at you. You experience them with your inner senses, not your physical senses, meaning your clairvoyant eye, or inner eye of imagination; your clairaudient ear, the inner ear of intuition; or your clairsentient body, your inner feeling sense.

The art and skill of sensing your guides with your inner senses increases with practice. The more you practice perceiving these subtleties with your heart and not your head, and the more you acknowledge and trust that the guides are with you, the clearer their presence and guidance becomes. Eventually as you get used to using your inner senses, you will simply know guides are by your side at all times. It will become normal for you, and should be, because as spiritual beings it *is* normal.

Remember my first guide, Dot? When I first connected with her, I experienced her as a bright blue dot that hovered above me when I closed my eyes. The minute I opened my eyes, she disappeared. Most spirit guides connect with us in this way, at least in the early stages of contact, and it can feel as though you are imagining the whole thing. Dot's blue light and presence was real, but I perceived her with my inner, clairvoyant eye, and not with my physical eyes, that's all. Once I understood that, I completely accepted her presence and was happy she was with me.

The same goes for "hearing" your guides. When it first occurs, you may experience this as an "inner voice." In other words, you may sense out of nowhere that someone is whispering or talking to you, which makes it easy to believe at first that it is your own voice. But it is not the same as the sound of a physical voice. While it may sound very similar to when you speak to yourself, unlike your own inner ego voice (which is often the harsh internalized voice of all the critics and negative influences you've met with in your life), the voice of your guides is calm, kind, reassuring, and full of love as it speaks to your heart and true self. The sweet inner voice that indicates the presence of your guides is not just different from your internal ego voice in tone, but in content as well.

Your guides, unlike your ego, offer new suggestions, fresh ideas and options, and surprising solutions to your questions and challenges, while your inner ego voice just repeats its own limited perceptions, and/or exaggerates and emphasizes your problems as if there are no solutions.

I spoke to a woman named Susan at one of my guides workshops who complained that she felt stuck and was unable to connect with her guides in any way. "I asked my guides to help me with my difficult marriage and to offer me guidance to lessen our struggle, but all I hear in response is my own voice," she lamented in frustration. "I'm not hearing my guides at all."

"Are you sure?" I asked. "What did your 'own voice' say?"

"It said to stop focusing on my husband and to consider going back to school."

I sat quietly with her for a moment and then asked, "Is this something that you generally suggest to yourself regarding your marital problems? Or something that you've thought about before?"

"No, not really," she answered. "I've never thought about school as a solution to my marriage troubles," she said. "I've thought about couples counseling, therapy, even separation, but never school."

"So how does this suggestion *feel* to you? Would you like to go back to school?"

"Well, while it feels as if it isn't answering my question, I do love this idea anyway. I'd love to go back to school and have wanted to for years," she said enthusiastically. "In fact, I've always wanted to go on to graduate school, but then I got married and forgot about it."

"In that case, I answered, "it seems to me that you *did* receive some excellent guidance after all. Just not the kind you expected."

Still doubtful, Susan wondered aloud, "Do you think so? Even if I felt that it was just my own voice talking?"

"Maybe it sounded like your own voice, but was it an idea or thought that you'd normally have, or was this something entirely different?"

"It was very different from the normal internal conversation I have with myself about my marriage, which is why I thought I was making it up."

"That's the nature of guidance," I assured her. "It's so subtle and natural that you can mistake it for your own voice if you're not careful. But it does surprise you. That is the best way to know it's guidance and not your ego talking. More importantly, ask yourself: Does the guidance you received appeal to you?"

"Yes," Susan said. "In fact, the more I consider it, the more sense it makes. I'm eager to grow in my own life and have felt resentful at times that I've postponed my own dreams to be a good wife and mother instead of being myself. This is partly the reason I'm so unhappy. If this suggestion is coming from my guide and not me making things up, then yes, I feel very connected—and I'm ready to listen to more guidance."

It's curious to note that we have all kinds of crazy notions of how guides should sound. What are yours? What expectations do you have? Are you waiting for an apparition from the Middle Ages, complete with a Celtic accent, to pop in? Of course, guides may come that way, but mostly just to entertain you. They aren't people. They are divine energy. They present in various ways to get our attention, and in time you will begin to see the more colorful side of them. That is something to look forward to and is very fun. But for now, it isn't how they sound or present that matters. It is what they offer and how it leaves you feeling that does.

A true guide will always leave you feeling reassured, more relaxed, inspired, encouraged, breathing deeply and smiling in some tiny way. This is another indication that a high vibration guide is on the job. Your spirit is happy they showed up, and this is why you smile. It's spirit-to-spirit recognition.

> *A true guide will always leave you feeling reassured, more relaxed, inspired, encouraged, breathing deeply and smiling in some tiny way.*

## ASK YOUR GUIDES . . .
## THEN LISTEN TO THEIR ANSWERS

Your spirit guides' most important assignment is to help you reconnect with your soul purpose and live an authentic, meaningful, safe, deeply loved, and loving life. Talk to your guides directly, in your heart, about the things you need. They are listening. In talking with your guides, you're simply sounding out your options, just as you'd bounce ideas off a trusted advisor. The more you speak to them and tell them what you need, the more they support you.

When I was learning to see guides, my teacher encouraged me always to look beyond the surface and more deeply into people and things. Once you train yourself to do this, you begin to tune in to the essence of things—including yourself. From there, it only takes a small leap to start seeing your guides directly.

When I lived in Chicago, my next-door neighbor was a man named Monty who had the reputation of being eccentric and emotionally unstable. He was a known hoarder and recluse, often staying indoors for weeks at a time and talking to no one.

All of the neighbors talked about Monty and laughed at him. The kids in the neighborhood called him crazy. Judging by his behavior, it wasn't surprising that they did; he did seem that way. But over the years I got to know Monty very well and found him to be one of the most intelligent, sensitive, sentimental, humorous, loving, compassionate, and deeply spiritual people I have ever met in my life. I felt honored to know him and loved him with all my heart.

Monty wasn't crazy. He was a shy introvert who loved and lived for his memories, which is why he held on to everything that crossed his threshold. He was completely devastated after his life partner passed away from lung cancer. Monty found solace in reading books. When he finally sold his house and moved on, many of the neighbors snickered at the mountain of stuff he had to get rid of—and it was truly a mountain. Yet, sadly, they only saw the outer man and missed the diamond of a soul that he was inside.

When I was first learning to connect with my guides, I often asked my teacher Charlie what they wanted me to know, and his response was always, "Don't ask me. Ask them."

I was reluctant to believe I could ask them directly and get the right answer. He would entertain none of my reluctance. "They are your guides," he laughingly reminded me. "They speak in a way you can receive. It's just a matter of making a leap of faith and trusting your spirit instead of looking to mine. I've opened the door to this world for you, but you have to walk in on your own."

Looking back, I am so grateful Charlie empowered me to trust my own connection to my guides rather than letting me rely on him. I could have used him for a crutch and been dependent on him for my connection, but that would not serve me. As the great teacher he was, Charlie wanted me to learn to trust myself and assured me that I could. "Just try it," he said. "It will work." I did, and it did.

When it comes to spirit guides, you're building a relationship with loving forces who offer their help with affection and friend-ship. Like all good friends, they always listen and reserve judg-ment, never try to control you or tell you what to do, and won't flatter you or cater to your ego.

## TAKE THE LEAP

In 2014, I taught a weekend workshop on connecting with guides, and in my class was a reserved and somewhat intellectual woman who was both an M.D. and a practitioner of Ayurvedic medicine. When I invited the class to connect with their guides, she raised her hand and said, "I don't think that I'm connecting with my guides. I think it's all just me and that I'm very smart."

This is such a common suspicion that I invited her to come to the front of the class and work with me to get past it.

Hesitating for just a moment, she stood up and boldly walked to the front of the room, but the minute she turned and faced us, her confidence evaporated, and she burst into tears, overcome by an unexpectedly intense wave of fear and anxiety. After being so rigorously trained by her family and by her scientific education to discount anything other than rational information, she was petrified to openly acknowledge and express her inner guidance.

I had compassion for her. So many of us have been taught to only obey outside authorities. If so, it may feel scary, even rebellious to become our own authority. To her credit, this morass of confusion didn't last long. Just as quickly as they arrived, her tears vanished, replaced by a confident new light in her eyes and a smile on her face. She wanted to do this and had for years.

Watching this spiritual empowerment taking place, I asked her to share with us her conversation with her guides, and what her "smart self" answered in their place.

"I asked them how I can be a better doctor and healer," she said. "Their answer was, 'Be yourself.'"

"Is that your 'smart self' speaking?" I asked.

"I think so," she responded.

"Really? Well, let's have more conversation to find out. Ask whoever is speaking what 'being yourself' means."

She did, and after a brief pause said, "My inner voice says, 'Be honest, be loving, and be caring.'" After a moment, she added, "It also says I should tell people that I have intuitive abilities that help me understand their wounds—especially those around loss of love and support in the family—and to let my patients know that I can use my ability to help them heal."

The entire class felt a definite shift in her vibration as she spoke these words, and how completely different they were from her words only a few minutes earlier. These guided words were clear, simple, powerful, and transmitted the feeling of truth. The class nodded in agreement as I asked her, "Is this your normal 'smart self' or something else?"

She hesitated and then said, "No, this isn't my normal 'smart self' talking. Maybe deep in my heart I'd like to be that personal with my patients, but as an M.D., it's too risky. My 'smart self' would never be so open and forward. I just try to let my patients know that I love them in how I treat them, but I'd *never* say so."

"Can you feel the difference between this inner voice vibration and that of your normal 'smart self,' even if they both sound like your own voice?" I asked.

She nodded and said, "If I were to be honest, I'd say there is a definite difference between this voice and my 'smart' voice because of how it *feels* to me. This voice is calm and truthful, whereas my smart voice can be more defensive and heavier. It's a subtle difference, but it's there. I've heard but ignored this inner voice all my life, although I have felt it. And in fact, it *does* feel like I'm being guided the more I express this voice out loud. It feels like the voice of my grandmother, who I knew and loved as a child. She often told me that love is what heals. Do you think that she could be my guide?"

"Ask," I said, smiling and thinking of Charlie.

Now that you've learned the ways your guides communicate with you, let's move on and learn how to communicate with guides through writing.

# CHAPTER 12

# A Step Further:
# Writing to Your Guides

Another great way to communicate with your guides is to write to them. It's simple to do. First, write your questions and concerns in a journal or notebook, as if writing a letter to your guides, asking them for advice on these matters. Then, relax, imagine that your guides are replying, and write down what you imagine their responses to be.

Guided writing (also known as automatic writing) works well and the answers will definitely surprise you and be other than your own habitual thoughts.

As you prepare to write to your guides, choose a specific time of day when you'll be relaxed and uninterrupted. You want to set up an appointment with your guides much as you would set up an appointment with a counselor. If you're harried or distracted, you won't be receptive to their responses.

If questions or issues arise before your writing session, jot them down and save them until your appointment. (Don't be surprised, however, if by writing time, the answers have already dropped into your heart.) When it's time to get started, sit down, shut the door, turn off your phone, and ensure that you have complete privacy.

Notice that I said "privacy," not *secrecy*. This is a crucial point that I want to address because many clients have told me that they feel the need to hide their efforts at contacting their spirit guides from those who are close to them because they fear their friends and loved ones wouldn't approve and would judge them negatively. They don't feel safe enough with some people to admit they are contacting spirit guides for fear of ridicule or censure.

In contrast to privacy—which is a positive choice—secrecy implies shame, as if trying to connect with your guides is somehow not okay. You never want to make contact with your guides in this frame of mind, because when you're feeling shameful or secretive, you risk attracting low-vibration entities. These guides don't have much to offer you. You want to attract high-vibration guides who can serve you well.

Set the tone for success by feeling positive, confident, and comfortable asking for guidance and divine spiritual support, calling in only the highest guides to help you. Rest assured that your intentions will be heard and respected, and only the best helpers will respond.

Don't waste your time trying to get approval from a closed-minded person who is not aware of the spirit world. You won't. Just accept that people are at different levels of spiritual perception and to each their own. One day, all souls will awaken and eventually seek guidance, just as you are now. It may not happen in your lifetime, but it will happen in the lifespan of your soul. In the meantime, let your soul priorities remain between you, your guides, your angels, and God. No one else has a vote.

This point reminds me of a period in my own life when I was openly judged and ridiculed by my then husband's family for connecting with my guides. As traditional Catholics, they regularly prayed to angels, saints, and the dearly departed for help, yet talking to guides was outside of their comfort zone. I was raised Catholic, too, but I had also been raised to expect my spirit helpers to talk back, and they did.

At any rate, it was impossible to keep my work with guides private because I was a published author on the subject. Nevertheless, I was wise enough not to discuss it when we were together. Having had such great spiritual teachers (thank goodness), I knew not to take my in-laws' negative attitudes and judgment personally, so

I ignored their raised eyebrows and rolled eyes, and carried on with my work.

Over the next 20 years, one by one, nearly *all* of these family members privately contacted me, asking me to help them talk with their guides. Not surprisingly to me, almost everyone also asked me to not mention their contact with me to the other family members.

This just goes to show that even the most negative or suspicious attitudes can shift and change—and probably will. It is never your job to change anyone's opinion or take their attitude toward working with guides, intuition, or anything spiritual personally. Don't even try. Instead, be discreet, do your thing, and let other people's negative projections and fears roll off of you like water off a duck's back.

## CALL IN ONLY THE HIGHEST GUIDES

When you write to your guides, state your intention to work *only* with high-level spirit guides. One way to do this is to say a short prayer before opening your notebook. Ask the angels to protect you. Ask to speak with guides who possess unconditional love and are of the highest vibration. You can also light a small votive candle to acknowledge the light of your spirit and to signal that you are only receptive to guidance that supports your highest good and the highest good of all concerned.

You may wonder whether to write to guides by hand or use a computer. In most cases, I recommend using a pen and paper because it's more organic. I have encountered people, such as my friend Charles, who hate writing by hand because of their penmanship. My friend David, who is just beginning to connect with his guides, has ADD and gets confused when trying to write by hand. He finds that working on a computer is far more comfortable, so it's perfectly fine to work on a computer if it is less stressful.

When writing to your guides by hand, you have two options: 1) either use your dominant hand to write the question and your other hand to write the answer, or 2) use your dominant hand for both but mentally change channels. The way to do this is to imagine that you pose the question, but your guide writes the answer. (Of course, if you use a computer, you'll type both your questions and your answers.) Your guides don't care which method you use, and they're going to show up when you ask them to, so just do what feels best and keep in mind that the key is to write quickly and get into a flow.

Once you've set your intention and are ready to start writing, introduce yourself and ask for guidance in this way: *I am [your name], and I am asking my spirit guides for assistance and support at this time.*

Be polite and respectful, and remember that you're asking for guidance and not turning your life over for the spirit world to run. Word your questions appropriately and avoid "Should I?" questions; instead, simply ask: *What guidance can you offer on [fill in the blank]?*

Approach your guides gently and don't bombard them with too many questions at once. Stick to three or four at a time. Keep your questions simple and direct. Your guides are intimately connected to you and are far more familiar with your struggles than you know, so there's no need for details. For example, you might write, *I'm struggling with finding satisfying work and feel blocked and frustrated. What guidance can you offer about the nature of my blocks, and what steps can I take to move forward?* (The guides are smart, so trust them to read between the lines.)

After you write your question, lift up your pen for a moment, open your heart, and turn your listening inward. Trust your body, relax, and then, holding the pen loosely, begin writing again when you feel the urge. Same goes for typing on a computer.

Your guides will gently nudge you to write, so don't worry about your hand being "moved" as if on its own. Although there were times when my guides were so enthusiastic and I was so open that it felt like a great force had taken over, usually (at least in the beginning) the urge to write is subtle, so when you feel it, begin. You may only get a few words, or you may get pages of guidance, depending on how receptive and calm you are and which guides show up. If you're genuinely open to insight and are willing to grow, a lot comes in.

You'll know that you're receiving high guidance by the content—as subtle as it may be—because even when you write ideas that have crossed your mind, the vibration will resonate as supportive and new.

If, on the other hand, you receive guidance that makes you highly uncomfortable, or goes against your moral code, or tells you to do something that is clearly not loving, *throw it away or burn it immediately.* A low-vibration entity may have slipped in and offered a useless opinion. Treat it like you would any lousy advice, regardless of who it came from, and just ignore it.

Remember that, when seeking guidance, you're not just looking for someone to agree with you. Real high-level guides will support your soul's growth and inspire you, and if your requests are genuine, the channel will serve you well. They will never tell you what to do or insist you do anything. *Never.*

> *Real high-level guides will support your soul's growth and inspire you, and if your requests are genuine, the channel will serve you well.*

To succeed at guided (or automatic) writing, be consistent but not obsessive. Check in with your guides once a day if you wish, but don't spend more than a half hour on this exercise. It's best to take guidance in small doses and then let it settle in. Savor it; think about it; assess if it leaves you calm, grounded, and uplifted; and then turn it over to your spirit for final analysis.

A client named Bernice used the pen-and-paper method to ask for guidance in her struggle with her weight. Her question was simple: *Why do I carry excess weight and what can I do to shed it?* She then sat quietly, ready for information, and after 30 seconds, the urge to write kicked in and her pen took off. She felt her guides transmitting answers so quickly that she could hardly keep up.

First, through Bernice, a guide wrote that in a past life, she was a Polynesian princess and that her weight was a source of power and pride; many of her people loved and respected her weight as a symbol of power and prosperity. Her guide wrote that Bernice missed this special attention and wanted people to admire her again, which is why she'd been reluctant to shed the excess pounds.

Next, a new guide came in. It strangely felt as though the channel had quickly changed, and the tone of her writing shifted. She wrote that her insulin levels were too high and that a vegetarian diet and frequent meals would ground and calm her nervous system.

Her writing changed again, signaling a third guide's input. This guide wrote that she'd been loved and celebrated for being a "good girl" throughout her childhood, and part of that praise was earned by being a good eater who cleaned her plate. She finished by writing that her weight would find proper balance when she stopped living for approval from others.

After that, the urge to write ended just as quickly as it began. Reading what she had written, Bernice marveled that although the information she had downloaded had never crossed her mind before, she felt that on a deep, soul level, it was accurate. She then went on to use the information she received to make positive changes in her life.

First, she had her insulin levels checked, and they were, indeed, dangerously high, just as her guides had indicated. As for becoming a vegetarian, well, since Bernice was a Midwestern meat eater, she initially scoffed at such a notion. Still, because she was feeling so lethargic, she eventually gave it a partial try. Over the next four months, Bernice dropped unwanted pounds, eating less and less meat by the week.

And finally, to garner positive attention for something other than eating, she joined a choir at her church, where her gorgeous voice earned her the opportunity to sing solos that really showcased her talent.

When I asked Bernice how she felt about the Polynesian-past-life part, she replied, "Well, who knows? I'm losing weight, so I won't question it!"

Similarly, another client Tim learned that there is no limit to the direction that can be received through guided writing when, within weeks of starting, he found himself writing the novel he'd long struggled to begin.

Another client Mitch asked his guides for advice on his love life, and the written response he received was *sandwich shop,* which he dismissed as absurd and threw away. Three weeks later, his buddy at work said, "Want to grab some lunch? There's a new sandwich shop two blocks from here that just opened up." Oblivious to the connection, Mitch walked in and was immediately smitten by the cashier, who seemed equally interested.

They flirted, and as she handed him his lunch, she said, "We close at five in case you're free this evening." They set a date to meet for a drink, and it went really well. It didn't occur to Mitch that he was guided there until after their third date. That night, just as he was drifting off to sleep, he suddenly remembered what he'd written weeks earlier and immediately apologized and thanked his guides for their counsel.

## YOUR TURN

When writing to your guides, take a breath and relax. Don't worry that you won't make contact. They *will* write back, but it may take a few minutes—or longer. In fact, it may even take a writing session or two before you hear a response. Just try to be patient. They'll respond—I promise!

To practice writing to your guides, simply follow the steps below:

- **Step #1:** Find a quiet, uninterrupted space, and before you begin, light a small votive candle and say a short prayer to ask for protection from low-level energies.

- **Step #2:** State your intention by writing, *I seek to converse only with guides of the highest vibration.* Next, introduce yourself by writing, *I'm [your name], and I'm asking for assistance at this time.*

- **Step #3:** Proceed to write your questions, one at a time, and then lift your pen and relax.

- **Step #4:** Hold your pen still but loosely in your hand and be ready to have the guides take over and respond to your questions by writing back. Expect suggestions from your guides to freely flow into your mind and then onto the paper. Don't censor what you write or doubt yourself. Remember that guidance is subtle and will feel natural. When the flow stops, put the pen down and take a few breaths. Then, reread what you've written.

As a final note, I suggest that you keep all the writing from these sessions in the same journal or notebook and don't discard any of them (unless, of course, they leave you feeling uncomfortable, in which case, burn them). The guidance you receive may not be what you expect or want, or you may not understand it immediately, but you should keep it anyway. In my experience, most guidance makes sense in time, if not right away, so it's good practice to set your writing aside and refer to it later. If that doesn't work, ask your guides for more information at another writing session, and then, if their response *still* isn't clear, let it go.

Now that you've learned ways to communicate with guides through writing, let's move on and learn how to clairvoyantly see your spirit guides.

# CHAPTER 13

# Learning to See
# Your Spirit Guides

Seeing your guides is perhaps the most challenging way of connecting with them, since they exist on an entirely different, nonphysical, vibrational plane. It can be done, only not with your physical eyes, but with your inner clairvoyant eye. It takes a little cooperation between you and your guides to succeed. On their side, guides must densify their frequency enough so that you can perceive them. At the same time, your own vibration must rise to a certain level to activate your sixth chakra, otherwise known as your "third eye" (the inner eye you imagine with), located in the center of your forehead. This is the "eye" that sees your guides.

People who have very active imaginations and can easily visualize things with their inner eye are most likely to see their guides. If you aren't a person who finds it easy to visualize, don't worry. We all have an inner eye, and it worked quite well when we were young. In fact, that's the reason why so many children are able to see guides and angels, although they're usually referred to as "imaginary friends." Sadly, when we begin to attend school, we are conditioned to stop using our inner eye; instead, we're encouraged (or forced) to turn our focus outward, which gradually disconnects us from our ability to see the spirit world within.

The good news is that with a little effort and some good old-fashioned patience and practice, you can reactivate this natural channel and attune to the spirit world once again. When that happens, you will begin to clairvoyantly see your guides. Use the following exercises to help you reopen your inner eye:

## EXERCISE #1: BE IN THE HERE-AND-NOW

First, look closely at your surroundings and notice every detail you can about what's right in front of your face. This may sound contradictory: Why concentrate on physical reality when you're trying to see the spirit plane? Most people are so caught up with replays of the past or imaginings of the future that they don't focus on the present; consequently, they end up not seeing anything clearly.

Seeing your guides is a hyperacute ability to clearly focus on what's right in front of you, only in another dimension. So it makes sense to begin by practicing seeing every detail around you in this dimension first.

When looking around the room, don't do what I call a "drive-by" glance, where you skim the surface and miss the details. This is how most people observe life, so it's no wonder they miss the subtle nuances that exist, including the spirit guides standing right next to them.

This quick glance does no good at all. Instead, slow down. Relax. Breathe. Then single out one or two items right in front of your eyes. Study them for details you didn't notice before. Is there a particular color, for example, a pattern or texture that you missed at first glance and now clearly see?

Taking a closer, more in-depth look at life is what students in a drawing class, for example, are asked to do, because this trains their eyes to look beyond the surface and into the essence of their subject. This is the exact same skill needed to activate your clairvoyant eye and see your guides. As you look, say aloud both what you see and what you sense.

For example, "I see my ficus tree in the corner of the room. I notice that several of its branches on one side have lost all of their leaves, while there are many new green sprouts growing on lower branches. I notice that the leaves are fuller on one side of the tree than the other as well, tree branches clearly reaching toward the sunlight. I see a renewal of leaves since I moved the plant closer to the window a few weeks ago, noticing how the spirit of this tree has positively responded to the change. It is no longer an inanimate dying object in the corner, but a lively and vibrant, thriving spirit in my home."

As you do this, more and more of what was hidden moments earlier slowly becomes more visible.

## EXERCISE #2: DAYDREAM

If your life is overly hectic, with nonstop, jam-packed days, daydreaming might be challenging to do because it requires a little more time and inner focus than rushing about allows.

However, if you're willing to make the inner space for daydreaming, you'll succeed. As children, we all participated in "woolgathering," as it used to be called, and when doing so, we often left our bodies and connected to (and even played with) our spirit guides. I believe the most soul-damaging instruction we may have received as children was to "stop daydreaming!" When we did, we disconnected from the healers, angels, and spirit friends who were helping us. Daydreaming is our gateway into their world. When we were made to stop, the gate closed.

Fortunately, although the spirit gate may have closed, it is never locked. It may need a little "oiling," however, which you can accomplish by taking the time to daydream as you did when you were a child. Letting your mind wander frees your focus from the outer physical plane and expands your ability to perceive the spirit realm of energy.

Shortly after moving into my present apartment in Paris, I was repeatedly reminded by my well-intending expat American friends that the French aren't particularly warm, especially toward foreigners. Therefore, I was advised not to expect the same level of friendliness when connecting with them that we Americans are used to experiencing with one another. I was especially encouraged to be extremely proper with my building concierge and never to be too familiar with her under any circumstances. While I took this to heart, I also trusted what Charlie taught me about not judging by appearances. Rather than being distant and cordial as advised, I decided to be myself and trust whatever unfolded.

One day while at the market, I came upon a magnificent flower stall. Suddenly and out of the blue I spotted a spirit guide hiding among the flowers themselves, urging me to buy a bouquet for my concierge. This struck me as odd and even inappropriate, since we had only spoken a few times since I had moved into the building and barely knew one another. Still, I followed the guide's suggestion, selected a gorgeous bouquet of blue peonies, and had them wrapped as a gift for her. Once home, I stopped by the concierge to collect my mail and, feeling a tad self-conscious, presented the bouquet to her, saying I felt she would enjoy them. To my surprise, my concierge burst into tears, confiding that her mother had just passed away and her heart was broken. Blue peonies were her mother's favorite flowers, so she couldn't believe this was the flower bouquet I had selected. Sobbing, she held the flowers to her heart and proceeded to tell me her entire life story, including the fact that she was Spanish, not French, although she had lived in Paris for most of her life. Fifteen minutes later, she and I had bonded. I was so grateful that I had not allowed appearances to keep me from following my guide's suggestion and was able to be a messenger of comfort that day.

To daydream, it's best to be in a grounded, calm, relaxed state. If you're upset or unsettled in any way or for any reason, first call on the ministry of angels to help calm you. They will.

Once you are settled and calm, start by imagining what your spirit looks, feels, and sounds like. Imagine your spirit is happy. Imagine seeing your spirit in three dimensions and in color, and with as much detail as you can muster.

Some people tell me that they don't see at all with their inner eye. If you're one of those people, know this: It's okay to see in other ways, such as with words. I may ask you, "What color is your spirit right now?" You may close your eyes and see the color pink, or you may just hear and sense the word "pink" popping into your head. That, too, is considered seeing on a clairvoyant level.

At this early stage of the game, trust what you see, however you see or sense it. In time it all comes together, and you will both see and sense the subtle realms in full rainbow color. Begin at the beginning and trust this natural clairvoyant eye will wake up with practice.

Imagine the life you really want. What are you doing? Where are you located? What are you wearing? Who are you with? What sounds do you hear? What can you touch? You may, for example, imagine having an artistic job, working in your art studio or atelier. You may see yourself in a loft-like room, collaborating with other people, a large whiteboard and markers in front of you. You may be surrounded by other imaginative, innovative people, all brainstorming a creative project with you in an atmosphere of enthusiasm and camaraderie. You may hear uplifting music playing in the background, perhaps your favorite rock 'n' roll, for example. The room may have a huge window, or large sliding doors leading to an outside garden filled with bright plants and a place to sit and relax, eat lunch, or meditate. There may be a mid-size friendly office dog sitting at your feet. You may see and hear yourself laughing with your co-workers or having a joyous and exciting back-and-forth conversation as wild ideas fly through the air, each one inspiring the next and the next. You feel so happy to be there. This is your dream job.

Enjoy a daydreaming exercise such as this for several weeks. It awakens your inner eye, raises your vibration, trains you to become aware of the presence of your guides, and opens the door for these dreams to come true.

I had a client named Sarah, who imagined seeing her spirit for several weeks. Every time she did, she saw herself riding a magnificent chestnut horse at full gallop across the countryside, her hair flowing wildly in the wind. (The scene was a far cry from her job as an intake administrator at a city hospital!) She began to feel that the horse itself was her guide, and with each daydream, she focused less and less on being on the horse, and more and more on where the horse was taking her. Several weeks of daydreaming eventually led them both to Provo, Utah.

Sarah, who lived in Cleveland, knew nothing about Provo and thought that it was silly to have her horse take her there. She kept an open mind about it, however, and you can imagine her surprise when, 10 months later, she was introduced to a chiropractor named Fred, who was from Provo, at a health-care conference. He told her that he was starting the first alternative health-care center in the Cleveland area. After a fairly brief conversation, he asked if she'd be interested in taking "a wild ride" and managing the center for him.

My client's daydream began to make sense, and she accepted his offer, starting the professional adventure of her life! Her guide was the horse, so to remind her of how she got this dream job, she placed a small bronze horse on her desk.

Sarah was able to master this exercise because she was patient and consistent in her daydreaming practice. She didn't give up after one or two tries as most people do. Daydreaming can be a powerful creative tool for seeing our guided future. Not all guides appear in the form of a human. Some show up as animals, as Sarah's did. Others may appear as bright lights. Some communicate an image along with a scent, like the image of a cigarette along with the scent of tobacco, or the image and scent of a rose. I know it sounds crazy. But that is just the way it is. It is best to have no expectations when clairvoyantly seeing your spirit guides and enjoy the surprises that come.

My sister Cuky often sees one of her guides—our deceased great-aunt Emma—not as she looked in life, but as a pool of water that appears in the corner of her bedroom. And when a client named Marvin began to sincerely concentrate on seeing his guides, he only saw clouds of white feathers, as though a down pillow had exploded. He accepted that this was his guide and named him "White Feathers."

Similarly, my client Dahlia initially saw her guide as a light blue heron that sat across from her and conveyed messages to her telepathically. The blue heron eventually morphed into a radiant bright blue being, whose name (my client learned telepathically) was Erin. Sometimes she sees the heron, and sometimes she sees Erin . . . It's always a surprise.

## IMPORTANT TIPS TO REMEMBER

- Guides keep it simple. They prefer giving short specific messages, often in image or metaphor form, instead of long-winded "talky" lectures.

- The highest guides tend to leave you with a light, refreshed, encouraged, positive, and loved feeling.

- Be consistent. Practice seeing your guides at the same time every day, such as when you first wake up or are about to go to sleep and have no distractions. Your ego mind is less vigilant at these times and your spirit awakens, making it easier to see beyond the veil.

- Keep regular daydreaming appointments with your guides. They will do the same. Please make an effort to show up on time.

- If you practice seeing beyond the physical world as a matter of habit and ask your spirit to reveal what is hidden, it will.

## Try This

### INNER SANCTUM

Sit in a comfortable chair or lie down on your bed. Then close your eyelids and imagine a movie screen lighting up in your mind's eye. Ask your spirit to project itself onto the screen, then relax and get ready to enjoy the show. If your mind or body feels restless, imagine your spirit sitting next to you, as if you were both in a movie theater, watching the screen together.

Next, ask your spirit to project the most beautiful place imaginable onto the screen, a place where you can meet your guides anytime you wish, your inner sanctum. Then, breathing comfortably in through your nose and out through your mouth, trust whatever pops up on the screen. Be curious and accept whatever appears without question.

Perhaps what you see in your mind's eye will be familiar. It may be a favorite spot from childhood or a place you traveled to in the past and enjoyed. Yet it could also be a place you've never seen before. Even if it makes no sense, trust that your guides are choosing the setting that works best for your connection.

For example, my client Thomas's childhood kitchen appeared on his inner screen, with a babbling brook running right through the middle of it. When he asked his guide to appear, she popped out of the stream, sat at the kitchen table, and then dove back in. Perplexed at first, it later occurred to Thomas that his favorite memories from childhood were of baking cookies with his mom in the kitchen and of fishing in a small stream with his dad. Having these scenes converge in his imagination as the perfect place to meet his guide was something he never would have thought of on his own.

If nothing appears on your screen, don't worry. Your inner eye may simply be a bit slower to activate than you'd like. In that case, it's okay to help it along a little. Using your imagination, decorate your meeting place in any way you'd like. Once you've done this, close your eyes and ask that only the highest, most helpful, creative guides appear here in your inner sanctum and take a seat across from you.

> *Even if it makes no sense, trust that your guides are choosing the setting that works best for your connection.*

Be patient, as you may need to try this several times before you have success. However, if you persist, your guides will appear. And again, they may "appear" in words, not visions. Accept whatever comes and remember that guides don't necessarily take a human form. They may manifest as symbols, for example. And don't be surprised if they also appear in different ways at different times.

Monique, one of my clients, bemoaned her inactive inner eye, but it lit right up when she was invited to decorate her inner sanctum as she wished. She chose to meet her guide in a cozy, oak-paneled room with a crackling fireplace, two thick armchairs in plaid velvet, and floor-to-ceiling bookcases filled with tomes that contained the answers to every question in the Universe. At her feet was an antique red-and-gold oriental rug; two thick, leather footstools; and a large, sleeping yellow Labrador retriever. There were standing lamps behind the chairs with colorful, stained-glass shades, and a 10-foot-tall floor-to-ceiling oak door that was closed shut to the outside world to give her and her guides privacy.

When she asked her guide to appear, instead of seeing a person, she saw a book fly off a shelf and open on the footstool. Accepting it, she then asked her guide about her husband's mental health, since she suspected that he was developing dementia. In response, another volume flew off the bookcase, and when it opened, the word "chelation" (defined as a process for removing metals and toxins from the body) appeared in her mind's eye.

In response to the message, Monique took her husband to be tested for toxicity, and they discovered that he had very high levels of minerals in his body, a condition that can mimic early dementia. Later, she happily reported to me that, soon after undergoing chelation therapy, his mental acuity began to slowly improve.

Let's review the things that you can do *daily* to start training your inner eye to see your spirit guides. Remember that you only need 10 to 15 minutes each day to practice these exercises. Of course, more time is okay, as long as you have the time and your ego keeps quiet!

- Start paying close attention to what's in the here and now.

- Return to your childhood pastime of daydreaming. Freely imagine what your spirit guides and the guides of others might look like.

- Keep your eyes relaxed and almost closed, and let your inner eye do the looking.

- Accept whatever image comes to mind, even if it makes no sense right away. In time, it will.

Now that you've learned various ways in which to see with your spirit guides, let's move on and learn how your guides get your attention.

# CHAPTER 14

# Spirit Speak

Spirit guides are subtle, so instead of speaking to us in direct language, they may contact us in other ways. They often use riddles, metaphors, symbols, dreams, and even jokes to speak to us. So not only must you become adept at picking up on subtle vibrations, but you must also recognize that the spirit world has its own language, and it's up to you to learn it.

Don't let this scare you. Your guides don't want to trick or confuse you. In fact, their method of communication is often better received and more humorous than a direct message.

I had a client, a flight attendant, who had a real sweet tooth. One morning at 4 A.M., as she was preparing to make the 40-mile trek to the airport, she heard in her mind, "Isn't it a good day for doughnuts?"

Used to talking to her guides and loving the thought of a fresh doughnut, she said out loud, "Yes, but I'm running late. I can't stop this morning."

Putting her bag into the car, she heard it again. "Isn't it a good day for doughnuts?" Laughing, she said, "Yes, it is. But I can't stop. I'm late." Just as she was about to enter the highway, she saw a doughnut truck pulling into the gas station next to the turnoff.

Again, her guides piped in. "Isn't it a good day for doughnuts?"

"All right, I give up. But I have to hurry." Pulling into the service station behind the doughnut truck, she turned off the ignition and saw that she was just about out of gas. She gasped as she realized that she could have run out on the highway and missed her flight altogether. The guides said in unison: "See, isn't it a good day for doughnuts?"

My client Wayne was in the shower one morning, getting ready for work, when he heard, "Get out of the fast lane." He imagined that it was a metaphoric message from his guides to slow down and take it easy. He was soon to learn it was much more. On the road for his 25-mile commute, he entered the fast lane as he always did. He instantly blew out his front right tire and nearly lost control of the car.

"Fortunately, I held on to the wheel and maneuvered out of the fast lane and crossed three more lanes to the side of the road without getting hit or hitting someone else," he told me. "It was a miracle. I got out of the car, inspected the tire, and saw the thinnest shred of rubber dangling off the rim. Then I remembered what I'd heard in the shower. I said to my guides gratefully, 'I guess you weren't mincing words today.'"

He said that as he started walking toward the exit ramp, seeking help, he looked down and saw a nickel and a penny. Bending to pick them up, he said aloud, "Oh, six cents." It dawned on him that his guides were having a little fun with him. "Six cents. Sixth sense. I get it. Thank you again. Now, please send help."

Learning spirit speak is a trial-and-error process that requires patience and a sense of humor. Guides love to make you laugh. The more you do, the higher your vibration. They love to feel this vibe from you, so they play with you whenever they can.

I was teaching a class on communicating with your guides at the Omega Institute in New York, and, as an exercise, paired up the students and invited the class to try speaking to their guides directly. Expecting profound revelations, one frustrated student raised her hand. "I'm not getting this at all. All I hear from my guides is 'Jelly beans. Tell your partner to have fun with jelly beans.' And that's just ridiculous."

The minute she said that, the student she was working with gasped and said, "Oh, my God! I've been wondering all morning if I should get a new puppy to fill up the loneliness in my life, because the woman who lives next door offered me one from her dog's new litter. His name is Jelly Beans! So I guess that answers my question."

Sometimes your guides come to you in symbols. A client who was constantly bombarded with images of butterflies asked me why.

I suggested that every time she encountered a butterfly over the next six months, she should write down in her journal precisely what was going on. Once she started documenting the appearance of butterflies, she realized that they showed up within one hour of her asking the Universe and her guides for reassurance that she was on the right life path. They were her guides communicating that all was well.

Another woman in one of my classes told me that every time she was about to make a mistake, Elton John's song "Don't Let the Sun Go Down on Me" popped into her head. The last time she heard it, she had just gotten engaged to a man she was crazy about—or at least she was crazy about his looks and his money (he was a handsome professional athlete). When she got in her car the next day, she turned on the radio and heard Elton John singing the song.

She screamed and turned it off, but she knew that it was a sign that all was not okay. After a very turbulent six-month engagement, they called it off. One of the last things her now ex-fiancé said to her during a stupid fight was, "And another thing—I hate Elton John."

A client who was just beginning to work with signs and symbols shared this story: One day, just as she was about to go shopping with a girlfriend, she heard her guides say, "Can't go until you shuffle your cards." She thought, *What a funny idea,* and dismissed it as she continued to get ready. A few seconds later, she heard it again, this time in a playful voice. It dawned on her that maybe the guides were referring to the brand-new deck of tarot cards she'd just purchased and had looked at earlier that morning. Not wanting to shuffle her cards right then, she ignored the message, grabbed her purse, and moved toward the door.

Again, she heard loud and clear, "Can't go until you shuffle your cards." She suddenly smelled something funny. She looked at the closed glass door to her office and noticed the room was filled with smoke. She opened the door and found a glass votive candle that she'd lit earlier still burning. The glass had become so hot that it was now causing the table to smolder. She blew out the candle and snuffed out the burning embers.

"This could have burned the house down," she said aloud. Then she saw that right next to the candle was her deck of cards. Grateful to her guides for the warning, she picked up the deck and shuffled. "Thank you," she said. "Let me know anytime when you want me to shuffle the cards." Then a card dropped from the deck. It was the ace of hearts, which means "You are protected by love."

Once you begin connecting consciously to the unseen world, you can learn to speak its language. It's full of sounds, symbols, riddles, and jokes, all of which are selected to mean something to you. Approach the spirit world as you would an exciting unknown land. Admire its scenery, enjoy its native customs, and accept the hospitality of its inhabitants, your spirit guides. Before you know it, you'll be fluent in their language.

> *Once you begin connecting consciously to the unseen world, you can learn to speak its language.*

## YOUR TURN

In a small pocket notebook, start keeping track of objects, impulses, images, phrases, melodies, ideas, and even random thoughts that seem to pop up unexpectedly and recurrently in your life. After two weeks, look back through your notes. Is there a pattern? Do you recognize any further meaning or any hidden humor in these messages now that some time has passed? Is someone trying to tell you something?

## Guides connect with you through

- Dreams
- Signs
- Songs on the radio
- Books falling off shelves
- Podcasts
- Other people
- Metaphors and riddles
- Symbols
- Overheard conversations
- And more!

Now that you've learned various ways in which your guides get your attention, let's move on and meet your guides individually.

# PART IV

## INTRODUCING YOUR SPIRIT GUIDES

# CHAPTER 15

# The Spirit Guides
# of the Nature Kingdom

Now that you've opened yourself up to receiving spiritual guidance and have practiced some basic techniques for communicating with your guides, let me introduce you to some of the different spiritual beings you may be hearing from.

As you become more attuned to the spirit in all things, the first guides you may encounter are the nature spirits. Grouped together, the nature spirits are called elementals. Among the elementals are the spirits of earth, water, fire, and air. They're sometimes known as gnomes, sprites, sylphs, devas, and salamanders (which are not anything like the small reptilian creatures). Although they may sound like the stuff of fairy tales, they are very real and are the spirit forces that look after every living thing.

The nature spirits are wonderfully therapeutic, and when you raise your sensitivity to their presence and ask for their help, you'll immediately begin to feel their support. When you learn to identify them and become open to receiving their gifts, the natural world will then become a place of healing and excitement for you.

> *The nature spirits are wonderfully therapeutic, and when you raise*
> *your sensitivity to their presence and ask for their help,*
> *you'll immediately begin to feel their support.*

## THE EARTH SPIRITS

The first of the nature kingdom are the earth spirits—also known as devas—beginning with the trees, flowers, and of course, Mother Earth herself. The earth is an incredible living, breathing spirit, majestically supporting all of the life on this planet.

Affectionately known as Gaia, she is the organic mother of us all. When we become sensitive to her energy, we instantly feel physically stronger and more supported.

Connecting with the earth spirit is known as "getting grounded," a term that's casually tossed about, but whose true meaning is rarely fully understood. It's the act of allowing our spirit to be nurtured by Mother Earth. When we're disconnected from her, we feel scattered, weak, easily pushed around by life, and cut off from support. When we raise our sensitivity to her and become conscious of her, our life calms down and our basic sense of security kicks in.

Not one of us can live without Gaia's force beneath us. If you ever doubt her power, just conjure up the magnitude of a big earthquake to bring you back to reality. At the same time, she can also be astonishingly gentle—nothing is so restorative to your body and bones as a massage from her.

When my daughters were four and five years old, I took them to Hawaii for the first time. When Sonia hit the beach, she could hardly contain herself. It felt so delicious and soothing to her that she threw herself onto the sand, grabbed it by the handful, squeezed, smelled, and even tried to eat it. She rolled around in the wet sand for hours and never tired of it. As I was putting her to bed that evening, her heart was so joyful, and she felt so grounded and connected to the earth that she gave me a full-body hug and said, "Mom, before today I used to love you like a dot. Now I love you like a circle."

If you feel drained, disconnected, unsupported, and unloved, tap into Mother Earth's spirit and let it nurture you. Ask her to enfold you with her endless arms and pull you back to her breast. Gaia's spirit is so powerful that connecting to her can help reduce anxiety and fear and can even ease one of our most significant modern diseases, chronic fatigue syndrome.

One of the ways to feel the healing power of Mother Earth is to have a session with a massage therapist or energy bodyworker. Because I travel so much, I easily become ungrounded and need a therapeutic healing session right after I get home to help me reground and reconnect to my body and Mother Earth once again.

My current favorite practitioner, an American named Greg Sax, frequently comes to Paris from New York, and whenever he is here, I always book a session with him. He uses many wonderful healing modalities, including energy work and Chinese acupuncture. Still, the most grounding and powerful treatment is when he quietly holds my feet at the end of a session and lets Gaia's healing life force enter my body, filling me with her vitality and power. He does this for several long minutes, saying nothing, just allowing the earth spirit to do the work. Nothing in the world is more grounding to me than this.

There are many other healing techniques for connecting with the spirit of Mother Earth. Reflexology, which involves putting pressure on certain zones on the hands and feet, can work wonders, for example. But as with all therapies, it only succeeds if the practitioner is skilled at channeling earth energy to the client.

You can tell if this connection is happening the moment the practitioner touches you. You either feel it or you don't. If the practitioner is in their head and not connected to the earth, which may be the case (they're only human, after all), their touch may be agitating and cold. In that case, end the session. It isn't worth continuing because the spirit of the earth is what brings about healing. If it isn't present, there is little healing to be had.

Using crystals also aids in connecting with earth spirits. I am a big believer that you will be naturally drawn to the crystals that work best for you if you want to use them. Go to any crystal store and pick up various crystals inside. The spirit of the crystal that is perfect for you will let you know because you will *feel* it.

Along with nature spirits of the earth, the spirits in flowers also work to calm and balance your emotional body—the first layer of energy surrounding your physical body—which goes through a lot of wear and tear in a day, a week, or a lifetime. This energetic body can become weak, thin, and ripped, leaving you vulnerable to all kinds of emotional and psychic distress. Flower spirits calm and heal these afflictions.

Tapping into a flower spirit doesn't take too much effort. Simply smell a rose, appreciate an orchid, or sniff a sachet of lavender to see what I mean. If you're feeling flat, weak, or uninspired, call on the flower and plant fairies to restore your balance and bring your emotional body back to balance.

Spiritual energies in flowers have such an immense capacity to heal the emotional body that they have been developed into essences and essential oils. They are available in health-food stores as well as on the Internet. Each specific plant extract or flower, or combination of plants and flowers, calls up a particular spirit to bring relief in some way. For example, holly relieves you of being critical, lavender opens and calms the heart, and violet builds confidence.

Perhaps the most remarkable example of the power of working with plant and flower fairies can be found in a spiritual village called Findhorn Community in northern Scotland. By paying close attention to the nature spirits and celebrating and revering their world, this experimental community has been able to grow huge vegetables, plants, and flowers in soil devoid of proper nutrients. Although no one quite knows *who* connects with and honors the fairies at Findhorn, its inhabitants are regularly rewarded with vast gardens.

You, too, can directly connect with fairies if you grow a garden, even if you just nurture a few potted plants. The next time you find yourself mindlessly watering the azaleas, stop and feel their energy and appreciate their strong yet gentle, spirit. Talk to your plants and flowers and even play classical music for them. Experiments have proven that plant spirits respond beautifully to kindness, and when receiving it they'll grow like crazy.

If you *really* want to feel some psychic support, take this a step further and hug a tree. I'm completely serious when I say this.

Look as loony as a lark if you must, but take the risk and throw your arms around the next oak or elm in your path. Place your heart up against the bark and see how you feel. If that's just too over-the-top and you can't bring yourself to enjoy that experience, at least plop down at the foot of a tree and connect with its majesty through its roots as you lean against it.

## THE WATER SPIRITS

The next in the nature kingdom are the water spirits, also known as undines. The water spirits are potent and cleansing, and they work to wash away the old and outworn feelings trapped in your emotional body. Water spirits can be ferocious, as the world witnessed during Hurricane Katrina in 2005 and the 2011 tsunami in Tōhoku, Japan, among other disasters when the force of the water caused massive destruction and death. At the same time, this very same force indirectly united the world in loving cooperation to help those who survived.

The world's awareness is beginning to heighten regarding the power of water spirits by the increasing frequency of water-related natural disasters in general, such as recent hurricanes, floods, and tsunamis. Global water shortages and droughts (even the fascination with designer water) are also bringing the world's attention to the influence water spirits have on our daily existence and how much more respectful we need to be of them.

Interestingly, people connect most readily with water spirits in dreams, claiming that some of their most disturbing or refreshing dreams involve water. For instance, every time my sister dreams of water, it's a warning that some decision she's about to make isn't wise. I have a client who dreamed of drowning in a sudden flood, only to be suddenly laid off from her job three days later. In both cases, the message delivered through the water theme was that each of them had something they needed to let go of, whether they wanted to or not. Connecting to the water spirits refreshes your perspective and can keep you from becoming stuck in a rut, as anyone who has enjoyed a walk on the beach can attest.

There are several ways to benefit from the cleansing and relaxing power of water. The first is to drink water—lots of it, if available. The more water you drink, the more you clear your physical body of debris, with emotional debris following right behind.

To attract water spirits, place small bowls of water with flowers in them around your home. You can even install a small fountain and invite the water spirits to refresh all energies dwelling there. I've seen fountains costing as little as $14 at Walmart and Target, and the fact that they're no longer a pricey item for the privileged indicates the growth of mainstream sensitivity to the healing power of the water spirits.

Bathe, take showers, swim. All of these activities invite the water spirits to clear and cleanse your energy and release the past.

Another way to connect is to carry a small spray bottle with fresh water and spritz yourself throughout the day, especially when you've experienced a challenging moment or fall into a mood of self-doubt. The water spirits will work on your behalf to keep such negativity or doubt from settling in and will help restore your energy to balance.

Be creative and trust your own inspiration when it comes to connecting with the water spirits. Pay attention to ways in which they connect with you as well. For example, if your home sprouts a leak, or your pipes burst, the water spirits are getting your attention, letting you know some unaddressed emotional blockage needs to be acknowledged and cleared.

## THE AIR SPIRITS

The air spirits, which can be felt in gentle breezes as well as fierce tornadoes, are of the mental plane. That means that when you connect with them, you energize, calm, and clear your mind and soul. The first and perhaps most primal connection happens when you simply take a deep breath. When you do, the air spirits enter and interact with your own spirit and bring you into the moment, stimulating your mind, improving your ability to focus, and allowing you to create.

On the other hand, when you hold your breath, you disconnect from the air spirits, stifle your own spirit, and cut yourself off from the creative flow of life. One of the best practices for inviting in support of the air spirits is to begin each day with a series of 5 to 10 deep, cleansing breaths before you even get out of bed. As you breathe, ask the air spirits to clear your mind, refresh your blood, invigorate your organs, and inspire you so that you can greet the day with enthusiasm and clarity.

Connecting with the air spirits—the sylphs—is also a good idea whenever you find yourself feeling fearful or anxious. Stop, breathe, and relax; breathe and relax; breathe and relax. With practice, this quick exercise will calm you immediately and quiet your thoughts.

It's helpful to call upon the air spirits when facing major decisions, undergoing interviews, negotiating with others, or giving speeches. They help to prevent your mind from becoming muddy or confused, keep your thoughts flowing, and tune you in to the refined frequencies of your other spirit guides. Since they're also the gatekeepers of telepathy, they provide the access line to all other entities within the spirit community.

## Calling in Air Spirits

In addition to breathing, calling in the air spirits can also be easily done by ringing a bell or a chime and asking them to come to your aid. Call the air spirits when you are working on a writing project, sending e-mails, or trying to come up with original words for any reason, such as giving a presentation, a talk, or a speech. Air spirits are particularly helpful with creative projects because the word "inspiration" means "breathe in." It is how inspiration comes.

Also, try ringing chimes and bells to clear the energy in rooms where there has been an argument or a fight, or where you sense any sort of tension or negativity in the air. Churches ring chimes and bells to raise the vibration and call in the helpers. You can do this, too. Just ring chimes or small bells for two full minutes as you walk through space you want to clear, and you will definitely feel a breath of fresh air blow in shortly after that.

## THE FIRE SPIRITS

The last of the nature spirits are the salamanders, the dancing energies that spark, crackle, and mesmerize all at once. The fire spirits excite our passion, initiative, and creativity, and connecting with them helps raise our sense of can-do-ism and eternal youth. Fire spirits need to be called in when we've lost our luster; when we find ourselves in a mental quagmire of blame, excuses, or self-pity; or when we are stuck and cannot get moving. There's nothing like a visiting salamander to shake us free of a habitual funk.

Have you ever observed how gazing into a fire evokes a sense of timelessness and romance, not just with respect to lovers, but with respect to life itself? When connecting to the fire spirits, forgotten dreams, desires, and passions come alive. This is due to a healing spark between the fire's spirit and yours.

Fire spirits can also surprise, shock, and, if necessary, clear the slate. I've witnessed more than a few of them burn a person's home or business to the ground, leaving those involved instantly reduced to a tabula rasa.

In 2019, fire spirits erupted in Australia, California and the Amazon rain forest. In 2020, they returned to the Amazon, and swept through forests in several Western states, including California, Oregon, and Washington. They are devastating and soul crushing, to be sure, and the losses from these raging fires are beyond words. True to their purpose, the fire spirits will not stop until they get us moving, in this case to take the actions needed to address climate changes.

When you call the fire spirits forward, be attentive to their dance, their crackle, and their frenzy. Salamanders ask you to step lightly, be flexible and inventive, adaptive and responsive. It's best to be humble when calling on them and *never* take them for granted.

To connect with the fire spirits, light a fire and put your intentions into it, either by writing your intentions down on paper and burning them, or singing them into the fire. This asks the fire spirits to get you going.

My client Sophie had been single for more than eight years following her divorce and was ready to start dating again. She felt she needed a boost of confidence to help her open up to new people. This was a perfect reason to ask the fire spirits for help. She wrote down her intention and called on the fire spirits to assist her in making the emotional connection she sought. Then she lit the paper on fire and threw it into the fireplace. Four days later, while picking up her daughter from summer day camp, she had a lively conversation with the camp director. They immediately hit it off, and from that day forward she could hardly wait to pick up her daughter at the end of each camp day. By the end of the six-week summer session, the director asked Sophie out on a date. One thing led to another, and a year later they were married.

"Talk about quick results," she wrote in an e-mail telling me of her upcoming wedding. "Calling in the fire spirits really worked fast!"

Always remain with a fire until it's been extinguished or has burned down to embers. Fire spirits like to be watched. If you ignore the fire, they may decide to get your attention by destroying everything in their path!

The greatest of all fire spirit guides is the Holy Spirit, represented by the eternal flame. This is why virtually every religion utilizes some aspect of fire in their symbolism and ceremonies. Calling on the Holy Spirit to revitalize and heal your spirit is one of the most potent requests you can make. We do this by lighting candles and setting intentions, asking the Holy Spirit to hear our prayers and grant our wishes, either in temples and churches or in our homes.

When I was growing up and attending Catholic school, I regularly went to mass. I loved the ritual of lighting candles to call up the Holy Spirit and the Holy Family to burn brightly in my heart and to watch over me. This weekly fire ritual kept me feeling connected to God and the Holy Spirit, and helped the fire of faith and courage burn brighter within me.

### Did You Know That . . .

- Earth spirits are also known as gnomes, fairies, tree devas, or elves, and provide grounding and attend to emotional healing.

- Water spirits are called naiads, sea nymphs, undines, or sprites, and are responsible for the cleansing, refreshing, and clearing of our spirits.

- Air spirits are sometimes referred to as air devas, builders, zephyrs, or sylphs, and can be called upon to calm us and to help with focus and mental clarification.

- Fire spirits are known by metaphysicians as salamanders, and can inspire passion, new life, blessings, creativity, and spiritual healing.

## YOUR TURN

The best part of connecting with nature spirits is that you begin to sense how wonderfully supported you are and how much your spirit is a part of the many domains of spirit all around. The nature spirits are eager to serve, to please, to inspire, and to support, and will do all this if you give them due respect and reverence. Just remember that they're there and they'll bring you many beautiful gifts. Don't forget to enjoy them!

Connect in some way with the earth, water, air, and fire spirits at least once a day to keep you healthy and your life force balanced. Try these simple exercises to get you started:

- Connect with the earth spirits by going outside. If you're lucky enough to be in a natural setting, sit quietly and focus on the buzz of life sprouting forth from the ground. It's even more effective to lie down on the earth, on top of a blanket if you'd like, and breathe in her spirit through every pore. If you live in the city, go to the nearest patch of green to make your connection.

- Connect with the water spirits when you shower or bathe by asking them to wash away toxic energy hanging in your aura. Appreciate their healing properties and ask them to clear your body, mind, and aura of all negativity and psychic debris.

- To call the air spirits, breathe in through your nose slowly, then, thumping your palm on your heart, exhale with full force while saying aloud "Ha!" This activates your spirit, opens telepathic channels, and shoos away all negative mind chatter occupying your brain. It's a great quick fix to get you instantly realigned with your spirit and brings your full attention to the moment.

- A safe way to ask fire spirits to bring movement, passion, and creative excitement to your life is by burning candles, lighting incense, or building a fire in your hearth. Ask the fire spirits to wake your courage and potential, and to keep you from falling asleep at the wheel of your life or forgetting who you are. And remember: if you burn candles, watch over them; if you use a fireplace, check the flue and safety doors; and if you burn perpetual candles, place them in a sink or bathtub when you leave the house. Do not walk away from a burning fire. The fire spirits are known to dance out of their containers and set things on fire when unwatched. These wise precautions simply reflect a healthy respect for the spirit and power of fire.

## THINGS NATURE SPIRITS CAN DO FOR YOU

### Earth spirits

- Get you back into your body and out of your head
- Reconnect you with the earth
- Tune you in to nature and help you become a part of life
- End your sense of isolation
- Make you stronger

### Air spirits

- Open your mind
- Inspire you to adopt new beliefs
- Help you release the past
- Offer the motivation and open-mindedness to learn new things
- Activate your creativity

### Water spirits

- Help you open your heart
- Motivate you to let go of resentments
- Assist in healing your emotions
- Help you receive more love
- Offer the strength and help increase self-love so you can forgive and move on

## Fire spirits

- End inertia
- Elevate your energy
- Initiate new beginnings
- Jump-start new projects
- Help increase your willingness to take risks
- Lead you to an adventure

Now that you've met the nature spirits, let's move on and meet your runner guides.

# CHAPTER 16

# Your Runners

Recently I was telling a group of friends about the spirit guides known as "runners" while on our way to a reception in Downtown Chicago. It was a cold, rainy Friday during rush hour, and I was sharing how much easier life is when I call on my runners for help. One friend, Craig, snorted in disbelief and challenged me, saying, "Well, call them for a parking spot, then. And make it close to the reception so we don't have to walk in the rain or pay for a garage."

No sooner were the words out of his mouth when a car pulled out from a metered spot directly across from the reception hall.

"See what I mean?" I said. "And better yet, it's one of those meters that we don't have to put money in since it's past six o'clock!"

When the reception was over, Craig once again tested me: "Okay, parking meters are easy," he said. "Let's see what your runners can do about finding a table for all of us at a good restaurant on a Friday night without waiting. Now, *that* will make a believer out of me."

"Where would you like to go?" I asked. He chose a trendy French bistro called La Sardine, in the middle of the Fulton Market area, not far from where we were.

"They're usually packed, but since we're close, let's ask the runners for help," I said.

We approached the restaurant, and sure enough, the house was packed.

"Table for four," I said, smiling.

The hostess asked if we had a reservation, and just as I said no, her phone rang. After taking the call, she turned to me, smiled, and said, "You're in luck—a party of four just canceled."

And that was just the beginning, as the runners were working overtime that night. As a delightful topper to the evening, our waiter showed up with a tray of sumptuous desserts we hadn't ordered. "A gift on the house," he said. In one night, my runners made a believer out of Craig and sprinkled magic throughout our entire evening.

## WHO ARE YOUR RUNNERS?

Runners are handy guides for all situations, and the first ones you may want to invoke for practical matters. My teacher Charlie taught me to call them runners because that's precisely what they do: run ahead and help you find things that you've lost or misplaced; or connect you to something that you seek, such as apartments, items on sale, or even parking spaces.

Runners are spirits who are very close to the earth and the natural world. They are usually indigenous souls who once inhabited the area where you reside today. For example, people living in America will often have Native American runners, since they're connected to the territory where you are (not to your ancestral roots). Similarly, you can be an African American living in England or Scotland and have a Celtic runner, or you can be a Chinese Australian living in New Zealand and have a Māori runner. A runner's loyalties are to the land, not to you.

What these guides do best is sprinkle magic in your life. The more magic you feel, the more you open your heart. The more open your heart, the better your vibration and the happier your spirit. When your soul is delighted, everyone you meet feels it, too. That's why runners' work is so important—it keeps us believing in the goodness of life and of our world.

> *The more open your heart, the better your*
> *vibration and the happier your spirit.*

I've called upon my runners for help all my life, and they've never let me down. And sometimes they even help me find things I didn't know I'd lost! For instance, once, after working late in my office catching up on paperwork, I had an overwhelming urge to look through the wastebasket before emptying it. I grabbed a handful of papers I'd tossed in the night before and found an envelope containing two weeks' worth of bank deposits, which I'd forgotten to drop off the day before. If not for my runners, I would have thrown those checks away and been seriously out of luck.

Runners rarely communicate with words; instead, they just nudge you without your necessarily knowing why. When I felt compelled to check the wastebasket, I simply acted without thinking. My runners didn't run through my brain with the suggestion, "check the trash before you take it out,"—they just grabbed me and pushed me to do it.

In 2014, while visiting Paris before I actually moved there, an hour before I had to leave for the airport to go back to Chicago, I decided to do some last-minute shopping at Galeries Lafayette, one of the main department stores in the center of the city. In particular, I was hoping to find my mother the perfect scarf for Mother's Day, which was coming up in a few weeks, and knew the huge selection here would give me the best chance of finding what I was looking for in such a short time.

My mother is very particular about the colors she wears, so I wanted to find something that would please her. That meant finding a scarf in ether mandarin orange, soft pink, or white, common enough colors and her favorites, but not necessarily the ones in season that year.

Thinking myself crazy to be doing this with so little time to spare, I ran into the scarf section of the vast store and glanced around at the mountain of scarves on display. Then I groaned.

There were scarves as far as the eye could see, but none in the colors I was looking for.

With only 10 minutes to go, I was about to give up and buy her chocolates at the airport. Suddenly, I felt the urge to take the escalator to another floor and look around. Not even sure where I was headed, I found myself in another, smaller section filled with scarves and accessories. Right there, on display on the counter, was the perfect mandarin-orange, pink, white and gold scarf, as if waiting for me. The gold was an added bonus color because my mom also loved anything gold. Eureka!

Racing against the clock, I convinced the store clerk to take the scarf off the display and sell it to me on the spot, telling her it was for my very selective mother. Being a fashionable Parisian, she understood right away and was all in to help me. In record time, I purchased the scarf, had it beautifully packaged, and was out the door and in a taxi to the airport.

"Thank you, runners," I said out loud as we sped down the highway. "My mom will absolutely love this gift." And she did.

Your runners watch out for you. They are there, waiting in the wings, ready to help you at a moment's notice. My friend Ella lost an heirloom necklace her grandmother had given her shortly before she died. Not believing in her guides, she called me and asked if I could help her. Usually, I would have tried, but my vibes insisted that I give the assignment back to her. "Not this time, Ella," I said. "My vibes say that you should send your own runners to look for it."

"You know I don't believe in all that," she whined. "Can't you please help me find it?"

"No, I can't. But if you ask sincerely, your runners might." I advised her to ask politely because runners are a touchy bunch. They're great scouts and detectives, since they're so closely connected to the area, but they tend to be proud, so you must appeal to them respectfully and not boss them around.

Ella moaned in protest, but she eventually gave it a try. "Please help me locate my grandmother's necklace," she pleaded, sitting defeated on the sofa after exhausting every hiding spot she could think of.

Ten minutes later, she got up, and without thinking, opened her sock drawer, and fumbled around, not knowing why. Suddenly she felt a lumpy sock, stuck her hand into it, and found the necklace. *How on earth did it get there?* she wondered. Then she remembered that she'd asked her husband to hide it just before they went on a weekend trip several months earlier since she wasn't comfortable leaving it in her jewelry box. He'd buried it in the sock drawer, and they'd both forgotten about it. But the runners didn't. They watched him hide the necklace and took Ella right to it once she asked politely for their help.

You can ask your runners to help you find just about anything, including a parking space. Charlie taught me this trick years ago: he told me to send my runners ahead to save me a great parking spot every time I got into the car—and not just any spot, mind you, but the *best* spot. As long as I asked politely, it worked like a charm.

I taught my friend Debra about runners and parking spaces years ago, and she's embraced their existence completely. Each time she turns on the ignition, she envisions where she's headed and what kind of parking spot she desires, and then asks her runners to secure it for her.

One day she invited me to lunch, and as we approached the restaurant, the sky blackened and suddenly unleashed a torrential spring downpour. "No problem," she said. "I'll send my runners to get us a good parking spot so we won't get soaked." Sure enough, as she drove into the restaurant's parking lot, a car that was parked about 20 feet from the door pulled out, leaving a great spot for us. "That's my runners for you," she beamed.

No sooner had she said that when another car parked only *10* feet from the entrance pulled out. I turned to her and said, "Now, that's *my* runners for you!"

We both squealed with delight as we enjoyed our dry lunch.

> ## Did You Know That . . .
>
> • Runners save time, frustration, and confusion, and help allevi-
> ate sadness resulting from loss.
>
> • They come in all shapes and sizes.
>
> • They're quick and waste no time helping when asked.
>
> • They're strongly connected to the earth and nature and were
> scouts in past lives.
>
> • They don't speak; they just act if you ask politely.
>
> • They're practical.

Not only do runners find lost things, save seats on planes, and turn up parking spaces, they help you locate items that you need but can't quite get your hands on. This was especially true for my client Myrna, who has size-11 feet and could never find stylish shoes in her size. Used to having salesclerks roll their eyes at her and make rude comments about her feet, she nearly gave up until she discovered runners in one of my classes.

The first time she asked her runners to help, she was led to a new store in the mall where she found a pair of elegant black leather boots that she loved. Hopeful but used to disappointment, she asked the salesman if they came in size 11.

"Normally they don't," he replied, "but just today, I received two pairs of elevens."

As she tried on the boots, which fit her perfectly, Myrna chatted with the salesman and discovered that he understood her frustration, since his wife also had size-11 feet. Consequently, he said that he'd found every designer and shoe store in the area that carried size 11s, and even knew when they arrived. He gave her the store list along with the boots, promising relief to Myrna's 20 years of shoe-buying frustration and low self-esteem resulting from her being repeatedly told that her big size was simply not available.

Runners know how difficult it is to accomplish all that we want to in a lifetime, and they're excellent assistants who keep us from wasting time and energy. They can be generous and indulgent as they work, too.

For instance, a client named Steven was running late for his flight from Denver to New York, was caught in long security lines, and was fearful he would miss his plane. Sending his runners ahead, he rushed to the gate only to be told the jet bridge was closed and it was too late to board. Just then, another agent walked off the jetway. Seeing Steven, he said, "The bags aren't fully loaded yet, so we can put him on."

Together, they ran down the jetway and knocked on the plane door. Steven then boarded the flight, where he was led to the last remaining seat on the plane—in first class! So, not only did his runners come through by getting him on the plane, they upgraded him to boot.


YOUR TURN

Next time you need to find or secure anything, ask your runners to help you. It can be your keys, a parking spot, a seat on a fully booked flight, an unusual item in a store, an apartment, reservations at a restaurant, seats to a sold-out play or concert, a lost item. Anything.

Call them by saying out loud:

*Runners, help,*
*please come quick.*
*Help me with [fill in the blank].*
*Thank you in advance, runners. Now go!*

Then relax and follow all hunches, nudges, and clues the moment you feel them, without hesitation or resistance. Runners will lead you directly to where you need to go to find what you are looking for, and *fast*. Once they succeed, make sure to thank your runners for their service. They love to help but want to be appreciated for it. As we all do.

Try it today. You will be delightfully surprised how quickly the runners respond.

## Call on runners to help you find

- Parking spaces
- Keys
- Lost objects
- Seats on airplanes
- Seats in restaurants
- Items when shopping
- Apartments
- Houses
- Cars
- Travel bargains
- And plenty more!

Now that you've met your runner guides, let's move on and meet your helper guides.

# CHAPTER 17

# Your Helpers

A friend of mine named Natalie grew very interested in her family's history when she turned 50. It became her nearly full-time pursuit to find out all she could about her relatives, past and present. She began to piece together the clan's genealogy but ran into a dead end when an estranged uncle wouldn't share any of his information with her. This frustrated Natalie, but she wasn't deterred.

One day she was relaxing in her living room when she suddenly felt the presence of her deceased father whoosh down and pass before her eyes. The feeling was so strong that Natalie was compelled to get up out of her chair, walk directly over to her computer, and Google her father's name on a genealogy site—something she'd never done before (or even thought about, for that matter). She began scrolling through the results that came up, but none of the data appeared to have any connection to her family.

Not wanting to waste her time sifting through this mountain of information, and not quite sure what she was looking for in the first place, Natalie arbitrarily decided that she'd only look at page 16 of the search results, and if there was nothing relevant to her family there, she'd stop. Expecting to find nothing, she was stunned to see a listing for her father at the very top of the page. The entry was followed by a nearly complete genealogy of the entire family, dating back several generations. What she'd been trying to compile on her own was there—in its entirety—right before her eyes! That "whoosh" that Natalie experienced had most certainly been her father's spirit acting as a helpful guide to assist her in answering her questions about her family.

The purpose of helper guides is precisely what it sounds like: to help make your life easier so that you can enjoy it. By serving you, they raise their own vibration, enjoy the afterlife a little more, and allow their own souls to grow. Very much like the ministry of angels, helper guides assist you with specific tasks, special projects, or hobbies, and they come in several categories. Quite often, as in Natalie's case, they're deceased family members or friends who speak to you from the Other Side, offering their help because they love you. Helpers can also be dead experts in the field in which you are seeking help. For example, expert writers can appear and help with writing. Musicians on the other side can help with musical compositions and lyrics. Doctors can help with medical issues, even dentists with dental challenges.

Helpers are especially handy in areas where they had some level of expertise when they were alive. For example, I have a guide named Mr. Kay who was my speech teacher when I was in grammar school and one of my most beloved and understanding instructors ever. His spirit shows up whenever I make audio recordings, helping me avoid stuttering or make other mistakes, just as he did when I was in speech contests back in school. To my amazement, most of my audio work is nearly perfect the first time it's recorded, something I could never accomplish without Mr. Kay by my side.

Helper guides will lovingly show up to lend a hand when you're stumped, blocked, or discouraged, which was very much the case when Dan, a recently widowed father of seven-year-old twin boys, came to me for a reading. Not only was he devastated by the loss of his wife to breast cancer, but he was frustrated because he didn't have anyone to care for his sons so he could return to work. He'd tried two nanny agencies, but neither of them had provided him with the kind of care that could fill the void in his family's home . . . or their hearts.

By the time he showed up at my office, Dan was desperate. Luckily his helper guide came through, and from the message I got, I was sure that it was his wife. When he first asked, "What can I do?" all I heard in response were two words: "first communion."

I asked Dan, "Are you Catholic?"

"No, I'm not," he said. "My wife was an Episcopalian who loved her church, and she often went with the boys, but I'm non-committal when it comes to religion, so I only went occasionally."

"Do Episcopalians have first communion?" I asked.

"I think so," he answered. "Why? Do you think I should have the boys make their first communion? What does that have to do with finding someone to care for them so I can get back to work?"

"I don't know," I replied, "but your wife is suggesting just that."

"Well, that would be just like her," he said as his eyes filled with tears. "I don't think it will help with my problem, but I'm willing to follow her wishes. I just don't make the connection, though. Can you ask her to explain?"

When I relayed his questions, I got the same answer, so Dan accepted the message and went to his wife's church, where he enrolled his sons in first communion classes. During the boys' lessons, he met other parents and shared his story with them. A woman named Donna told him that her recently widowed mother was moving from Utah to live with her family the following week and would soon be looking for a job. She assured Dan that her mother, who'd been a homemaker all her life, would be the perfect nanny. A week after arriving from Utah, Donna's mother showed up at Dan's door, ready to work, love, and nurture all three of them. The connection was unbelievable, and five years later, she's still with them and has become the anchor of their family.

It's important to note that helpers don't necessarily have to *do* something to be helpful. I think in many ways their greatest gift is letting us know that life goes on beyond death and that the spirit doesn't die, even when the body does. Losing the fear of death helps us live our lives to the fullest, which is perhaps the helpers' greatest mission.

My dear friend Joan, one of the best astrologers in the world, who lost her life to brain cancer over 12 years ago, often shows up to remind me to pay attention to current astrological aspects and their impact on my life, such as an upcoming Mercury retrograde period. These are signs I would generally ignore, but with Joan nudging me, I do check from time to time, and having this awareness in mind has helped me make better-timed decisions. Joan, always the practical Capricorn who suffered no fools, also pops in and points out when I am tolerating or engaging with people who are clearly not good for me, another historical blind spot of mine. I can just sense her raising her eyebrows and shaking her head "No!" when I'm about to feel sorry for someone who is just pulling on my heartstrings and manipulating me. Thank goodness for Joan. She keeps my emotions sober and lucid.

My deceased brother, Bruce Anthony, who was a great musician when alive, also regularly shows up in my life, usually when I'm teaching workshops, suggesting songs to play during meditations, group exercises, and for the spontaneous dance parties we have each day. Bruce loved to dance, celebrate, and play more than any other member of my family. His spirit loves helping me in class, and he does his part to make it a good time for everyone else's spirit. I love his presence and am grateful he pops in to all my classes. He is a huge support for me.

My father's spirit also regularly helps me, mostly when it comes to fixing things around the house. This was his specialty when he was alive and continues to be his best contribution from the spirit world as well. When the washing machine in my Paris apartment broke down, it caused me all kinds of stress because getting something fixed here can be quite the ordeal. Just as I was about to look on the Internet for a repairman, my father popped into my thoughts, saying, "Wait. I'll send someone."

Trusting him, I turned off the computer and carried on with my errands for the day. At noon, I heard from an American friend, Allen, who had been living in Paris for over 20 years, asking me if I wanted to meet for coffee as he was in my neighborhood. Shortly after I sat down with him at a café an hour later, I told him about my washing machine breakdown. "Don't worry," he said. "I have just the guy for you. Luckily he just moved back to town last month. I've known him for years. He's honest, competent, and cheap. I'll reach out to him right now and see when he can come over to help you." Five minutes later, it was all arranged. The machine was fixed for 20 euros later that night. The best part was that the repairman's name was Paul, the same as my father's. He is now my trusted handyman. Thank you, Paul. Thank you, Dad.

Similarly, my mother communicates with *her* mother (my nana) all the time through her dream state. The two were separated during the war when Mom was a child, so she's thrilled to have reconnected with Nana in her dreams. Sometimes they go to a beautiful place where they listen to gorgeous music and dance and sing together all night long, while other times Nana gives her tips on sewing and making patterns, a creative passion they share. She even tells jokes, which my mother remembers and shares with us. And sometimes she's just *there,* giving Mom her love and company.

In addition to deceased family and friends, helpers can also be spirits who've had no relationship with you in this life, but who had strong connections with you in previous ones. They often show up to help you grow in areas in which you've worked together before. For example, I have two beloved helper guides named Rose and Joseph, who help me a great deal with my mission in life as a six-sensory teacher and a healer. I feel them with me as I encourage people to open their hearts and to love themselves and life more. I'm sure I knew these spirits in past lives, and our work together, even then, was to guide, counsel, and direct people in very much the same way that I do today.

As I've mentioned before, I also work with the Pleiadean Sisters, guides who help me when I give readings, especially at the point when I'm directing people to their soul path or higher purpose. According to these sisters, I've been their student for lifetimes. They're essential to my work and I rely on them greatly for direction with all of my clients.

### Did You Know That . . .

- Helper guides love to help and have the perfect skills to do it.

- They were human at one time, and their vibration and frequency are still very much connected to the human plane.

- They usually communicate telepathically with you in words or short messages that you pick up in your mind.

- They like to connect with you in your dream state, usually in some sort of friendly conversation.

- They rarely elaborate on their input.

- They share the knowledge and skills they learned while human before they move on to higher frequencies.

- They help the planet through you by sharing what they've learned.

You may attract helper guides who come to you simply because they love what you're working on and want to share their knowledge and expertise with you. Their relationship to you will be more impersonal since they're not connected with you from the past. They're often sent to you by the ministry of angels, who know that a particular helper can draw from their past lives to help you in an area where you may be stuck or not know what to do.

These helper guides may be doctors who assist you with your physical health or money managers or bankers who help you attract or better manage your finances. They may even be odd-job workers or fix-it wizards who help you repair things, such as the mechanic guide who recently helped jump-start my friend's car when it stopped running in heavy traffic on a two-lane bridge in New Orleans.

As I said earlier, my father was a master handyman, and for as long as he lived, he could fix anything that broke down, including televisions, vacuums, refrigerators, DVD players, air conditioners, and washing machines and dryers. Amazed at his skill, I once asked him where he learned to be so handy, to which he replied, "I didn't actually learn from anyone. I simply follow my inner guide who tells me what to do, and together we seem to figure it out." Dad must have had quite a talented group of helpers since he always got the job done!

Note that some of your helpers stay with you all your life, while others are more temporary and only step in for a short time to assist with a particular project or assignment. If you're willing to listen to guidance, these guides will stick around and see things through to the end. If, on the other hand, you ask for aid and then perpetually ignore it, they'll step away. They're there to help, but they'll never force you to accept their assistance, so if you insist on doing everything your way and never consider their input, they'll respect you and pull back.

The key to connecting with your helpers is to quiet your mind and trust what comes in, rather than allowing skepticism or logic to shoot down their suggestions. You may hear their instruction in only one or two words (or a few more if you're lucky), and often they'll only repeat their direction once, so as not to interfere with your free will. It's up to you to pay attention so you don't miss it.

Diane, a realtor, was a student in a class I taught in upstate New York who shared an excellent example of the benefits that unfold if you're willing to listen to your helpers without hesitation or resistance. It seems that one day she was on her way home from an open house when she got a call that a new house had just been put on the market. She decided to drive past it to see what it looked like, and when she arrived, she felt an instant attraction to the place. Suddenly a distinct voice said, "Buy it," loud and clear.

Diane already owned two houses and was financially stretched to her limit, but her helper guide again insisted, "Buy it." That's all she heard, but it felt right, and that was enough for her.

"Okay, I will," she said aloud, adding, "but you need to help me."

When she went home and told her husband what had happened, he was not happy. "What about your plan to buy a dream cottage near the ocean?" he asked.

Yet Diane didn't back down. She couldn't believe her resolve—she rarely trusted her gut so clearly and hardly ever challenged her bullying husband, but in this case, she was adamant about her decision to listen to her helper. She realized that she was tired of missing moments of opportunity out of fear and hesitation and was ready to give her intuition a chance. When she expressed her unwavering intention to listen to her guide, her husband backed down, which was something that had never happened before.

That night Diane told her son, Ryan, who was newly married and renting Diane's second home, about her plan to buy the property. To her surprise, Ryan asked, "Mom, would you mind if I bought the house rather than continue renting from you?"

Ryan had never indicated that he'd wanted to move, let alone buy a house of his own, yet the minute he said it, it resonated with Diane. Together they made an offer on his behalf, and three weeks later, the house was theirs.

The best part of the story was yet to come: Since Ryan moved out of her second home, Diane was now free to put it on the market. In a matter of weeks, it sold for *triple* what she'd paid for it. She had more than enough money to buy her dream cottage by the ocean, which she and her husband found shortly after. While this may all sound far-fetched, it's actually a classic example of the benefit of having helper guides: in less than two months, a whole stream of related desires was made possible because Diane accepted their help.

Dreams are often the portal through which your helper guides connect with you. My client Allie for instance, was certain that her helper was her deceased dad. Their relationship hadn't been very close when he was alive because he'd buried himself in his work as an investment banker, but this changed soon after his death. She began having dreams in which he offered her financial advice, and this eventually evolved into a daytime connection where she even heard his voice in her head.

> *Dreams are often the portal through which*
> *your helper guides connect with you.*

Three months after her dad passed, Allie started receiving nudges out of nowhere to invest in an apartment, an idea she'd toyed with in the past but it wasn't a current priority. She knew her dad's spirit was suggesting this, and, boy, was he insistent. She ignored these flashes for a few weeks, but the feelings intensified until she finally gave in and started looking.

Six weeks into looking, Allie saw a terrific apartment at a fabulous price and spontaneously made an offer to buy it. She offered quite a bit less than the asking price, another decision in which she felt her father's spirit was influencing her. To her shock, the buyer, apparently eager to move out of state quickly, accepted the offer that same day, and before she knew what hit her, she was a first-time homeowner. Within two years the area where she lived appreciated tremendously, and her modest investment nearly doubled in value.

"That is exactly what my dad had always wanted for me when he was alive," she said. "No wonder he plopped the idea to buy into my head when he did, even though he had passed. I wasn't even interested in buying at the time, and now I have a prime piece of real estate and a home I adore. I feel closer to him now than I did when he was alive."

In helping his daughter, Allie's father also helped his own soul. That is precisely how it works with helper guides.

Sometimes helper guides work in pairs, or even in groups of three or more. A few years back, my friend Butzi and I met for coffee early one morning at our favorite French café by the Seine to brainstorm new creative ideas for our businesses, as was our monthly ritual.

This particular morning, I told him of my new wish to create an amusing, short video demonstrating how much our angels and guides help us. Even though Butzi had never heard of angels and guides before meeting me, and flat out said he didn't believe in their existence, we nevertheless suddenly found ourselves improvising a funny script based on some of my experiences. We wrote it down in 10 minutes flat.

Butzi then asked me if I had ever done any acting, to which I replied, "No, but I can try. After all, when it comes to this script, I wouldn't really be acting. It's how I live."

Once that was established, it felt as though a different guide stepped in, this one a Hollywood producer. One idea poured in after another. Before our coffee was finished, in addition to the script, we had a plan for a friend of Butzi's named Sami to film the video in my apartment, with another friend of Butzi's named Caspar cast as the angel. In 30 minutes total we were guided in how to create the entire thing.

Three days later, Butzi, Caspar, Sami, and I met in my apartment shortly after breakfast, and in two hours, without a bit of rehearsal, we had filmed our little script on the first take. It was a purely guided effort on all of our parts, and we had a gloriously fun time doing it. After a day of editing, I posted the video on my Facebook page just to see if anyone else would find it as amusing as we did. Within days this silly film took off, and before we knew it, it started going viral. As of today, our project has over 1.25 million views and growing. Not bad for a group of amateurs! I can only attribute this success to the assistance of our collective helper guides who were laughing along with us as they directed us every single step of the way in making this happen. It was too easy to take the credit ourselves. You can watch the video, called "One of those days? Ask Your Guides!" on my Facebook and YouTube pages. I hope you enjoy it as much as we and our guides enjoyed making it.

## Try This

Do you have a creative idea or inspiration you would love to manifest, but need help to make it happen? Write down your idea and share it with a creative and supportive friend. Then call in your best helper guides to assist in making it happen.

Write down all the crazy notions that pop up as you brainstorm, and don't censor a thing. The more open and receptive you are, the more your helpers can get their suggestions to you.

## CELEBRITIES IN THE SPIRIT WORLD

The most exciting helpers tend to be deceased famous people. And if you wish, you can actually invoke such past masters to help you. For example, I often call on the renowned medium and spiritualist Edgar Cayce to help me with my work as a psychic, especially when dealing with problems related to health and past lives. In many cases, he's helped me understand these issues better than any other guide.

My friend Julia Cameron, the well-known writer and playwright, invokes Rodgers and Hammerstein to help with her musicals, and John Newland, the famous director, to help her with her plays. Similarly, a client of mine who's a young female scientific researcher regularly invokes Nobel Prize–winning chemist Marie Curie to help her with her experiments.

Celebrity helper guides are wonderful for aiding with creativity, as evidenced by a rock star client of mine who once told me that, while working on his first solo album, he felt as though he were being fed specific musical inspiration from both Prince and David Bowie. And after hearing his music, I was sure that he was helped, as it carried such similar celestial energy to that of both musicians.

My mother began studying painting through correspondence classes when I was a young girl. She was so intent on becoming proficient at it that she progressed rapidly, and before long, she started entering contests. Whenever she got stuck on a project, she sat down and prayed for help. In response, a Renaissance painter named Fra Angelico showed up in her dream state to give her specific tips on how to improve her work. He guided her through one particularly difficult painting and did such an excellent job at instructing her that she won a national contest with it!

Invoking famous people to help you may seem like a bold or outrageous idea, but why not? These souls took their talents to a masterful level and are more than willing to share what they've learned from the Other Side. My daughter Sabrina, who struggled in school with math and science, had no inhibitions about asking for the very best tutors to aid her, including Einstein (whom she called on regularly). Did he answer? Well, she passed her classes, aced her SATs, and got into an excellent college, so I'd say yes.

If you need assistance in a particular area and can call to mind a famous person who's crossed over into spirit, simply call out their name and request their support. To better succeed, focus on a picture of that person if you can find one; if not, write down their name, meditate on their spirit, and then request that they come forward to help you. There's no need to beg, since they're in spirit and don't have egos anymore. Just ask for help, plain and simple, and be as specific as you can.

Here's a word to the wise: Sometimes people tend to act a little starstruck around famous people and make themselves small in their presence—even dead ones, believe it or not. Just remember that on a soul level, we're all part of one spirit and one family that simply resonates at different frequencies. Helpers (even famous ones) don't see you as small: you're magnificent. They know this and want to help you discover it, too.

When asking famous people on the other side for guidance, remember that their role is to support your creativity and inspire you with your ideas, not give you theirs. This is tricky because you may feel theirs are better. What these guides do is awaken in you the same creative confidence they tapped into while working on their expression and pursuits. You may sense the expertise of such accomplished guides overseeing your artistic development, but they won't override it. You are the creative one in this lifetime, and your best personal creative expression is what they are here to bring out in you.

## CALLING IN YOUR FAMOUS HELPERS

Make a list of deceased celebrities and famous people in your fields of interest and write down their specialty next to their name.

Jane Austen _____Writing novels

Duke Ellington_____Composing music

Johnny Cash_____Writing song lyrics

Maya Angelou_____ Writing poetry

Frida Kahlo _____ Painting

The list can be as long as you like. Carry this list with you wherever you go. Whenever you have a creative need for support, consult the list and see if there is someone you can invoke for help.

If yes, do so right then and there. For example, if you are calling on John Lennon, say "John, I need to write my girlfriend a love song. Can you help me, please?"

Then take a breath and imagine him in the room with you. Have a mental conversation with him and listen to what he has to say. Use your imagination and keep your ego mind out of the conversation. Be open and expect guidance from John and it will come.

You can do the same with any expert guide you call upon. Talk to that guide as if talking to that person directly, like a dear and trusted friend, only in your imagination. Speak to your guide out loud if possible and write down what you hear from your expert.

My client Pam, a therapist, called me one day, more than a bit rattled, and told me Prince had just visited her over breakfast. "I feel as though I am losing my marbles, except that it was such a lively exchange. I was daydreaming with my cup of coffee early this morning, and suddenly he popped into my mind. We had communicated for thirty minutes. I didn't even listen to his music when he was alive. Why would he come to me of all people? Do you think I'm crazy?"

I didn't, of course, and said so. In my world this is perfectly normal. I thought she was lucky. I would love to have breakfast with Prince.

As for why he came to her, I asked, "Are you working on anything? Any creative project, for example, that Prince might want to help with? Maybe he's looking for a way to help himself by helping you?"

"I'm working on a project concerning isolation and how it causes so much trauma. Do you think he is here to weigh in on that?"

"I'm not sure. Ask him," I answered. "Seems like he was very isolated by fame and maybe that is even how he died. A direct conversation is best. Have one."

I never heard from Pam again, so I am not sure if she continued to communicate with Prince or not. I do know that spirits such as Prince show up at times to assist on projects of yours they are familiar with.


## YOUR TURN

To invoke your helper guides—famous or familiar, friends or family, personally known or otherwise—focus on which areas you'd like help in and then ask for the highest level of expertise to assist you. It's wonderful to call in deceased family members or friends, but be careful—just because they're out of body doesn't necessarily make them instantly enlightened.

If they were talented in a certain area when they were alive, your loved ones can be helpful from the spirit plane in that area as well. But if your mother was a hopeless gambler, for example, don't seek her help on debt! By contrast, if your grandmother was happily married to the same man for 60 years before she died, she might be a great resource to help you with relationship challenges. Just remember to use common sense and manners when asking for help, just as you would when asking people for help on this plane. Open your heart, quiet your mind, and listen for their guidance. It *will* come.

## Helpers can help you

- Finish a task
- Choose an outfit
- Find information to complete a project
- Pick the best person for a job
- Bring your attention to information you need
- Offer solutions to problems
- Navigate while driving
- Fix things

Now that you've met your helper guides, let's move on and meet your healer guides.

# CHAPTER 18

# Healer Guides

Some of the most beneficial guides you'll ever connect with are your healers, who come in two forms: 1) those who have been healers, doctors, or caretakers in past human incarnations and focus on healing your body; and 2) light beings who come from very high energetic frequencies but may never have been in human form, who heal your spirit.

As a rule, healer guides use every means possible to attract your attention, including communicating telepathically, appearing in your dreams, nudging you physically, and causing other sensations in your body. They may also send agents to bring you messages and have been known to go to great lengths to direct you to the right place at the right time. They'll use any clever maneuver they can.

These beings are subtle at first, but they turn up the volume and intensify their efforts according to the severity of your situation, doing everything in their power to get through to you. And unlike your helper guides, you don't have to ask for their input, partially because you may not be aware that you need it. They've made a soul commitment to guide you throughout your life.

Members of this group don't interfere with your choices, but they do let you know when the choices you make aren't in alignment with your health and well-being. For example, my client Tom was recently diagnosed with type 2 diabetes. He said that for more than 15 years, every time he reached for a second piece of cake or a third bottle of beer, he'd feel a slight physical tension and a small voice in his left ear saying, "Too much, too much."

He dismissed it as just being his conscience nagging him, but deep down, he sensed that it was something more. The voice felt as though it wasn't coming from inside, but rather from someone next to him. And because he was slender and didn't indulge all that much, no one else ever suggested that he cut back.

When he received the diagnosis, he asked, "How did this happen?"

His doctor replied, "Who knows? It could be genetics, or maybe bad habits. Or too much of the wrong thing in your diet— amounts that are okay for others, but not you." Hearing the words "too much" was no surprise to Tom, because his healer guides had been telling him that for years.

## HEALERS WARN YOU

Healer spirits not only warn you when personal choices could cause harm, but also alert you to environmental problems as well.

A friend of mine, Louise, highly intuitive herself, was ready to begin a new chapter in her life a year after her partner of 30 years unexpectedly died. She decided to rent a beautifully renovated vintage house in the Cherry Creek neighborhood of Denver that was owned by her longtime friend and architect, Fred, who wanted to help her move on.

However, 10 days into her new living situation, she began to feel deeply exhausted and nauseous like never before. At first, she attributed this to stress and anxiety caused by the move itself. But something told her it was not that. Moreover, every time she went by the state-of-the-art laundry room just off the kitchen, she felt something was "off." Even though the laundry room was a renter's dream on the surface, her intuition told her it was unsafe to go near it.

Because Fred had been so helpful in offering the house and moving her in, Louise didn't want to say anything at first, hoping she was imagining things. One night, however, Louise abruptly woke up from a dead sleep after having a nightmare that she was buried alive and couldn't breathe. That was all she needed. She *knew* without a doubt that her guides had sent her a warning in this dream, and she needed to act on it, fast. She called Fred in the morning and said, "Something is really wrong in the house, maybe the laundry room, Fred. I need you to come and look at it."

Fred was both surprised and impatient with Louise, thinking he had just done her a great favor by inviting her to be his tenant, and now all she was doing was complaining. Clearly annoyed, he asked Louise for specific details. Was the washing machine broken? Was the dryer not working? What exactly was the problem?

Louise didn't know the answer to his questions and couldn't explain the cause of her unease. The only thing she could tell him was that she had been warned by her guides and was not going to ignore this. Fred needed to check the place out. He pushed back, saying Louise was "imagining things," and being "too sensitive," and urged her to let it go. It did no good. Louise was not going to be dismissed. She was so insistent that there was indeed a problem that she said she couldn't stay in the house one more night and was going to a hotel. She would not return until he brought in a home inspector to check out the laundry room and assure her everything was safe.

Exasperated, Fred scoffed, "Okay, Louise, but this is ridiculous. This is a completely renovated home. There are no problems."

Louise then went a step further. "I want to believe you, Fred, but I need written proof from the inspector that this is true and not just take your word for it. I hope you understand because my dream and the way I feel inside the house tell me otherwise."

Fred was ready to kick her out by now, annoyed that his "nice friend" had turned out to be the tenant from hell. Except, when the inspector tested for problems, he discovered that there were not only high levels of mold in the laundry room, but also signs of a carbon monoxide leak. "Let's put it this way," he told Fred. "I wouldn't want to live here, and you are lucky your tenant discovered these problems before a real disaster occurred for you as the landlord." The problem was so big that the laundry room needed to be torn out completely and redone. Fred was shocked and apologized.

Vindicated, Louise was let out of her lease and moved out the next morning. At the risk of losing a friend, she had trusted her healers and knew they were only trying to save her life with their interference. It sometimes takes courage to listen to your healer guides, but Louise knew from experience they were reliable, and she needed to listen, even at the risk of looking like a fool. Better that than getting sick, or worse.

## SPIRITUAL REFERRALS

Healers sometimes work indirectly by placing you in the presence of people who will give you information that you need to stay healthy, such as a new screening test or treatment, or even something as simple as the right doctor. The events often seem accidental, but they aren't; there's intelligent orchestration involved in putting you in the right place at the right time to get what you need.

For example, one day, I made an appointment to have a facial, which I seldom do, but rather than going to the neighborhood salon, I was guided to drive two suburbs away to see a woman who worked out of her home. I'd known her for years as a client but had never considered using her services before my healer guides said, "Go to Erica," in my mind just as clearly as if someone had spoken to me out loud.

"Erica?" I asked. "Isn't she a bit far away for just a facial?"

"Go to Erica," I heard again, and so I went.

Erica was delighted to see me and couldn't have done a better job on my skin. As she worked, I told her about the constant battle my younger daughter, Sabrina, was having with migraine headaches, severe bellyaches, and sleepless nights, the cause of which none of her doctors could pinpoint. This had been going on for years and had made her life miserable.

Erica told me about a noted nutritionist who might be able to help. This approach had never occurred to me, and I felt tremendous relief that I could now do something to aid my daughter.

Taking this tip as a message from the healers and the real reason I had been sent to Erica, Sabrina and I went to the nutritionist, who determined that my daughter was allergic to wheat and dairy products and cut both of them from her diet right away. Her symptoms immediately subsided, and she experienced relief within days.

Guides are often useful in assisting with ailments that confuse medical doctors, and they try to help our earthly healers as much as possible. This was the case for my client Loraine, who, at age 36, was the picture of health, and a fitness fanatic. An avid runner, very conscientious about her diet, and devoted to other healthful behaviors, she couldn't understand why gradually her health began to deteriorate. To her horror, in the course of one year she went from being a vibrant young woman to nearly incapacitated for no apparent reason. Her energy dwindled, leaving her almost totally bedridden; her hair fell out, her vision blurred, and her mind wouldn't focus.

Diagnosed variously with depression, Epstein–Barr virus, chronic fatigue syndrome, lupus, and even bipolar disorder, she underwent test after test. Nothing conclusive was discovered and her condition worsened.

In the meantime, she lost her job, and ended her relationship with her partner due to the stress her illness created for both of them. She had no will to keep going. In desperation, she came to me for a reading, hoping that I could help.

"Am I losing my mind?" she cried as she sat down in my office. "I can hardly get up to go to the bathroom, and the doctors tell me that I'm just depressed. Will this ever go away?"

I asked both my healers and hers what the problem was. They were very clear and direct: "Diet," they answered.

"Diet?" she scoffed. "How can that be? I eat nothing but vegetables and fish. I have a great diet, better than most."

"The guides say 'diet,'" I insisted.

"But I eat no red meat or sugar or processed food, so how can that be the problem?"

"Maybe it's the fish," I answered.

"How can it be the fish? Fish is good for you."

"I don't know," I said. "Ask your doctor about it. Maybe he knows something that we don't."

Loraine started to leave. She was disappointed that neither my guides nor hers could get a better read on her illness, and she let me know it.

I was let down, too. I'd hoped to give her something more helpful from the guides, but I never have control over what they say. Still, their message was so clear that I felt it would eventually make sense.

"I'm sorry you're disappointed," I said at the door, "but don't rule out what came through. Just ask your doctor next time and see what he says."

A week later, Loraine called back. "Sonia!" she exclaimed. "The doctors finally know what's making me so sick! It's mercury poisoning from all the fish I've been eating. After you suggested this in my reading, I decided to check it out, even though I thought you were way off. I made the appointment with my doctor, and after some more tests it turns out, you were right! I've been eating fish like mad because I thought it would help me get better, while it is the very thing making me feel worse by the day. Thank you so much for suggesting I look at my diet once more. Maybe I can finally turn my health around."

"Don't thank me," I said. "Thank your healer guides. They're the ones who pointed out the problem."

Healer guides don't only warn about environmental dangers and monitor your physical health. They also diligently attend to your soul, which can get sick and fragmented due to depression, drugs, alcoholism, trauma, and abuse, especially in childhood. They work on your energy field as well, which can become depleted due to a weak identity, low self-esteem, exhaustion, or poor personal boundaries.

My client Noah suffered for years from depression and substance abuse. His struggle took a considerable toll on his life: his wife left him, he went bankrupt, and his kids stopped talking to him. It wasn't that he wasn't trying to sober up and, in his words, "grow up." He tried medication for depression, 12-step programs, and went to group therapy. In his heart, however, he felt more comfortable blaming everyone else for his choices than getting real with himself—that is, until his drinking buddy and fellow self-pity addict suddenly died from a brain aneurysm.

Devastated, he saw the emptiness of his wasted, self-destructive years and went to bed crying. And for probably the first time in his life, he asked for help from "someone out there," and meant it.

Noah fell into a deep slumber in which he entered what some call a "lucid dream." He found himself standing next to a very tall, handsome bearded man in a long red-and-gray coat with black boots. They both looked down at Noah's sleeping body, then the spirit-Noah said, "I'm sick of myself. Is there any cure for that?"

The man gave him a profoundly heart-penetrating smile and replied, "Forgive your past, be of service, cleanse your body and mind of toxins, serve God, and know that we are here to help you."

Noah woke up, still hearing the man's voice in his head, and for the first time in his life he felt as if someone cared about him and could help. With that, his crazy lifestyle was over, and he ended his self-destructive behavior. Some profound wound within him had instantly healed.

He called it a miracle, and I do, too. At the age of 46, he sobered up and went back to school to become a teacher, something he'd strongly desired but lacked the courage to do before. Noah was no longer floundering and causing pain to others. He was back on his path and in the flow.

I've witnessed many such miracles through the grace of God and the assistance of a powerful healer guide. The most important part of their work is to teach you to have faith so that you can step out of your own way and allow the Universal Divine forces of heaven to come through you to heal your body, mind, and soul.

## HANDS-ON HEALING

Years ago, my friend Lilly, who'd recently moved from Bulgaria to Chicago, suffered a cracked tooth and found herself in great pain and distress. Needing a dentist fast—and one who could speak Bulgarian at that—her options for immediate help were limited to a practitioner who had a less-than-stellar reputation. Desperate for relief, Lilly decided to go ahead and work with this person, but before she sat down in the chair, she began fervently praying to her healer guides to come to her assistance.

> *The highest purpose of your healer guides is to heal your heart and fill you with self-love.*

Closing her eyes as she opened her mouth, she suddenly saw in her mind's eye a tall, fiery-looking shaman with red flames for hair who announced himself as Zonu. Reassured by his presence, Lilly asked him to guide the dentist to do a good job in repairing (and hopefully saving) her tooth. Seconds later, another guide appeared, a woman named Madame Q, who conferred with Zonu.

The next thing Lilly knew, these two were working together, guiding the dentist's hand as they took over the procedure. Only 20 minutes later, the dentist—to her own astonishment—announced that she was finished. In that short time, she'd managed not only to save the tooth but also to rebuild it to perfection, something she'd never succeeded in doing before.

Not surprised, Lilly knew that this success was due to Zonu and Madame Q's help. She nevertheless thanked the dentist profusely and said, "I had no doubt that you'd be able to do a perfect job for me."

The highest purpose of your healer guides is to heal your heart and fill you with self-love. All other healing follows this.

At age 37, my client Julie had just emerged from an acrimonious five-year divorce battle in which she lost her home and the custody of her two sons. No sooner had the ink dried on the divorce decree when she was dealt another devastating blow: she discovered a lump in her right breast, was diagnosed with stage 4 breast cancer, and was given a bleak prognosis, with little chance for survival. Still reeling from the toll of her familial troubles, she found this news almost too much to bear. Pulling herself together, she immediately began aggressive treatment, including a double mastectomy, radiation, and chemotherapy, but not only did her treatment leave her broken and sick, but it also wiped out her will to live.

One night as Julie lay drained from nausea and grief, she decided that it wasn't worth trying to live. She'd lost her body as she knew it, her boys, her home, even her identity as a wife and mother, and felt that there was nothing left. Despairing, all she wanted to do was die.

When she eventually fell asleep, she dreamed that she was surrounded by 10 beautiful women of all ages who were gently singing lullabies, combing her hair, and rubbing her feet and toes as if she were the most precious child on Earth. Starting to cry, she asked why they were so kind to her.

The eldest one smiled and said that they'd come to help her heal and begin to enjoy her life once again. Julie responded that she had nothing to live for and that she was a complete failure, but the woman simply smiled again and kept combing her hair and singing to her.

Allowing herself to enjoy their loving care, Julie began to relax on a profound level, and the next thing she knew, it was morning. It seemed as if all that remained of the dream was a lasting warm sensation in her chest, yet there was something else. Remarkably, she felt peaceful and wanted very much to live. It was as if those women had lifted the weight of her grief out of her body.

Not looking back or feeling ashamed anymore, Julie dove into her healing with a vengeance. She changed her diet, joined a support group, and got a therapist and a coach. Two years later, she was proclaimed cancer-free. That was seven years ago. "Those women worked a miracle on me," she told me.

"They were your healers," I answered, "and yes, they did. They opened the door for you to love yourself, and *that* is what healed your body."

---

### Did You Know That . . .

- Healer guides will always leave you feeling peaceful, self-loving, and self-accepting.

- They are gentle, noncoercive, and forgiving.

- They speak to your heart, not your ego; to your eternal essence, not your mortal self.

---

If you suffer from a lack of faith, it means that somewhere along the way you got disconnected from your loving Divine Source and Creator. Like a beautiful flower without a garden to grow in, life without faith becomes a struggle to survive. This is perhaps the most considerable drain on your health—body, mind, and soul—and something that you should ask your healer guides to restore. They'll respond by opening your heart, quieting your mind, and raising your vibration.

Your healers can do remarkable things for you, but *only* if you follow their direction and cooperate by loving yourself. Start by knowing that in each illness lies an opportunity to learn, love, and honor yourself, and to accept God's love. When this Divine affection isn't blocked, healing can occur.

The fact that you have the power to help yourself heal doesn't imply that your illness is in any way your fault. Each soul takes on challenges for reasons that no one else can judge or fully understand. When combined with environmental toxins, emotional stresses, and karmic soul lessons in which you must face the consequences and repercussions of poor choices in past lives, this life, or beyond, it's virtually impossible to determine a simple reason for any imbalance. All illnesses are lessons, either for the person who experiences them or for those around that individual.

The first lesson the healer guides share is: "When it comes to illness (or life, for that matter), don't judge—not yourself, not anyone, not ever!" And the second lesson is: "Forgive—first yourself, then everyone else." If you're willing to take these two steps, you'll clear the way for these beings to do their work.

It's important to note that your healing guides aren't a substitute for seeking professional medical, psychological, and emotional care when you need it. In fact, another one of their important jobs is to steer you to find the right professional help. They did this for me after the birth of my second daughter, when my body collapsed into profound chronic fatigue. No matter how much I slept, I kept feeling worse. I went to endless doctors and underwent countless tests, to no avail.

I asked my healer guides for help, and then the next day I went to a bookstore to pick up some books for my daughter Sonia. While I was there, a book on hypothyroidism fell off a shelf and almost onto my head. Needless to say, it got my attention! I'd been tested for the disorder before, and at the time my doctor said that my thyroid hormone level was borderline and not a problem. But after reading the book, I knew that something wasn't right.

My healers then made me aware of a holistic doctor, whom I visited for a second opinion. My levels were still marginally okay, but he put me on a very low dose of natural thyroid hormone anyway, and that did the trick. One month later, my energy level rose, and I had my life back. Once again, the healer guides both pointed out the problem and led me to the right doctor for treatment.

My experience with the book isn't unusual, as that's one of the most common means through which these guides communicate. My teacher Charlie told me that if a book is recommended to you once, it might be a sign from the healers. If people mention it to you twice, then it's definitely a message from them. And if you hear about it three times, they're screaming at you to pay attention!

Healer spirits are overseen by the healing angels and work on a very high frequency, with the highest degree of love and compassion. Similar to your helpers, many of these guides have also been in human form at some point, so they understand the particular challenges of the human experience and what causes people to become sick and imbalanced. Many of them are from the lost civilizations of Atlantis and Lemuria and come to share the knowledge that they acquired in their past incarnations. All the ones I've worked with have been tireless, devoted, and felt very privileged to help.

As is the case with all guides, however, they can't *make* you well and balanced; you must do that for yourself. They work under the motto, "God helps those who help themselves." They are your partners in health—and if you follow, they'll lead the way.


## YOUR TURN

To invoke your healers to open your heart or mend your body, you must first find compassion and love for yourself and be willing to be healed. With your cooperation, they'll know exactly what to do.

To invoke healers on another's behalf, open your heart to theirs and send the same unconditional love and compassion to them. Don't focus on the illness, since to do so would be like watering a weed to make it grow. Instead, focus on 100 percent wellness according to God's plan.

In both cases, the next step is prayer, to which healer guides respond immediately. Myriad studies confirm that those who pray and are prayed for heal more quickly than those without this aid.

My favorite healing prayer is:

*Divine Mother God, Father God, and all healing forces of the Universe, restore me to balance in body, mind, and spirit.*

*Remove everything from my consciousness and body that isn't in perfect alignment with your loving plan for me.*

*I give my full permission and cooperation to all healing forces of Divine and loving nature to serve my well-being.*
*Amen*

## Healers can help you

- Heal your body
- Heal your emotions
- Mend a broken heart
- Heal from past trauma
- Heal from past-life karma
- Forgive others
- Improve your self-esteem
- Fight exhaustion
- Lift your mood
- Fix your finances
- Release shame
- End addictions
- Grieve peacefully
- And much more

Now that you've met your healer guides, let's move on and meet your teacher guides.

# CHAPTER 19

# Teacher Guides

Some of our soul's most devoted guides are our spiritual teachers. These spirit guides resonate at a very high frequency and work closely with us to raise our awareness and understanding of our true nature as spiritual beings, concentrating their efforts on helping us discover our purpose in life as well as to work through our karma, or life lessons. In fact, the word "karma" means "to learn" and implies a classroom.

Unlike runners and helpers, these guides have little or no interest in the day-to-day affairs of our lives. They don't concern themselves with questions such as "Will I get married?" or "Should I buy a new car?" Instead, their attention is directed to freeing you from the limitations of your ego and expanding your awareness so that you can fully embrace your unlimited potential to live in joy as a Divine being. They're also committed to guiding you in how best to learn to love yourself unconditionally so you can eventually extend that love to others. They are here to teach you the value of serving your fellow human beings. They help you to open your heart and to release and dispel illusions, fear, judgments, resentments, false ideas, self-imposed limitations, and feelings of unworthiness.

Often, the same teacher guides oversee your soul's journey from one lifetime to the next. They group together to make up your soul's school, with each period you spend on Earth representing another level of advancement—much like being promoted to the next grade in school here on the physical plane. Some teacher guides have lived past lives as mortals, and as such, are sympathetic to the difficulties that humans face as they learn how to advance in life. They've often been wise men and women, mentors, or holy ones, and choose to continue this work on the spirit plane. They have infinite love, patience, and compassion, and often show much humor as they strive to help keep you aligned with your soul's desires.

Although these guides may have taught you in past lives, they still must wait for a signal from you before they step forward and begin working with you again. Some may even have been instructors you've known in this life, now crossed over to the other side. I've spoken with many psychics, mediums, and other spiritual messengers over the years, and nearly all of them have at least one influential teacher who's passed over but who remains a prominent guide in their soul's work. These continuing relationships are soul contracts that run deep and long and are not interrupted by death.

Two of my lifetime teachers, Charlie Goodman and Dr. Tully, both passed into spirit many years ago, yet they continue to work closely with me from that plane. I feel their guidance as clearly as when I sat as a shy, young student in their respective classrooms all those years ago. Looking back, I am sure that wasn't our first time meeting one another or working together.

Charlie, my first teacher, taught me almost everything I know about the spirit world and was the first to introduce me to the proper protocol in working with many of my guides. I'm very aware of his presence whenever and wherever I teach classes, and even now, as I write this book. His particular calling card was (and still is) a laugh like a tumbling waterfall, with energy to match. His chortles remind me over and over that, on a soul level, all is well at all times and that I should never get too worked up about anything.

I loved Charlie, and I'm grateful that I've been able to stay connected to him after his death. He knows my strengths and weaknesses, and every time I veer off my path because of insecurity, fear, judgment, impatience, self-righteousness, or anger, I hear his laugh shattering the spell I've fallen under. With it, I know he's bringing me back to center.

Dr. Tully, my other primary spiritual teacher in this life, was much less personal but had no less of an impact on my learning process. He demonstrated, again and again, the direct correlation between my thoughts and my experiences. His detached style was part of his power, and through him I learned to be less emotional and more objective in my response to the world, a painful lesson that I was grateful to learn (and with which I still need help). His powerful voice is his calling card; it cuts through my mental chatter and silences my emotional reactivity immediately. He taught me to tame my mind rather than entertain its confusion. He's also the one who showed me that my soul's purpose in this life is to be creative and to accept full responsibility for the life I create.

> *Much of our contact with teacher guides occurs while we sleep or daydream, as we're all too often preoccupied with day-to-day dramas in our waking lives to remember our higher callings.*

My most impressive spirit teacher guides are known as the Three Bishops. They've been with me for several lifetimes, and I am confident I studied with them when I was a French priest examining ancient mysteries in the Middle Ages. The Three Bishops guide both me and my clients in matters of life purpose, clearing karma, forgiving, and releasing what is challenging to forgive and accept, as well as the importance of developing integrity and character. They're quite direct when pointing out poor choices and where mistakes were made. Although the Three Bishops don't mince words, their delivery is exceptionally loving and often humorous as they speak to the highest potential in both me and my clients.

Perhaps you can think of someone who serves as your teacher in spirit. Some of these guides may still be alive and not only direct you in waking consciousness, but also visit you in your dreams or connect with you while you're in reverie. Much of our contact with teacher guides occurs while we sleep or daydream, as we're all too often preoccupied with day-to-day dramas in our waking lives to remember our higher callings. They also visit us during meditation, which is an ideal way to have direct contact while in a conscious state. Their assistance will most likely continue after their deaths.

In my years of work as a spiritual teacher, I've had quite a few students report seeing me in their dreams or having me pop into their awareness out of nowhere. Some even see me in spirit standing before or behind them as they struggle with issues. I'm not surprised. Spirit isn't defined by the physical body, so mine can be in two places at once. I must admit that when I wake up in the morning, I often feel as though I've been busy all night helping and teaching my students, and these reports confirm it!

## IT'S ALL IN THE FAMILY

Spirit teachers on a soul level can be our friends on this plane as well. Teacher guides, more than any other type of guide, surround us on all levels and all planes, even the physical one, at all times, even though we may fail to recognize most of these guides as teachers. In fact, many of our most demanding spiritual teachers are our own family members or close friends. One of my greatest teacher guides is my mother, a Holocaust survivor who, at the time of this writing, is 90 years old and still going strong. No other person has taught me how to feel, sense, see, trust, and work with spirit on all planes more than her. No spirit has challenged me as much either, teaching me such difficult lessons as detachment, patience, tolerance, humor, and surrendering control. She is truly my master teacher on those fronts. I am grateful for all her lessons and recognize her to be one of the greatest blessings in my life.

Spirit teachers may be dear friends whom you love and who lift you up when you are down. My friend Lu, whom I've known since I was 14 years old, is such a teacher. Not only does she help me every single time I call or see her, but I also frequently get help from her in my dreams. When sleeping, I visit her regularly, and we have long, deep, soul-healing conversations, which I value as much as my phone and in-person connections. In this case, I'm the student visiting my teacher at night, sometimes having classes till dawn. I wake up exhausted when this happens. This may be why you sometimes awaken fatigued in the morning as well. Maybe your spirit was pulling an all-nighter learning or instructing others, too.

Do you recognize a family member who may be one of your spirit teachers? It might be someone who inspires and supports you (like my mom) or someone who drives you up the wall (like my mom). Maybe a good friend—or even a "frenemy"—is serving your growth as a teacher guide. Not all teacher guides are easy to be with, because growth is difficult.

With all this in mind, see if you can now identify spirit teachers that you missed before, and appreciate them in an entirely new light.

## TEACHER GUIDES INVITE GROWTH

You can tell if someone is your spirit teacher if they push your buttons and/or cause you to want to look inward, open your mind and heart, do something different and better than before, and in the end be more loving and creative all the way around, both toward yourself and with others. If they're still of this world, you may very well be their spirit teacher guide at the same time.

It may surprise you to think of some of your teacher guides as living people, or even to view yourself as a possible teacher guide to others, but we all have an ancient soul history, and we're evolved—even masterful—in some areas, while we still have a long way to go in others. Both Charlie and Dr. Tully taught me that our spirits are both instructors and students of one another at the same time because we're all connected like cells in a body—all showing each other how to grow on different levels.

## TEACHER GUIDES SEND YOU TO SCHOOL

Other teachers no longer walk the earth, or never did. Some are ancient, wise spirit guides who long ago acquired the spiritual awareness and discipline to quiet the mind and make direct contact with the Divine. These elevated, gentle, loving, and incredibly patient beings show up when you begin to question the nature and purpose of your life and want to live in a more meaningful way. Having worked hard for so long to dissolve their egos, many of these spirit guides choose to remain anonymous.

Teacher guides work indirectly, often making you aware of and motivating you to attend specific lectures, workshops, seminars, and spiritual gatherings. Years ago, when I became overwhelmed by my marriage, kids, and work, I asked my teacher guides to direct me to what I needed to learn so that my life would flow easier. The very next day, I was made aware of a personal growth workshop called the Hoffman Quadrinity Process, a six-day intensive program where I could learn creative new strategies for living in my spirit. It turned out to be one of the best classes I've ever taken. (Check it out at hoffmaninstitute.org.)

Since then, my guides have sent me on to other classrooms, including workshops on the Enneagram, breathwork, kundalini meditation, singing therapy, and cooking classes. My teacher guides have lovingly made me aware of all of these opportunities to grow my soul and raise my vibration over the years, and I'm sure they will be sending me on to others in the future. At least I hope so.

I also believe most of the students who have shown up in my workshops were sent by their teacher guides, just as my spirit guides sent me to my earthly teacher guides' classrooms. In this way, we are all helping one another grow on all levels at all times.

## RAISING GROUP CONSCIOUSNESS

Many spirit teacher guides focus on shifting the mass consciousness to a higher frequency and have been doing so since the 1950s with great success. The relatively low number of "hippies" in the 1960s has now expanded to millions of people interested in spiritual topics, thanks in large part to these guides who've brought meditation, relaxation, massage therapy, and intuitive exploration to a broader audience. They're also responsible, along with healer guides, for bridging the gap between science and religion, mainstreaming spirituality, creating fellowships such as 12-step programs and group therapy, and opening the door to alternative and holistic healing, all of which are pathways to higher learning and healing on a soul level.

---

### Did You Know That . . .

- Teacher guides are coming to us en masse now in virtually every area of learning and expertise.

- They reach out to us as our world is being seriously challenged—especially in our spiritual understanding of things.

- They serve their primary purpose in helping you shed any false identity that you may have connecting you to your ego.

- They lead you to live fully and truthfully in your spirit.

---

You'll know that your teacher guides are with you when you're no longer content with how you handle your life and want to learn more. At the age of 40, Max was the picture of success on the outside: a handsome, single airline pilot with looks, money, and glamour. He was also the only son of a doting—but in his mind, demanding—old-school Italian mother. On the inside, however, he felt miserable, conflicted, and bored, and saw his life as meaningless, resulting in a low-grade depression.

He regularly cheated on his girlfriends and was sexually promiscuous and inconsiderate as often as he could get away with it. He verbally abused and disrespected his mother and put his own needs and convenience alone over anyone else's as a matter of course. His fellow employees had little regard for him because of his arrogance and rude behavior and avoided including him for dinner while on layovers between flights.

One day, sitting alone in an empty airplane in Cleveland as he waited for the crew and passengers to board, he closed his eyes to relax. Suddenly, he felt as though a higher presence had come to visit. It seemed to open a door in his mind that had been nailed shut. He heard no voice and he saw no ghost from Christmases past. He just felt an inner opening that used to be blocked and saw clearly where he was headed given the path that he had been following. His negative behavior suddenly loomed large and he felt ashamed and sad. It was as if a benevolent force had freed his eyes and his heart, and he instantly realized that his life lacked satisfaction because he was so selfish and self-centered.

Max was so appalled at what he'd become that he had trouble concentrating on flying that day. Fortunately, he made it to Chicago (where he was based), but after that, he was unable to continue his flight schedule. He called in sick because that's how he felt.

What followed was his dark night of the soul. With his teacher guides ever present, his new awareness kept expanding back through his life to the day that his dad had died, when Max was only 11—the day that his heart had slammed shut and he'd decided to think only of himself rather than go through the pain of loss again.

Realizing all this, he cried out, "What shall I do?" but he heard nothing. The next morning, still off from work, he went for a drive in the city and ended up at a tiny, hole-in-the-wall New Age and self-help bookstore. Until he walked in and looked around, he'd never known there were such things as self-help books; to him, the word "spirit" only meant cocktails. He was fascinated and spent three hours browsing. Then he bought 10 books, some on the soul, some on purpose and direction, and some on meditation, including my book *True Balance*.

Max's spiritual journey began the day his guides led him to the mirror to see what he'd become. He was then directed to resources for a more authentic existence, first through the bookstore and from there to classes, workshops, intuitive sessions with mentors and other instructors, and eventually to me.

His soul's growth was slow but steady: His teacher guides introduced him to a group of volunteers who helped kids in developing countries who were in dire need of medical care. Time after time, Max flew them to the U.S. for treatment. It was so fulfilling that he cut his job to part-time and put most of his energy into this service. By helping these suffering children, he opened his heart and learned to love again, fully and without defenses. His guides taught him well.

Max realized the teacher guides' highest purpose: to teach us to open our hearts and see the world and ourselves with love, to recognize that we're all one family in spirit. If we injure others, we hurt ourselves; if we aid others, we help ourselves.

## LEARNING FROM THE MASTERS

In addition to receiving soul instruction from our present and past life teacher guides, we also often feel connected to one, two, or even three master spiritual leaders. This group is known collectively as the Ascended Masters or the Brotherhood of the White Light, and they work with us both personally and impersonally to raise our consciousness. The most well-known have walked the earth, such as Jesus, Mother Mary, Quan Yin, Buddha, Mohammad, Wakan Tanka, and St. Germaine, to name a few.

Many people, including me, are deeply drawn to one of these Universal Avatars as their master teacher. I have a client who's so connected to Mother Mary that she prays a rosary to her three times a day. This woman is the most loving soul I've ever met, having been a foster parent to more than 14 children over the years, and adopting 8 more. She believes that it's Mary—the mother of us all—who gives her the endless energy, patience, and faith to pursue this path so joyfully.

Maurice, another client, talks to Jesus about everything in his life, and I understand his devotion. Having lived through a house fire in which he lost his family and was burned on over 40 percent of his body, he said that Jesus taught him to forgive and get on with his life. He now tutors children with disabilities and feels at peace with the painful past and is fulfilling his purpose.

My own master teachers are Mother Mary, Jesus Christ, and Mary Magdalene. These three have been my guiding lights and sources of love and strength for as long as I can remember. These teachers are in my life to show me the power of unconditional love for self and others, non-judgment, forgiveness, and compassion for all human beings. In my heart, I believe I have been following their guidance and love since they walked the earth. Suffice it to say I carry their love in my heart and feel it in every breath I take. I talk to my masters daily and pray nonstop for both personal and world healing. This is a constant mantra in my heart.

Who are your master teachers? For several of my dearest friends, it is Buddha, and their devotion to his teachings is a profound way of life. They make offerings, go to Buddhist retreats, and meditate several times a day with great love and joy in their hearts.

As far as master teachers go, I believe "all roads lead to Rome," so to speak, and we are all on a soul journey back to spirit, back to God, back to the light, and no matter who is our leading guide, we will all arrive in the same place of eternal love in the end.

## SCHOOL'S IN SESSION

You know that you've entered the classroom of a teacher guide if your heart softens, and you become quieter, more inclined to listen than talk. You're under their influence if you desire to read more on spiritual matters, become called to a fellowship or community intended to help you grow, or seek spiritual instruction in some direct way. You're especially following a teacher guide if you feel called to serve humanity in a sincere, selfless manner.

These lessons are adapted to what's right for your soul. These beings know, as should you, that one size doesn't fit all when it comes to spiritual growth. One person's guides may send him to church, while those of another may take her away from the church and direct her to a more personal relationship with God and the Universe.

Teacher guides especially want you to know that there's no one *right* way to grow. You must listen to your own heart, follow your inner guidance, be willing to be uniquely yourself, and run your life based on self-love and acceptance rather than fear or a desire to please others.

Don't ever worry about calling on your teacher guides too often. You're their number one priority through dark nights and confusion. When you ask, they'll step right in.


## YOUR TURN

In a quiet space, first request that your Higher Self open your heart by taking a deep, relaxing breath, then gently ask your teacher guides to reveal themselves to you. *What am I to learn right now, and how can you best help me to do so? What am I hiding from? What am I afraid of?*

Listen quietly, and if you're able to respond to this question out loud, let your heart speak as they guide you to the answer.

Your teachers, more than any other spirits, have impeccable standards for guidance. They don't isolate, praise, or flatter you, although they work hard to create a positive learning experience. They won't compare you to others. They'll only give suggestions, never ultimatums, but they *will* ask the most of you. They had you pick up this book, didn't they?

Teachers, like all guides, know precisely what you need. They'll guide you through a gentle learning curve and stay with you for as long as you require. Just remember, when the student is ready, the teachers appear. If you're ready, then so are they.

## Teacher guides can help you

- Grow in awareness
- Develop your intuition
- Learn to forgive
- Let go of the past
- Face your demons
- Release resentments
- Uncover your blind spots
- Acknowledge your shadow
- Overcome jealousy and materialism
- Love yourself unconditionally
- Increase compassion
- Ask for forgiveness
- Learn your soul lessons
- Love yourself and others unconditionally
- Overcome ego limitations
- Discover your past lives

Now that you've met your teacher guides, let's move on and meet your animal guides.

# CHAPTER 20

# Animal Guides

Some of our most important and influential spirit guides are the most obvious, yet are often overlooked: those of the animal kingdom. There was a time long ago when we humans were closely connected to the natural world and consulted animals for their wisdom and personal power. But even though we've drifted away, this connection has never left us, and different creatures are continually communicating with us both in the physical world and in our dreams as they attempt to guide our souls and spirit.

Animals are part of the teaching world. Some bring us the wisdom and skills to survive, while others show us how to morph and adapt, which can be very useful at times. They may be humorous and playful and teach us how to lighten up and laugh at life's challenges. Many are known for their loyalty and ability to love unconditionally, or perhaps they have a grounded detachment, remaining true to themselves rather than pleasing others. There are detectives and those with the capability to disappear. In one way or another, all of them have fantastic soul-awakening qualities and the ability to speak to us in their own manner.

Animals serve as spirit guides in three ways. First, they simply exist in our lives and communicate directly with us; second, they appear in our dreams, bringing messages through the astral plane. Third, by offering their spirits as gateways to access their unique power and energy, they help us accomplish our goals.

You can start connecting with your animal guides by seeing the spirit of the animals already present in your life. Begin with any pets you have (or have had) and focus on what their essence brings (or brought) you as a gift. My beloved dog Miss T, a black miniature poodle, was a gorgeous, devoted, sensitive soul who worked hard to love all my family members equally and unconditionally. One way she did this was by sleeping with each of us in shifts throughout the night. She would start in my room, then move to my daughter Sabrina's bed for a few hours, then finally migrate to my other daughter Sonia's bedroom where she'd stay until morning. She also sat with us one at a time: with me in my office when I did readings, and at the foot of each of my daughters' desks when they did homework, sometimes pacing back and forth between them. When she was present, we all felt much calmer and happier.

We each recognized how psychic she was and how she communicated with us, no matter the time of day. When I was awake, one look from Miss T would let me know if someone wasn't okay. On the rare occasion that she growled or snarled at anyone, I knew immediately that something about that person wasn't right and I should be on guard.

Once, when my daughters were toddlers, I hired a babysitter who came highly recommended and was very personable. But Miss T wasn't impressed. She barely tolerated the new addition and never took her eyes off her, letting us know that this person wasn't to be trusted. The sitter had worked for us for only a few days when we received a phone call from her frantic father claiming that she was a runaway and that he wanted her home. We'd *felt* that something was amiss, but our little dog *knew* it, and we sent the girl home.

Miss T was a tremendously playful spirit as well, dancing for us, doing funny dog tricks, and playing catch and hide-and-seek when we were down. Her gifts were endless.

A few years before she passed, I'd felt that this sweet spirit wasn't herself, but thought that it wasn't anything too out of the ordinary. Then I dreamed she told me that she was sick and needed to see a doctor. So, the next morning, I took her to the vet, but the doctor couldn't find anything wrong. Later that night, she sat at the foot of my daughter Sonia's bed and let her know that she needed help. Sonia pried her mouth open and found a small chicken bone lodged deep in her throat, which she removed. Miss T could have died, but the minute it was gone, she rebounded to normal. Miss T's sweet spirit still visits me from time to time. When I moved into my third and now present Paris apartment, I dreamed several nights in a row that Miss T was sleeping at my feet on the bed, keeping me company and helping me get settled. Each morning I woke up feeling so happy that her spirit was with me, especially since I was still getting acclimated to living in a new country and beginning my life all over. Her loving presence assured me that I was not alone and that I was being watched over.

Cats are also incredible teachers and communicate with our souls. I've never owned a cat because I'm allergic to them, but my brother Anthony had two tabbies, Summer and Winter Girl, who've kept him grounded and amused through many emotionally challenging times of illness and stress. His cats' antics and calming presence kept his heart open and happy when he could have easily shut down. In many ways, they were his healers, and he said so all the time.

Birds are another type of creature that will speak to you, and my client Marlon has relied on them for guidance. He was about to undertake a new business venture that involved opening movie theaters with his brother-in-law when he spotted an owl in his backyard two nights in a row. Knowing that these birds are predators who are active at night, Marlon felt that it was a signal confirming his suspicion that his brother-in-law would be sneaky and aggressive. Thanking the owl for the warning, Marlon declined to enter the partnership. Once he made that decision, the bird left.

Disappointed, Marlon's brother-in-law took on another collaborator. Eventually, he and the new partner began fighting over who owned what, and accounting cover-ups by both parties were revealed. The theaters closed and lawsuits were filed. Marlon's personal relationship with his brother-in-law, however, remained intact, thanks to the owl.

Birds can bring both warnings and encouragement. Shortly after my in-laws had a terrible accident many years ago, black crows suddenly filled the trees in front of the house and began to caw, as if to bring a message. I've always taken crows to signify power and magic, so I knew that their presence was significant.

For 10 minutes, the crows called out at full volume, and then they flew away. I don't speak crow, of course, but in my heart and soul I knew that they were telling us that my family would be all right. My in-laws did get better eventually, and to this day, I thank the birds for reassuring me at a time when things looked so bleak.

Another time, I was in a deep quandary over whether to switch publishers from Random House to Hay House, which I had been invited to do. This happened when I was in France, visiting the host family I'd spent time with years earlier as a young student. Uncertain if this would be a wise move, I asked my guides to give me a definite sign and then went to bed.

As if awakened by some higher force, I shot out of a deep sleep at five in the morning and looked out the window. Heading straight toward me was a large white dove, which flew in through the bedroom window and *hit me squarely in the head*! Knowing from my teachers that birds are messengers of the soul and from my Catholic upbringing that this white dove was the symbol of the Holy Spirit, I was immediately assured that making the change was something I must do.

Meanwhile, the poor dove got knocked for a loop and landed in a daze in the corner of the bedroom. She recovered her composure after a moment or two, then flew out the window and into the sunrise. I changed publishers and changed my life for the better in a million and one ways.

My nephew Jacob told me the following beautiful bird story. Feeling upset and missing his father on the first anniversary of his death, Jacob decided to go for a walk along a deserted Michigan beach near his home. As he walked, a magnificent bald eagle, the first he had ever seen in that state, seemed to come out of nowhere and soared above him. Jacob then looked down and saw a rose frozen in the ice. The events both shook him and strangely comforted him, and he knew that the eagle was a messenger from his father.

These are just a few examples of how closely animal guides can be connected to you and how they show up to teach you more about your spirit. Once you begin to notice these encounters, your mind will open up to the more significant ways that these beings offer direction in your life—and they don't even have to be alive to do so!

Once I was riding my bike along the Chicago lakefront and nearly ran over a huge, smashed rat. Swerving to avoid it, I knew that this disturbing sign had a particular and timely message for me. Two thoughts came to mind: 1) rats are less than savory, and 2) they live in my environment. Adding up the signs and evidence, I felt that the spirit of the dead rat was warning me of my undesirable community and the bad ending it could bring me if I didn't watch out. The more I thought about it, the more I had to acknowledge that there were several individuals I was connecting with at the time who didn't share my ethics and values and were, in many ways, quite rat-like. That rodent was a warning for me to step away from these people before something ended badly (as had happened to the animal), so I did.

A few months later, it came to my attention that one of these unsavory "rats" had stolen money and credit cards belonging to mutual friends and then left town to avoid prosecution. It was indeed an unfortunate ending, but due to the warning the dead rat had offered me, I was spared the drama.

> *Once you begin to notice these encounters, your mind will open up to the more significant ways that these beings offer direction in your life—and they don't even have to be alive to do so!*

## ANIMAL SPIRITS GIVE YOU POWER TO PREVAIL

My client Eleanor, an intuitive coach and grief counselor, has really been through the ringer in her life, having beaten cancer twice, suffered the death of her only son from a drug overdose, and lost her home due to a poor financial decision during the mortgage crisis in the nineties. She said it was so bad for a while that on many nights she literally prayed for her life to end because the pain was too much to bear and she saw no way forward.

On one particularly dark night, after crying for hours and hours, reeling with grief from the death of her only son, she finally fell into a deep sleep, during which she had the most extraordinary dream.

In it, she was walking in a field followed by a beautiful black and silver stallion, appearing over eight feet tall. Ahead were threatening clouds and lightning, and a terrible storm coming her way fast. She became afraid as she saw no place to seek shelter, but the horse nudged her from behind as if to get her attention. Calmed by his powerful presence, he somehow telepathically conveyed to her the message, "Peace. I am your protector. My name is Flight and I will carry you through this storm."

The next thing Eleanor knew she was on his back, galloping at lightning speed straight toward the storm, first on the ground and then suddenly in the air, as Flight sprouted wings, like Pegasus. They instantly soared above the clouds where she was showered with blinding sunlight and intense warmth, causing all stress to leave her body, replaced by deep relaxation and peace.

She woke up, still feeling the warmth on her skin. Eleanor was convinced that this was not an ordinary dream and that the horse, Flight, was her spirit guide. She felt so buoyed by this experience and Flight's presence that her deepest grief began to ease, replaced by a profound sense that all was well, even with her deceased son.

It was that dream that began her mission to learn all she could about spirituality, grief, loss, death, rebirth, and healing, which became her soul's purpose in life. She felt Flight with her every moment from that dream on. "He gives me the confidence and power to guide others through the dark night of the soul, as he did me. He is my anchor, strength, and friend. I would not be here or do what I do without him."

As that experience shows, animal spirits are at times powerful teachers and healers, and will help us through the worst.

## Notice this

- Watch how fish in an aquarium, or even only one swimming in a fishbowl, bring you a profound sense of well-being as they smoothly glide through the water.

- Turtles teach you how to withdraw from the world and retreat into your own being whenever you feel stressed and overwhelmed.

- Hamsters teach you how to work together with enthusiasm as they play on their wheels and sleep together in their cages.

- Kittens teach you to be spontaneous, light-hearted, and silly as they chase one another or bat a piece of string.

### Did You Know That . . .

- Animal guides are some of your most powerful spirit guides.

- They enhance your life and activate your creativity and intuition.

- They help return lost pieces of your soul and reconnect you to the natural world.

If your life is stagnant or in need of healing, you can request animal spirits to come and help you change your vibration and arouse your energy. Just remember that when calling these guides forward, it's the animal spirit who chooses you, not the other way around.

This chapter is only an introduction to these fantastic beings. There are many excellent books available on how to work with animal guides if you're interested in learning more. For now, be open to all creatures—those in your life, those who cross your path, those in your dreams, and the animal guides who serve as your spirit helper. They're to be loved, respected, and valued deeply for their help and service to your soul. If you allow it, they will serve you well.


## YOUR TURN

Do you own a pet, or are you around other animals? Start connecting to these guides by appreciating the unique spirit in your own pet or any creature you engage with regularly.

What lessons can you learn from them? What message or healing do you receive from them?

Next, begin to recognize where animals show up in your life in other ways. For example, have you noticed any birds lately? How about deer or horses?

Think about whether any recurring animals are presenting themselves to you in some way. Perhaps you keep meeting hawks, rabbits, or other wild beasts. Ask your spirit what these beings are trying to tell you and trust what you feel.

Keep a journal by your bed and note any visitations by animals or birds in your dreams. Tell someone you trust about these experiences, because whenever a creature gets your attention, it's bringing you a spirit message.

If you want to connect with your animal spirit, you must use your imagination. Here's how:

- Relax in a comfortable place where you won't be disturbed.

- Imagine going into a cave or an old, hollow tree, and emerging in a natural setting such as a meadow or field.

- Experience the peace and power of nature in this place.

- Ask your animal guide to appear in this beautiful place and speak to you. Trust whatever animal appears and how it chooses to communicate. You may sense, feel, hear, see, or simply know in your heart that it's present.

- Once you're connected to your guide, use your imagination and go back through the field or meadow to your cave or tree, and then step back into present reality. Take a moment to get grounded and slowly open your eyes.

- Once you know what your animal guide is, study it to learn all that you can about it. There are many books on animal spirits that you find in metaphysical bookstores.

- After you connect, thank your animal and ask it to send you a sign that it is indeed your spirit guide. The indication can appear in many ways: You may see its face on a card, in a picture, in a magazine, or on TV. You may even observe a live version. Be patient, and it will appear.

## Animal guides can help you

- Teach you their wisdom
- Wake you up to blind spots
- Help you move ahead in life
- Heal your soul wounds and help you move on
- Offer insights on your relationships
- Help you recover from loss
- Retrieve lost pieces of your soul due to trauma
- Show you a way forward
- Act as trackers and lead you to openings and out of danger

Now that you've met your animal guides, let's move on and meet your joy guides.

# CHAPTER 21

# Joy Guides

One of my most beloved groups is joy guides. These are the child spirits of the Universe, and their job is to keep *your* inner child alive and well. Sometimes they're children who've lived and then crossed over while still very young, but more often they've never been in human form. As you might expect, they have high, light, and joyful vibrations, and work to keep us from taking ourselves and the human drama too seriously.

Joy guides show up when they're least expected, usually when our egos are so drugged by our self-important suffering that we've lost all perspective and isolated ourselves from our usual support system. This isn't to say that all our pain is self-imposed. There are plenty of times when we face overwhelming challenges and heartbreaking loss, at which point our angels and healers rally to get us through. Even then, however, these delightful spirits appear to ease our pain, distract us from our sorrow with their comedic antics, and remind us to detach and get a breath of air for a moment. A little humor and charm can go a long way toward helping us get to the other side of sorrow, grief, frustration, and all other unhappy emotions and experiences.

But joy guides are most often inclined to appear when our egos have gotten the best of us and we're bent out of shape, such as when we work too much, give too much, and lose our balance. Joy guides are the conquerors of workaholism and the antidote to this nasty addiction. When they appear and interrupt us, our usual response is irritation. Their favorite method is to send in your kids, who want to talk, play, and laugh. This sometimes works, but if you brush them off or don't have children, the joy guides will activate plan B and use your pets to get you to take a break.

In 2017, a professor was doing a live interview with the BBC when suddenly in came his two small children, and finally, his frantic wife trying to shuffle them out—all while they were continuing the broadcast. It was so hilarious that it went viral, and the entire world burst out laughing. This was undoubtedly the antics of joy guides having a blast.

My friend Julia Cameron told me that when she's buried too deep in work and has become so absorbed that she's lost her sense of humor, her West Highland terrier Charlotte drags over her ratty toy and insists on a game of fetch. My dog Miss T did the same for me. Our furry friends are regular emissaries of joy guides. Have you noticed how many self-important Hollywood types who are buried under the weight of their fame carry silly little dogs with them? Chihuahuas, Maltese pooches, you name it—they're on a mission to relieve these actors of the burden of their egos.

If you don't have pets, joy guides resort to other means to capture your attention. They may ring the doorbell and run away or flicker the lights or surge the volume on your speakers. We're often annoyed by these acts. But joy guides are relentless, and the more you resist, the more they tease. You can blow your top and try to send them and their adorable helpers scurrying for cover, but you'll feel like an ungrateful creep if you do. They're there to relieve you of your ego, not fight for it. If you simply give up the battle and laugh, you'll regain your balance and escape the corner you've put yourself in.

Being spontaneous and silly pranksters, joy guides especially love the element of surprise. Just recently, a client told me a funny story about these spirits. She and her husband had been suffering in a miserable marriage, each spending a great deal of energy fighting and trying to control and correct the other's behavior most of the time. They agreed on nothing, continually argued, and spent the hours away from each other complaining about their spouse's outrageous behavior. One day it got so bad that they both said: "This has got to stop. We must divorce."

Finally agreeing on something, they very calmly (at least for them) began discussing how they intended to go their separate ways. As they were speaking, a fly flew in between them. While the husband spoke in a dead-serious tone about his need to be free, the insect landed on his nose. As he swiped wildly at it, his wife burst into laughter at how ridiculous he looked.

The situation was so absurd that he, too, had to crack a smile. And when he resumed his serious demeanor, the fly returned, landing right between his eyes. Refusing this time to acknowledge the fly's presence, he continued to rail while the bug strolled across his forehead. Again, his wife laughed uproariously, and in response, he slapped his head with such full force that she lost all control. He was doing to himself what she'd longed to!

Then it was her turn to air her grievances. As she started in on her laundry list of his transgressions, the fly landed on *her* face. She immediately went berserk trying to swat it away, only to have it dodge her as well. Her husband, of course, doubled over in glee. By that point, the silliness of it all was so infectious that she couldn't help but giggle, too. Their laughter escalated until tears rolled down their cheeks. They hadn't had that much fun together since they were dating.

Soon they were reminiscing about other shared moments of hilarity and spent several hours strolling down their memory lane of joyfulness. By the end, the husband said, "I'm sorry. I don't want a divorce—I just miss having fun with you." She felt the same way, so they called a truce and decided to give their marriage another try.

Will it work? I don't know. But with the joy guides present, at least they stand a chance.

### Did You Know That . . .

- Joy guides make you laugh so that your heart softens.

- They help you be more easygoing, generous, and accepting of others.

Joy guides have only one purpose: to help us get over ourselves and remember how beautiful life is. They especially connect to babies and small children, entertaining them with crazy antics, which kids often mimic. If you've ever heard an infant in the nursery laughing and having fun all alone, you can be confident that the room is full of joy guides.

My daughter Sonia had a great connection to these beings as an infant, and with their help, found all kinds of ways to entertain me. She was especially good at it on the days when I felt frazzled and overwhelmed when I was pregnant with my second daughter. At only seven or eight months old, she'd see her joy guides and laugh out loud with them, knowing full well as she did this that she was making me laugh, too. There were dozens of times when I was fully prepared to sit down and have an indulgent feel-sorry-for-myself session, but then she'd start to squeal and laugh and make such funny faces that I couldn't remain down in the dumps. Through her, I felt the spirits dancing all around, and we'd both giggle so hard that everything I'd worried about faded away.

Laughter, especially the ridiculous, intoxicating kind, is the calling card of joy guides. If you ever want to find an abundance of them, go to places that attract children and pets. But remember that joy guides don't just focus on kids and animals. As I mentioned, they also help lighten up overly serious adults and relieve extreme stress, especially in solemn gatherings where the pain and sorrow are often too much to bear. That's why you'll usually find them at wakes and funerals.

I once attended a funeral for a friend's mother. She'd been a jovial, outspoken woman who insisted on having the last word on everything. Her sudden death from a heart attack left her family and friends stunned and devastated. In the middle of the priest's solemn eulogy, a cell phone rang, but no one dared to acknowledge it. The priest scanned the congregation to locate the culprit to no avail, so when the ringing finally stopped, the eulogy continued.

Moments later, another phone sounded from a different part of the congregation. Again, no one made a move to silence it. The priest, again interrupted and gravely displeased, waited until the ring stopped, asked everyone to please silence their phones out of respect for the dead, then resumed speaking with a disapproving glare.

Then yet *another* ring tone echoed through space. This time the priest lost all patience and said, "For Pete's sake, what is going on with all these cell phones?"

Little four-year-old Emily, one of the deceased woman's grandchildren, raised her hand and blurted out, "I know! I think it's Grandma calling from heaven to let you know you forgot to say how much she liked chocolate ice cream."

Everyone, including the dour priest, burst out laughing. Their grief was relieved, and the eulogy switched from sorrowful words of loss to all the wonderfully funny moments that Grandma had brought to her loved ones. This was clearly a visitation by the joy guides, the practical jokers and comedians of the Universe.

As pranksters, one of the joy guides' favorite antics is to hide things, often in full view. Have you ever missed your car keys on the way out the door, your passport just before boarding an international flight, or your tickets on the way to the theater? Frenzied, you eventually find them in the corner of your pocket, or even clutched in your hand. That's the work of a joy guide, telling you to take a breath, relax, get grounded in the moment, and realize that everything will turn out well. They aren't malicious or nasty; they're just having fun with you to get you to lighten up.

They also love to hide jewelry, shoes, wallets, purses, library books, bathing suits, and cell phones, the report you've been working on—anything to get you out of being on autopilot and bring you back into your body and the life right in front of you. If you listen carefully, you can hear them giggling as they watch you race around like a chicken with its head cut off searching for the lost item.

You can save yourself stress and time if you simply acknowledge the joy guides and go along with the joke. Just say, "Okay, I get it. I need to lighten up. Thanks for reminding me." If you do, the missing item will magically reappear. Being eternal children, joy guides like to play hide-and-seek with your runners. They hide things; your runners find them. Just enjoy the game.

Besides keeping you from taking life too seriously, these spirits also connect you to what brings you happiness. They'll drag you into an art-supplies, toy, or music store, to a dance or acting class, a drumming circle, or a travel agency for the trip you keep postponing.

Joy guides are the voices in your head that say it's okay to give yourself little treats, such as a Saturday to play with your kids—or to frolic as if you were a kid, to hang out with friends over coffee and conversation, to break out a board game with the family instead of all staring at the TV in silence. They remind you to go for that bike ride, take the beading class, and hang out and read a good book, guilt-free.

Start appreciating the joy guides around you. Open your eyes, ears, and heart to them. "Get over yourself and get into your spirit," as my teacher Charlie used to say, by paying attention not to what's wrong with this picture, as your ego tells you, but what's *right*, as your spirit reveals.

Feed your inner child with creative, joyful pleasures, and these guides will come dancing in. They love to help you do this by bringing you presents such as unexpected flowers from a partner, or a spontaneous invitation from a sister to go to see a play. You might be gifted a dessert on the house at the restaurant where you are dining, or receive an unexpected upgrade on a flight. My mom enjoyed giving these spirits assignments by asking them (and telling us to ask) for presents openly and often. On the way out the door to school in the morning, she'd remind us to ask for gifts—and expect them. "You never know when they'll come," she'd say.

---

*Feed your inner child with creative, joyful pleasures,*
*and these guides will come dancing in.*

---

I followed her instructions then and still do today. Upon waking, I say this little prayer: "Divine Mother, Father, and God, I'm grateful for your presence in my life. Joy guides, I'm grateful for your presents and presence throughout my day. Thank you."

I love playing with my joy guides and am always open to receive their many gifts. Once when visiting my sister in Kansas, we took my mother's advice and went out to lunch, both of us actually expecting presents. We waited an unusually long time to be seated at the restaurant we'd chosen, but we were so engaged in conversation that we didn't even notice the time. Finally, the manager did notice, and she apologized and gave us each a gift certificate for a free dinner!

Happy with our good fortune, we strolled next door to an apparel shop. My sister found a beautiful pair of pants that fit perfectly but had a tiny bit of dirt on them—nothing a dry cleaner couldn't take care of. She showed the pants to the owner, who apologized and said, "If you buy something else, I'll just give you these pants. It's the end of the season and not worth the expense of cleaning." My sister chose a blouse and left with a complete outfit. Outside, we found two teenagers washing the car. When we asked what they were doing, they said that it was community service day. We offered to pay, but they refused the money. We laughed and sang all the way home—thank you, joy guides!

Joy guides really dive-bombed me on a recent trip home to Paris after teaching a workshop in Chicago. Exhausted, running very late due to traffic, and extremely cranky due to lack of proper sleep, I ran to the airplane gate in a fit of stress, barely making it before they closed the door behind me.

Ten minutes later, the flight attendant in charge made an announcement. All passengers had to immediately deplane due to a mechanical problem. Gathering my belongings, I rushed to the exit and walked to the lounge across from the gate, where I was told to wait until further notice.

I had just gotten comfortable with all my stuff around me when I heard an announcement that we were to once again head to the gate and quickly reboard as the problem was now fixed.

Happy to hear we were back on track, I gathered my things in a hurry and rushed to the gate, once more settling into my seat. The door shut once more, but we didn't move. Soon another announcement came on, the flight attendant apologizing profusely, saying, "False alarm, the problem still isn't fixed, and we must deplane again!" Argghhh! I was nearly ready to blow by this time, but what could I do?

Gathering my bags for yet a *third* time, I got off the airplane again and started back to the lounge. No sooner had I sat down when the lounge agent made a further announcement saying go back to the gate, and fast. I did but was *really* irritated by now. Thankfully, after boarding again, this time we took off and I slept the entire way to Paris. But as I was landing and gathering my things, I realized to my horror that I couldn't find my purse anywhere. This was a disaster. Where did it go? Did I lose it during the chaos of boarding and reboarding? I must have. And worse, how on earth would I get into the country without my passport? Moreover, I had no money or credit cards with me either. This was *not* good.

About to flip out with stress, I put my hand in my coat pocket and, to my immense relief, discovered my passport. What luck! Apparently, I had put it there when I reboarded for the second time, then forgot about it. Thank goodness I had done that (or my joy guides did). At least with my passport I could get into the country and go home. I called my helper guides, but the joy guides showed up instead. They were having fun watching me search around in panic.

Somewhat encouraged, I asked the flight attendant for help locating my lost purse, but he couldn't do much. An agent met me at the gate upon landing and, hearing my plight, escorted me to a taxi and handed me enough money to get home, which I greatly appreciated. He then said he would message back to Chicago to see if anyone had found my purse or turned it in, but not to count on that happening. On the way home, I said out loud, "Okay, joy guides, enough fun for now. Get some runners to help you and bring back my purse, fast. *Please!*"

By the time I got home an hour later, I received an e-mail from the agent who had helped me at the airport. He said my purse was miraculously found in the lounge and was already on the next flight to Paris. I'd have it back by tomorrow morning. What a miracle!

Rushing as I had been, and so cranky to boot just before the flight, this was indeed a wake-up call to slow down, be present, and go with the flow when things get disrupted. "Lesson learned, joy guides. I got it," I said. I could feel my joy guides clapping with delight as the deliveryman handed my purse over the next day, with everything in it just as I'd left it. It brought me such joy and felt like such a present that I laughed out loud. "Who has this happen like this, with such a happy ending?" I wondered. "Thank you, joy guides. Thank you!"

YOUR TURN

Summon your joy guides every day. Give them names. Appreciate their antics. Ask them for gifts and to help you see the humor in life. If you aren't sure what kind of gift you want to receive, then simply say, "Surprise me." They will. Help them to help you by remembering that nothing is worth losing your sense of humor over. Nurture your sense of humor by watching funny movies, videos, and cartoons. Joy guides remind you to enjoy the journey and to know that in the end, everything will *always* be okay.

## Joy guides can help you

- Regain your sense of humor
- Get through painful passages
- Gain a new perspective
- Laugh at yourself
- Ease up and go with the flow

- Take it easier
- Give up control
- Get over things that drive you crazy
- Appreciate human flaws
- Accept vulnerability
- Enjoy life more

Now that you've met your joy guides, let's move on and meet the light beings.

# CHAPTER 22

# Light Beings

Years ago, during a soul-healing intensive workshop in Kauai, a new and very powerful source of guidance made contact with me. I first became aware of this new spirit energy on the third day of the retreat in an afternoon meditation.

Relaxing to the beautiful music created by my friend Mark Welch, I instructed the class to gently close their eyes and concentrate on their breath as it flowed into and out of their bodies. Moments later, I lost all awareness of the group as I suddenly saw in my mind's eye what appeared to be an army of tall, blue, cylindrical beings approaching me with open arms and an intense amount of love. Their vibration was so high that I became completely absorbed by their powerful healing energy and the room disappeared. Slowly I felt my head tip back and my ego step aside as this throng of light beings approached and then burrowed into my body to speak to the group through what's known as channeling. I was conscious, but felt far removed from my own physical self, as though I were watching from some faraway place, as fascinated by what was happening as everyone else.

The guides introduced themselves as the Emissaries of the Third Ray, Second Octave of Love and respectfully asked for permission to address the group. Not sure what was occurring, but sensing the same intense vibration of deep love that I felt radiating through me, the group agreed.

The light beings then began to share a clear and urgent message. Through me, they told us how loved and precious we all are, but how we must change our vibration from one of fear to love if we hope to survive as individuals and as the human race. With great compassion, the Emissaries said that they were connecting through me to them (and back to me) to offer their assistance in helping us achieve this transformation. As they spoke through me, my voice took on an entirely different tone and cadence than my own. It was strange but not uncomfortable.

I was struck by how powerful their vibration felt as it coursed through my being. Their light and love were so great that it felt as if 10,000 watts of energy were channeling through a 200-watt circuit and threatening to blow me apart at any moment. Incredibly, what happened instead was that my heart opened to a degree I'd never felt before. I felt intoxicated because I was so high on this wave of love. Every cell in my body felt energized and renewed; aches and stiffness gave way to absolute peace and calm; all the worry and anxiety in my history yielded to perfect ease. With the assistance of these loving light beings, I felt at one with the Universe and with God.

They only spoke for a few moments but talking wasn't the most important thing. They conveyed such a tremendous healing vibration that words couldn't possibly communicate their message, and I later found out that everyone present felt the same way. By transmitting this powerful vibration of love, the Emissaries of the Third Ray expanded our heart chakras to a much wider level than any of us thought possible. We got the message because we *felt* it.

After channeling through me for several minutes, the Emissaries receded, thanking us for our attention and telling us that to feel their presence again, all we had to do was open our hearts and let them flow through our hands. Then slowly I returned to my own consciousness.

I'd channeled guides before, allowing them to speak through me, especially the Three Bishops, my teacher guides, but never before had I gone into such a deep, altered state or felt so physically affected.

After they left, we all sat in astounded silence. Everyone felt the shift in energy and the exhilarating freedom from fear. This vibration of full, loving power was so radically different from the frequency of consciousness we were accustomed to that we were speechless. There was no need to say anything . . . We were in bliss.

This first contact with the Emissaries was quite exciting. For the five years before this, I'd been feeling them trying to come through, but my vibration wasn't open and grounded enough for them to connect until that day. I wondered if I'd be able to make contact again, and so did the rest of the group.

The next day at our afternoon meditation session, the Emissaries of the Third Ray returned. As their unbelievably high vibration filled me with light and affection again, it nearly knocked me off my feet. This time, a spokesman stepped forward from this blue army of love and introduced himself as Joachim.

He greeted us with the same respect and affection as the Emissaries had before and asked our permission to speak. It was eagerly granted, and through me he began to convey what was again called an urgent message. Speaking slowly, deliberately, and with tremendous intention, he told us that the human race won't survive unless we shift our fundamental consciousness to a higher collective frequency. He said that the planet won't be able to support the levels of fear we're creating, and that great numbers of people consumed by terror would need to leave Earth in order to rebalance it.

He related that this wouldn't necessarily happen if everyone shifted their survival energies from fearing and withholding to loving and giving. They'd not only be fully protected and safe in this time of change but would also be the progenitors of a new race of higher beings. As he spoke, I again felt the profound peace and calm I had the day before, and so did the group.

Using my body and my hand, Joachim then demonstrated how to generate this powerful heart-chakra energy. He asked everyone present to open their hearts and extend their hands outward, intending a vibration of love to pour through them and into the world. Thus, he assured us, we could create and attract whatever we desired.

Feeling a potent vibration running through my being when I followed this instruction (as did others, I found out later), I understood how what he said could be true. This unrestrained flow of caring that the Emissaries of the Third Ray were helping each of us channel into the world was so compelling and peaceful that I intuitively knew it was the same vibration Christ had used to heal. If we tapped into this fully and called it home, then we, too, could perform miracles.

Joachim said that the Emissaries had come to help us usher in the miracle of unrestrained love that the world desperately needed right now. Then he and the other light beings led us in a heart-opening meditation that put us in an altered state for hours. We were told that having our minds quieted and our hearts opened was the beginning of a new kind of human, and they were here to show us, as they were showing others around the world, how to plant those seeds.

With a final blessing, Joachim withdrew, but not before assuring us that the Emissaries of the Third Ray and many other armies of light beings are available at all times to guide anyone ready to release fear and move into the vibration of love.

Joachim and the Emissaries have been strongly connected to me ever since. They told me that my spirit has agreed to be one of the midwives of the new emerging type of human beings, who will be rooted in love, not fear. My mission is to help people activate and expand their heart chakra and become energetically rooted in its caring. I believe it, because ever since I was a child, I've been preparing for this. Now the Emissaries come through during my public appearances to help me activate this higher vibration in everyone present. They and other light beings are contacting many others who are also receptive to shifting the earth to love, because with enough humans open to this, we will succeed. Remember, light beings are highly evolved entities from higher dimensions who assist in accelerating our evolution as a race on this planet to a higher more loving and balanced vibration.

> ### Did You Know That . . .
>
> - Light beings tell us that the Universe has a spiritual plan to ultimately raise the vibration of the earth to a higher octave of harmony and balance.
>
> - They are connecting with us more than ever before in order to bring greater understanding and love to us as we face the important changes now taking place.
>
> - They assist us as the earth purges itself of old negative patterns that have accumulated in our confusion.
>
> - They will guide us through these changing times.

## LIGHT BEINGS CONNECT WITH US ALL

Perhaps you've been contacted by light beings yourself. More and more people have been lately as these loving beings are descending in droves to wake us up and help us stop the insane, hurtful indifference toward and disconnect from our planet and one another that so many people are caught up in. They don't always beam themselves through a channel, as they did for me. They may show up in different but equally powerful and loving ways. For example, you may be introduced to a book on light beings, or accidentally tune in to a podcast on these loving entities. You may attend a crystal bowl healing session and sense their presence during that experience. They may even show up in your dream state.

These highly advanced beings are inviting in new technologies, new ways of saving the earth, new sensitivities in ourselves, and more engagement across cultures, all of which can invite in more love and light and cast off the darkness that seems to be consuming us.

You'll know light beings are working with you if you suddenly feel a deep and urgent need to forgive all ego-based hurt feelings and past injuries, and a desire to love yourself, others, and life with your whole heart and soul. You may also feel inspired by intense motivation and new ideas for helping the greater good instead of just yourself.

> *You'll know light beings are working with you if you suddenly feel a deep and urgent need to forgive all ego-based hurt feelings and past injuries, and a desire to love yourself, others, and life with your whole heart and soul.*

If you sense that you have been contacted by light beings, take a breath, open your heart, stay grounded, and welcome their energy. They are here to help our planet, and, through you and with your cooperation, they will. Of course, you have a choice, but the light beings are drawn to you because you are already receptive.

You may not experience the connection in the same way as I have, but you can and will be reached if you feel called upon to do your part in fulfilling their mission of healing the planet. When light being contact occurs, your heart eases and you begin to feel the life and spirit we all share. You can never again look at another person and feel separate from them or any hatred or lasting judgment toward them. This doesn't mean that you won't have your moments or get upset or irritated. It just means that these feelings and fear-based vibrations will no longer be significant enough to hold on to.

Initially, I hesitated to share my connection with the Emissaries of the Third Ray so early in my experience with them. Still, they encouraged me to do so, as their message is important: "Move away from fear as your root energy and embrace love in its place." I feel the urgency of this information and hope that you do, too.

Today I am witnessing more and more light beings making contact with people all over the world. Some are getting their message out directly via channeling experiences, such as my own, and others are communicating more indirectly. Light beings are awakening tremendous gifts of inspiration and genius in people, creating massive planetary healing efforts through them that at first seem impossible, but against all odds, are actually working.

Light beings have galvanized movements to clean our oceans, save our rain forests, plant more trees, and heal human trauma. Perhaps you are part of these efforts, led by the guidance and direction of these loving light beings. If you aren't yet, you soon will be.

When the time comes, trust and believe in your own noble impulses and your urges to help. Act on your inner calling, whether it is by recycling garbage, giving up using plastic bags, planting trees, walking or bicycling instead of driving, praying instead of cursing, loving instead of hating. The light beings are behind these urges and together we are turning things around. We all have gifts to share and are each here to make a positive difference in the world. Light beings know this and will put us all to use, inspiring us to donate our time or money to saving the bonobos from extinction, protecting the rain forest, funding stem cell research, supporting musical therapies for trauma, planting gardens in schools, or doing something else to help heal the world.

We are reminded daily of the horrific crises this planet faces, but at the same time, we know that light beings are among us, helping us turn these disasters around and heal the earth. To be sure, there are ignorant, dark forces trying to stand in the way of progress and healing, but they will not prevail. The armies of light are committed and arriving in wave after wave, awakening in us the desire and creativity to help ourselves. If you open your heart, you will feel this, too.

Above all it is important to know that light beings don't heal the earth or heal people; instead, they inspire *us* to do the work. So unlike other guides, we can't call on them for help; we just have to be open and wait for them to call on us. They will.

YOUR TURN

Open your heart to the light beings and invite them in—it's that easy. Ask for their help whenever you feel fear directly or in the form of anger, judgment, sadness, or any of its other disguises. With a slow breath, open your heart and extend your hands. At first it may feel as if nothing is happening, but don't be discouraged. Continue to breathe and keep your center open.

You'll soon feel their support as their beneficent forces are very strong. Try it right now and see if you sense them. If so, enjoy their healing vibration; if not, continue to breathe and release your fear.

Whether you feel it or not, the light beings are present. On a personal level, they'll inspire a profound sense of peace in you, no matter what's going on in your life. On a cosmic level, they'll motivate you to join the forces that want us to love ourselves and save this beautiful planet. I do hope that you'll join me and others in this effort.

## Light beings can help you

- Open your heart chakras

- Relieve survival trauma

- Activate brilliant creativity for change

- Recognize our shared human connection

- Usher in new technologies and inventions to save the planet

- Inspire new ways of learning

- Awaken new values

- Awaken the urge to contribute to the betterment of humanity

- Find the power and motivation to forgive completely

Below is a link to a 35-minute channeled meditation journey that calls in the Pleiadian light beings to help raise your vibration.

Visit https://www.hayhouse.com/downloads and enter the Product ID **1381** and Download Code **resources**. You can also visit http://www.soniachoquette.net.

Now that you've met the light beings, let's move on and have a word of caution about negative entities.

# CHAPTER 23

# Negative Entities

When opening up to your spirit guides, it's important to be grounded and discriminating so that you attract high-vibration guides who will assist your life—and not low-vibration, negative entities who only disturb and distort things and cause trouble.

Just as you wouldn't invite a stranger into your home and give him a measure of control, you shouldn't accept that all guides are useful or worthwhile without some initial scrutiny. Most are loving and helpful, but some spirits aren't of a high vibration. They're wandering around lost and confused and would love to grab you and try to run—and possibly ruin—your life instead of floating aimlessly through the ether. Most of these lesser spirits are harmless but annoying and can be easily recognized by their vibration.

High-vibration guides are subtle, patient, calm, loving, and don't tell you what to do. Instead, they make subtle suggestions, usually upon request, and leave you feeling peaceful and supported. Low-vibration entities, on the other hand, are pushy, bossy, negative, and will do everything in their power to control you, including flattering you, criticizing others, or psychically harassing you into doing what they want, which is to create drama and trouble.

They'd like you to believe that they're mighty forces that you must obey, but they really have no power and can be easily dismissed. To do so, you need only send them into the light with your intention and firmly ask them to leave. Unlike joy guides, who are playfully fun, make you laugh, and lift your spirit, negative entities are mostly nuisances who entertain themselves at your expense, and they sneak into your field of awareness when you aren't grounded or focused, causing you to feel stressed, anxious, or unsafe.

You can also identify low-vibration entities because they're very seductive. They try to make you feel more important, smart, or "special" than others. A high-vibration guide would never do that because it knows that on a spirit level, we're all the same, unfolding at different rates of consciousness. No one is special, because we're all connected. Negative entities speak to your ego; higher guides connect with your spirit.

Negative entities encourage you to blame others for your problems and feel victimized and sorry for yourself; they want you to keep your distance from others. Trustworthy guides, on the other hand, encourage you to look at your challenges and experiences as soul lessons, seeing that whoever or whatever is involved is only helping you learn to grow spiritually. They ask you to lovingly study and learn from all situations, and once the lesson is learned, to move on. They don't play the blame game, and they support you in viewing others with compassion and forgiveness.

Negative entities boss you around and hound you. Eager to wield influence, they have a harassing feel about them, which is in contrast to high-vibration guides, who are quite subtle and enter your world slowly and respectfully, and only when asked.

> *Negative entities speak to your ego;*
> *higher guides connect with your spirit.*

## WHAT ATTRACTS NEGATIVE ENTITIES

Fear of these beings scares many people from opening up to guides, preventing them from accessing spirit guides' profound spiritual resources. It isn't all that easy to attract low-vibration entities, and even if you do, they can be easily eliminated.

Nevertheless, it's useful to know what things *do* invite them so that you can avoid this nuisance altogether.

Perhaps the most compelling attraction is an addiction of any sort, be it alcoholism, drug addiction, rageaholism, or workaholism. An addiction weakens your aura, confuses your will, disturbs your spirit, and sabotages your creativity. It disrupts and attacks your energetic balance, much like having an invader in your home. When you're addicted, you're out of control, so it should come as no surprise that negative entities seize the opportunity to enter. The way to shut that door is to acknowledge the problem and treat it.

Another attraction is being chronically passive and unfocused in your priorities and goals. That doesn't mean that you must know what you want to do at every moment, but you need to at least be clear about what you value to keep from drifting into negative territory. If you're the type of person who wants to be led around by the nose and take no responsibility for your life, low entities will take advantage of you, just as people will.

Also, Universal law states: "Like attracts like." If you're angry, judgmental, aggressive, jealous, and mean-spirited, you'll pull in the same qualities on the unseen level. I'm not talking about having a bad moment or one episode of unpleasantness—that's human. I mean being chronically committed to being negative, an entirely different vibration that attracts low-entity energy.

If you're run-down, stressed, or in an emotionally weakened state, there's the slight possibility that you may pick up a negative entity in a public place, just as you would a cold. For example, I've had them attach to me on airplanes and in hotel rooms, restaurants, and even hospitals. These irksome energies lurk wherever there's a "down" or stressful vibration over a long period of time. Like stowaways, they grab on to higher vibrations such as you and tag along. They usually don't mean harm; they're just trying to get out of the limbo they're in.

---

### Did You Know That . . .

- Negative entities encourage you to be judgmental and critical of everyone and everything.

- They are weak energies and can never overwhelm the human spirit.

- They run away or head to the light the moment you begin to pray.

- They tell you what to do and give you the feeling you have no choice in the matter.

---

Signs that a negative entity has glommed on to you are: suddenly falling into a very bad or irritable mood; becoming extremely agitated; snapping at people; feeling surges of self-doubt, anger, or a loss of energy; and suddenly viewing the world in negative, hopeless, or cynical terms, especially when this isn't your normal behavior or outlook.

Hollywood has attempted to frighten us with its version of these beings and what occurs when they're present, but don't be fooled. Not only is what you see on the silver screen a fantasy, but it's also absurd. Negative entities are simply like flies attracted to the light, not like zombies from the *Night of the Living Dead*. And just for the record, I've never seen an entity possess anyone. They may give you a scare, but the human spirit is strong and not easily diminished.

Just recently I ran into a negative entity while getting a massage at a hotel spa while on a trip. The minute I shook the massage therapist's hand I had a bad vibe and felt like recoiling. Still, being "nice" as I had been conditioned to be for all of my female life, I followed the massage therapist into the treatment room anyway and hoped I was imagining things or was being overly sensitive.

Things didn't get any better five minutes into my treatment. Not only was my therapist not grounded, rushing into the room while talking on the phone (reason enough to end the session!), but she had a very negative, draining vibe, and every time she touched me I felt like cringing and pushing her hands away.

I denied what was happening for several more insufferable minutes, but each passing second made me feel more and more agitated, to the point of getting angry. Finally, I just asked her to stop and said, "I'm sorry this session isn't working for me." She was extremely annoyed, and snapped right back, "What do you want, lady?"

I nearly laughed, as her response was so aggressive and inappropriate for the situation. I quietly looked her right in the eye and politely said, "Nothing more, thank you. I'm done with this massage." Then I got up and left the room. I was kind and left quietly, but with determination. Some unhappy energy was hanging around the therapist and I wanted nothing to do with it, even if I looked like a weirdo in saying so. I didn't care.

I went into the changing room, quickly took a shower, surrounded myself with the archangels to clear my field, and hightailed it out of there. That's all it took to shake them off. Negative entities have no power. They just need to be called out and cast into the light.


## BANISHING NEGATIVE ENTITIES

If you suspect that you've attracted a lower vibration, don't be frightened. It's no different from a bug, and if you catch it early, it can be easily eliminated by simply raising your vibration with positive thoughts of things and people you love. And prayer. Prayer is kryptonite to negative entities. It sends them running in an instant.

Negative entities are dispelled the minute you pray. End of subject. Simply ask that all lower vibrations be sent to the light *now*, in the name of God, Divine Light, Mother Mary, Jesus, Mohammad, St. Germaine, or whichever master teacher you connect with. This should do it, no questions asked.

You can tell if a negative entity is messing with you if you have these symptoms:

- You are easily irritated or agitated
- You quickly and harshly judge others
- You think terrible things about yourself
- You feel hopeless all of a sudden
- You feel like you have "ants in your pants"
- You feel suddenly jealous and insecure
- You become unexpectedly angry and harsh
- You laugh at or feel happy about someone else's pain
- You don't like anyone or anything
- You feel drained or trapped

## SURROUND YOURSELF WITH LOVE

Practice not taking on what isn't your responsibility. If someone isn't feeling positive, then send that person love, but don't absorb their vibration. If necessary, simply step away from their bad vibes. Put up a white loving light in your mind's eye and let it serve as a shield to block all negativity.

Establish clear boundaries when asking for guidance or opening your psychic channels by insisting that that only the most loving, elevated guides be allowed to enter and influence your energy. Similar to using a filter to remove debris, setting boundaries before asking for guidance is smart and keeps your life flowing smoothly.

If you believe that someone is troubled by an entity, you can dispel it on their behalf by asking it to leave now and enter the light in the name of God. It must obey, as there's nothing greater than God.

Don't spend a lot of time dwelling on these low-level energies. Like hooligans playing tricks, they love to scare people and thrive on attention. Instead of falling prey to this, insist that they leave, which will dispel their meager power quickly.

I've written about entities because they're a nuisance and can cause trouble, but you shouldn't regard them as a big problem. Just be discriminating when opening yourself up to guidance and have some firm boundaries in place. This is good general life advice, by the way: if you're clear, grounded, have good boundaries, and remember to surround yourself with Divine light and protection, you'll always be okay.

## YOUR TURN

If you do suspect the presence of a negative entity, follow these steps:

- Stay grounded
- Pray. Say prayers of gratitude and appreciation and make requests for unconditional love and protection.
- Do the Cube of Space Ritual (page 58)
- Laugh
- Say 10 appreciative things about yourself out loud
- Establish your boundaries
- Take an Epsom-salt bath
- Recommit to your goals

This should eliminate your problem, and better yet, prevent a new one from occurring.

Now that you've met the myriad of guides available to you, let's move on and learn how to relate to them as friends.

# PART V

# RELATING
## TO YOUR
# SPIRIT GUIDES

# CHAPTER 24

# Guides Work with
# Earth Messengers, Too

Your guides' ability to get your attention can be impeded by your emotional state. If you're stressed, worried, or are experiencing any kind of emotional upheaval, it's nearly impossible for your guides to get through. And face it, this is when you need them most.

So what do your guides do? Rather than try to communicate with you or inspire you directly, they will often engage the help of someone around you to deliver their supportive messages. In fact, chances are that someone else's guides have used you to help one of their charges as well.

For example, have you ever felt compelled to pick up the phone for no reason and just call someone who tells you that you couldn't have possibly called at a better time? My client Jeff told me recently that he was on his way to his construction job at 6 A.M. last spring when he had the overwhelming urge to call his grandmother, whom he loved but hadn't spoken to in more than a year. His feeling was so strong that in spite of the early hour, he called her right then. She answered, crying. "Are you okay?" he asked.

"Oh, Jeff, I thought you were the vet, and no, I'm not okay. My cat Bob just died. He's been my best friend and companion for the past twenty years. Now I have no one. I feel just terrible."

Devastated by her grief, Jeff said, "I'm so sorry, Gram. But you're wrong about one thing. You're not alone. I'm free this weekend and I'm coming to see you. Hang in there, Gram. I'll be there late this evening to help you get through this." He left right after work.

Another client, Jesse, told me that she was sitting quietly one morning in a Starbucks, working on a report for her job when, quite out of character, she asked the woman sitting at the next table if she was a regular.

The woman said, "Actually, no. I just moved here from Indiana, and I've only been here for three days. I'm staying with my roommate from college and I'm looking for an apartment in this neighborhood. I'd love to live here, but I've been told it's tough to find something at this time of year."

Jesse laughed and said, "This is so strange. My landlord asked me this morning if I knew anyone looking for an apartment. She didn't want to go through the hassle of advertising. I've lived there for five years and love it. It's only three blocks from here. I'll give you her number."

The woman signed a lease before lunch. Then the two became great friends. The woman's guides had borrowed Jesse to help their charge.

As another example, consider my dear friend Bill. A Chicago television host and a bachelor who wanted very much to meet his heart's desire, he could hardly believe it when one day he got his wish. A beautiful woman, Angela, had come to interview him for a local magazine. The chemistry was undeniable. Yet, fearing it wasn't real, he asked his spirit helpers for some kind of sign to let him know that love was indeed in the air as he walked from work to meet her for lunch.

When he entered the restaurant, the maître d' gave him a rose. When he asked what it was for, the man said, "I don't know. Something told me to give this to you." Imagining the rose to be the sign he had asked for, Bill took it, and at the table, he offered it to Angela. A year later, they were married.

"The rose clinched it," said Bill. "When I received that rose, I knew that my wish was about to come true. And it did."

**Did You Know That . . .**

Every message that catches your attention has meaning.

## YOUR TURN

Reflect on a time when you were the spontaneous messenger and guide for someone, a time when you called just in time to save someone's day, said the right thing, or offered the right solution. What happened? When did it happen? How did it happen? Who was involved? What was the outcome? Did you feel the influence of the Other Side in this event? Tell at least one interested person about this experience and notice the effect it has on you.

In those situations, the other person's guides borrowed you for a moment and used you to deliver an important message. That's the beauty of this infinitely loving Universe. We're all interrelated and can be the helper and the one helped at the same time.

Now that you've learned how guides relate to us, let's move on and discover their names.

*We're all interrelated and can be the helper*
*and the one helped at the same time.*

# CHAPTER 25

# Your Guides' Names

One of the most popular questions clients ask me is, "What is my guide's name?" As you know by now, you're connecting to many guides, not just one, and when they leave their physical bodies (if they ever had one), most of them have no gender or name but exist on an energetic level. However, to help us better connect with them, they will sometimes take on a name and even a gender. They'll usually assume the identity in which they knew you in a past life to help you remember them and reconnect with them on a conscious level.

Other guides, especially those from other solar systems or nonphysical frequencies, will simply assume a name that best replicates their vibration. Usually, vowels and open sounds have a much higher frequency than consonants, which is why you hear of many guides whose names are airy and light—Ariel, Abu, or some other short, open sound.

Some guides are loved ones, family members, or friends who have crossed over and may still be operating energetically on the same or similar frequency as when you knew them. So you can recognize them, they often use their earthly name. When their name crosses your mind several times, you can be sure they're with you. When someone has recently passed, their name will obviously be on your mind often. To tell whether this is just because they're recently departed or because they're trying to communicate with you, try to see if you sense their spirit or any other signal that may be connected to them when their names come up. If you do, then they're most likely trying to contact you. If not, then you're probably thinking of them in the context of their recent death.

My client Edith was married for more than 40 years to Stanley, whom she loved very much and with whom she lived in upper Michigan. When he suddenly died of a stroke, Edith was inconsolable. Several weeks after the funeral, as Edith was barely regaining her composure, she felt Stanley's presence everywhere, but nowhere as strongly as on the back porch where he used to rock in his chair. She found a red cardinal sitting on the chair and said, "What are you doing on Stanley's chair?" The bird didn't move. She moved closer and said, "Why are you here?"

Edith remembered how much Stanley loved birds, so the incident unnerved her a little. The next day she again felt Stanley's presence and was drawn to the back porch where she found the same red cardinal perched on the chair's arm. Still, it didn't fly away.

This went on for 10 days. Finally, Edith said to the cardinal, "Stanley, is that you trying to tell me something?" The bird didn't move. "Is that you, Stanley? Really?" Then she poured out her heart, feeling that the bird was Stanley and was listening to her.

The most important message she delivered to the bird was a poignant goodbye to her late husband, which she'd been unable to do because he'd died so suddenly. The bird flew away after that and never came back. But the connection was made; Stanley was present and helped Edith move on.

Another client desperately wanted to connect with one of her guides to ask for help with her marriage. The minute she asked its name, "James" popped into her mind, followed by "with blue eyes and a way with words." Suspicious that it was too easy, she asked James if he could give her another sign that she had his name right and was indeed connected to a healing force. What immediately popped into her mind was, "Write your husband a letter to communicate. Don't talk." She pondered that thought for the next several days and then followed James's advice. She wrote her husband a 10-page letter explaining exactly what she wanted to change in their relationship, as well as what was working for her, and asked him to do the same. Then she mailed it.

Two days later, while she was still at the workshop, her husband sent flowers and a return letter saying how much better he understood her and agreed to work on the issues she had raised—all this from a man who normally stonewalled her verbally and emotionally. So James was her guide's name, she decided, and he more than proved himself to be a healing force, given the success of the suggestion he had offered.

Sometimes you won't get one name because you aren't working with one guide. As I mentioned earlier, I connect with three guides who speak as a trio and call themselves the Three Bishops. I'm also in contact with the Pleiadean Sisters, two beautiful angels who can sometimes be three or more, and they, too, speak to me in unison. My dear friend Julia Cameron, when working on a movie years ago, wrote to her guides often, and they always answered in the plural without revealing their names. Another friend calls her guides the Light Ones.

Sometimes guides will give you a name through automatic writing. When connecting in this way, ask your guide or guides, "How shall I address you?" and see what flows from your pen. The same goes for visualizing your guide in your sacred meeting place. When you see or sense a guide there, ask, "How shall I address you?" and listen for the answer.

You can also give your guide a name. This doesn't change or modify the connection. The name you choose endears the guide to you, just as pet names or nicknames do. To quote Shakespeare in a scene from *Romeo and Juliet,* and as I stated earlier: "What's in a name? That which we call a rose / By any other word would smell as sweet."

### Did You Know That . . .

If a guide is not a friend or family member who has crossed over, the best way to find out their name is to ask telepathically.

## YOUR TURN

To connect with your guide's name, close your eyes and take a deep breath. Then ask your guide to come forward. Once you sense your guide, ask, "How shall I address you?" Accept the first name that comes to mind. If no name comes, don't worry. Instead, name the guide yourself. Don't overthink. Have fun with this. Your guide will love the name you choose.

If you sense that you're connecting to a group of guides, ask their group name. Trust whatever comes through.

Once you've established a name or names, request your guides by name every time you want to connect; you'll get a response. Assigning names makes your connections with your guides more personal and keeps the channels to high energy open even more. Choosing a particular name doesn't matter as much as sticking to it. Names are merely calling cards of intention. By being consistent, you forge strong bonds and expand your ability to receive your guides' assistance. In time these guides will feel like old and dear friends.

---

*By being consistent, you forge strong bonds*
*and expand your ability to receive your guides' assistance.*

---

Now that you've learned the guides names, let's move on to understand the role they play in your life.

# CHAPTER 26

# Your Guides
# Are Not Servants

It's essential to understand the role your guides play in your life if you want to have a positive experience with them. They love to assist and are never, ever bothered when you ask for their help. But they cannot—nor do they want to—do it all. I learned this for myself when my best girlfriend Lu Ann and I packed up my car in Chicago and set off for Denver in the middle of January when, after a year and a half on my own, I decided to move back home.

As I drove down the driveway, Lu Ann asked me if I had a map. "No," I arrogantly answered, "I don't need one. My guides will lead the way."

An hour later, stopping for gas, I realized that we were in Milwaukee, having gone 90 miles in the wrong direction. As the gas attendant laughed at me when I asked if we were on the right highway to get from Chicago to Denver, I humbly bought a map.

No matter who your guides are or what their level of expertise, when opening yourself to their influence, it's essential to understand that they're available to assist you, not to take over your life and run it. Their job is to lovingly provide clues and direction that will ease your cares and lead you to greater personal growth on your earthly journey. As tempting as it may be to desire a higher power to take over and save you from all potential mistakes, it would most likely become insufferable. After all, we're here to learn, and the only way to do so is by trial and error. Your guides don't want to do your work; they just want to help you learn your lessons as quickly and efficiently as possible while enjoying yourself.

In other words, don't get lazy (as I did that day) and think you can turn your life on autopilot, not do your homework, and expect your guides to take over. High-level ones respect your free will and won't ever take over. All they do is support and assist you. Like the road map, they'll show you the best way to reach your goals, but they won't drive the car.

I must warn you, however, that there are low-level earthbound and ego-bound entities who will gladly run your life if you allow them to. I had a client named Denise who sought the help of a guide because she'd acquired a lot of debt and wanted a quick fix. Rather than asking for help in learning how to better manage her money, she asked her guide to tell her how to win big on the local riverboat casino, a plan another indebted friend had suggested.

Sure enough, a low-level entity piped right up and encouraged her to do just that. Convinced that she was being guided to easily win a fortune, she diligently went to the casino week after week on the urging of this reckless entity (and her wishful thinking), even though each time she did, she lost *even more* money. Not only did she not get out of debt as she'd hoped the guide would do for her, but she plunged more deeply into debt than ever. In six short weeks, she lost her house and had acquired more than $75,000 in credit card debt over and above the $50,000 of debt she'd had to begin with.

Telling her shocked and shattered husband that her guide was to blame did her no good. It didn't relieve her predicament or save her assets—not to mention, it made her look like a nut. Rather than being honest and admit that she had a problem, she blindly turned her power over to this entity, who manipulated her into further trouble. She lost everything.

This is not to suggest she was the hopeless victim of an opportunistic and exploitative guide. Denise wanted a quick fix to bypass any responsibility she held for her financial chaos. She asked for the trouble she got into.

The best way to work directly with your guides is to ask for their assistance, but realize that at best they will make suggestions, through either gentle nudging, inspiration, or sudden insight. Ultimately, it's up to *you* to decide whether or not to listen and act upon their advice. No matter what is offered, use your good judgment and common sense, and remember: until you choose to act or not act, nothing will change. Guides can't do things for you, change things for you, or make magic happen. They can only make you aware of the natural magic and benevolence of the Universe and urge you to align with it.

## Here are four basic questions to help you decide whether the guidance you receive is worthwhile:

- Is this guidance grounded and nonthreatening?
- Does it feel gentle and loving?
- Does it consider everyone involved?
- Does it help me without harming anyone else?

If you can answer yes to all four of these questions, then the guidance you're receiving is worth considering. If you cannot, then the guidance is probably coming from a low-level source and not worth taking into consideration.

In any case, don't let any guidance distress you. If it's negative in the sense that it conveys information that you'd rather not hear, doesn't jive with your perspective, or disappoints you, listen anyway. Guides are not in the business of flattering you or agreeing with you. They *are* in the business of guiding you, which at times may be tough to take. If the guidance you get is negative in the sense that it suggests unloving things about you or others, makes you feel threatened or attacked, diminishes your spirit in any way, or encourages you to go against your better judgment, rather than let it frighten you, shrug it off and give it no importance whatsoever. Either you've unwittingly allowed an earthbound entity to slip into your awareness and play games with you, or, more than likely, your own low self-esteem has taken on a louder-than-usual voice and is interfering with your spirit.

I spoke to a large crowd in Chicago, and while signing books afterward, I met a very distressed young woman who said that her guide told her she and her best friend would soon die in a car accident, and she wanted to know what I thought about that. I promptly told her I thought very little of such nonsense and that she should not waste another minute fretting about it. But I also told her that it didn't mean that she shouldn't be careful when driving. She was still obliged to use common sense whenever she got in a car. "Don't drink and drive. Don't speed. Obey the traffic rules and pray for protection whenever you get in a car," I advised. "And relax. You just had a low-level entity scaring you for fun."

She seemed visibly relieved, and I was relieved for her. There was no point in her being tormented by something as toxic as being told of her imminent death. No good guide would ever do that. Death is a sacred communication between you and God, and guides do not interfere with that. Nor do high-level guides torment you or anyone with such frightening information. If she were really in danger, or even asking for trouble, her guide would warn her to drive more safely, not predict her death.

All high-vibration guides recognize you as a beautiful, Divine spirit, beloved and precious, attending a tough and challenging classroom on Earth. They understand your challenges, have compassion for your struggles, and love and respect you very much. High-level guides feel privileged to assist you and do so in a positive, respectful, and compassionate way.

> *All high-vibration guides recognize you as a beautiful, Divine spirit, beloved and precious, attending a tough and challenging classroom on Earth.*

When speaking to your guides, don't ask them what you "should" do. Instead, ask them to guide you to your soul's highest good and help you make better-informed choices. By asking what you "should" do, you are, in essence, turning your power over to them, which they don't want you to do and will not accept. If you ask them to run your life in that manner, they will become detached and remove themselves from your frequency, and you'll have to start connecting with them all over again.

It's also important to recognize the difference between guidance and wishful thinking. Real guidance is subtle, considers everyone's best interest, and will always lead you to the high road of personal responsibility, spiritual growth, and integrity. If you receive "guidance" that bypasses any of that, be suspicious. It's probably not so much guidance as your own ego talking, trying to trick you into being enslaved to its drives.

I had a client who asked her guide if she should get a divorce soon after meeting a handsome man who showed her some attention at a wedding. Unhappily married to an alcoholic, but also codependent and a shopaholic herself, she wanted an easy way out of her situation. Her guide was quiet, but her unhappy brain immediately said, "Yes, leave your husband because this new guy loves you." Convincing herself that she had met "Mr. Right" and had Divine permission to leave "Mr. Wrong," she filed the divorce papers, ready to go after the new guy.

Shocked, her husband begged her not to proceed and even suggested marriage counseling, but she'd already set her sights on the wedding guest and wasn't interested. She was sure this was the right thing to do because her "guide" had said so. The divorce went through quickly, and she pursued the new man, who promptly informed her that he had no genuine interest in her whatsoever and told her to "hit the road." She was devastated and confused. "My guide told me to get a divorce!" she cried in my office. "I trusted him. How could he mislead me so?"

"No guide would or could make that call," I assured her. "Are you sure it was your 'guide' and not your personal agenda?"

"I think it was my guide," she answered meekly. "It felt like my guide when it told me to leave my husband." But when I asked her the four basic questions, she couldn't reply yes to them.

"Then I believe it wasn't your guide," I mused, "because it wouldn't make that decision for you or be so insensitive to your husband. Maybe it wasn't a guide at all. Maybe it was you wanting an easy out."

"Maybe," she answered, thinking over the mess she had made of her life by acting so quickly without thinking things through. "Maybe."

A clue to knowing when you're getting trustworthy guidance or getting low-level input from your ego or low-vibration entities is that true guidance, even if it's not exactly what you were hoping to hear, always leaves you feeling satisfied and peaceful. It "pings" or energetically resonates deep within your body, settles in, and feels right, no matter what the message. If it's not trustworthy guidance, it won't settle into your body. Instead, you'll find it rattling around your brain, like a loose ball bearing out of place. So listen to your body when it comes to guidance. Feel it rather than think about it, and soon you'll discern the difference.

Don't let the fear of low-vibration entities or the power of your ego prevent you from freely asking for assistance every time you're stuck. Your guides' purpose and intention are to help strengthen your direct connection to your highest good, and they're happy to help. The more you work with guides, the more your inner compass and intuition strengthens. This is one more clear indication that your guides are successfully working with you.

### Did You Know That . . .

- High-level guides will *help* but not run your life.

- They will inspire you but not make your decisions for you.

- They make subtle suggestions that harm no one.

- They are never pushy.

- They help strengthen your intuition.

- They leave you feeling peaceful and supported.

## YOUR TURN

To prevent any confusion when communicating with your guides and to distinguish between your guides and your ego, simply avoid the question "Should I?" altogether. Instead, ask, "Show me my best options." Then be patient and listen. By formulating questions in this way, the channel with your guides will keep strengthening and opening, and your ego and other undesirable energies will be silenced. Every time you ask, "Should I?" you're inviting an outside force to take over. High-level guides refuse to do that; it's disrespectful. But your ego will jump in and will run the show if you let it.

It takes practice and attention to communicate correctly and with the right intention with your guides. Here's a little default trick that will keep you on the right path: Every morning, say to your guides, "If I slip and say, 'Should I?' just know I really mean 'Show me my best options.'" That lets your guides know that you're not surrendering responsibility. You're just learning to be aware and may make mistakes. A week or two of this will most likely be enough to retrain you to ask for help correctly.

Now that you've learned the role guides play in your life, let's move on to connecting with them through oracles.

# CHAPTER 27

# Speaking to Your Guides Through Oracles

When I was 12 years old, I connected with my guides through an ordinary deck of playing cards. Although to most people they look like a simple tool to play games with, playing cards are actually descended from a numerological oracle handed down from the ancient civilization of Atlantis. Each card has a special meaning, which I learned from my mother while doing practice readings at our dining room table.

At first, when working with the cards, it was all I could do to remember their meanings, but after a while, something shifted, and I moved beyond their basic meanings and felt that they were talking to me. When I began working with my psychic master teacher Charlie Goodman several years later, he told me that my guides were talking to me through the cards. That made sense, because I was receiving far more than the basic meanings I'd learned.

I remember doing a reading for my best girlfriend (and a mild skeptic at the time) Vicky. While staring at several cards, I distinctly felt that she was about to get a new car. Two days later, her dad surprised her with a 1969 Plymouth Road Runner. Although I spoiled the surprise, I was thrilled that I hadn't gotten Vicky's hopes up for nothing. She was, too, as we hot-rodded around Denver all that summer.

The more I did readings with my cards, the more I felt a guide working with me as I did. I eventually came to know him as Joseph. The minute I'd pick up the deck and begin to shuffle, I would feel him beside me.

Playing cards are not the only way in which you can communicate with your guides. There are many oracles you can use. Whether they're tarot cards, pendulums, rune stones, the I Ching, or any of the other more modern versions of these ancient divination tools, all oracles create a direct link from your conscious mind to your Higher Self, your spirit, and all Divine forces in the Universe.

Oracles have been around for as long as humans have. Legend has it that the prehistoric cave drawings in central France were created by the ancient people of Lemuria as oracles to communicate with the heavens.

While you don't need to use oracles to communicate with your guides, they can make communicating with them a lot easier, in much the same way that using training wheels makes learning to ride a bike easier. Just as it's entirely possible to learn to ride without them, it's also possible to learn to communicate with your guides without oracles. But working with them does make the process, at least in the beginning, much more accessible.

There are many different types of oracles to choose from, and it's a matter of personal preference which one you're attracted to. I think all oracles are wonderful because they provide extra avenues for your guides to communicate with you.

Through oracles, the guides can point you in a particular direction, invite you to see things you've overlooked, warn you of personal digressions and external threats, and remind you of what's important, all of which makes your spiritual journey much easier to travel.

Oracles work because they give your guides a medium to use that you can understand, and when used properly, they work efficiently to connect you directly with your spirit guides and Higher Self.

Oracles are terrific tools to help you voice your guidance rather than merely have it rumble around in the back of your mind, muted and ignored. When working with oracles, the more you ponder their meanings out loud, the more guidance you tap in to from the higher realms.

My mother had a very dear psychic friend named Mary, who used playing cards as her oracle. Her deck was so tattered from use over the years that I was sure the cards were going to fall apart in her hands every time she picked them up. When she did a reading, she shuffled until she felt her guides' presence, and only then would she begin. Mary, a traditional Mexican Catholic, told me that her guides were St. Francis and St. Alphonsus. She read as soon as her "saints came marching in" by laying out the cards one at a time. She was very accurate; the cards for her revealed far more than their basic meanings.

Mary was the first person other than my mother to give me a reading using cards. She told me that her guides said I would be world-famous one day. I was 13 years old at the time, so it was quite an incredible thing to hear. Staring at the same cards she was looking at, I asked which card said that. She shook her head and said it wasn't the cards themselves, but St. Francis speaking to her through the cards. I don't know if I can be called famous, but my books *have* become well known throughout the world, as St. Francis predicted. To this day, every time one of my books gets published in a foreign country, I thank St. Francis and think of Mary.

It's important when working with an oracle deck, or any oracle for that matter, not to repeat a question just because you didn't like the first answer. If you try to manipulate the oracle rather than allow it to reveal its wisdom freely, the guides retreat, and the oracle loses its energy. It will simply not work for you.

> *When working with oracles, the more you ponder*
> *their meanings out loud, the more guidance*
> *you tap in to from the higher realms.*

To be successful with oracles, you need to be sincere, use common sense, be willing to learn, be respectful, and be open-minded about the guidance you receive. My teacher Charlie said, "When you're spiritually mature, oracles work wonders and guide you brightly through the night. When you're spiritually immature, they're possessed by low-level energies that mock you and make fun of you."

Many psychic and intuitive people prefer oracles as a means of connecting with their guides. I knew one woman, the late Hanna Kroeger, who lived in Boulder, Colorado, and was world-famous for her ability to accurately diagnose and treat physical ailments with the use of her oracle, a pendulum on a chain. Holding the pendulum steady over a person, she could immediately tell what the illness was, both on a physical and emotional level, and recommend the appropriate treatment.

My dear friend, Lu (the same Lu Ann, who went to Denver with me) often uses cards to connect with her guides. But even more useful and beloved by her is the I Ching, an ancient Chinese divination oracle. She consults it every morning to guide her during the day and uses it for readings. She keeps a journal of all her I Ching readings, and they've become a regular part of her morning conversation with her guides.

For reasons I don't fully understand, different oracles tend to attract different types of guides. The I Ching, rune stones, tarot, and divination cards tend to attract high-level guides who provide a great deal of direction and coaching.

The pendulum, however, can be hit or miss when it comes to the type of guide it attracts. Sometimes high-level guides come in, but occasionally low-level ones show up. I believe that's because a pendulum can easily be manipulated by the user's frame of mind and is, therefore, subject to confusion. That's not to say that a pendulum cannot be a great oracle to help you connect with your guides. Just know that it can be fickle, and it takes serious focus and concentration to attract the kind of guidance you desire when using it.

YOUR TURN

Whichever oracle you choose, just remember—these are tools to strengthen channels from your heart to your Higher Self and guides. They're neutral, just like a phone. You dial in the inquiry; the Universe returns your call.

## The rules are simple:

- Get familiar and comfortable with your oracle
- When applicable, protect it in a silk bag or purse
- Don't let anyone else use it
- Be sincere
- Listen, learn, and discriminate
- Don't ask the same question twice
- Turn the final analysis over to your Higher Self
- Enjoy yourself

If you follow these basic rules, all oracles can be a powerful means to dialogue with your guides. Oracles have worked for me, and I'm still learning from them. With the proper approach and intention, oracles will work for you, too. If you want to know more about them, there are many books available, including my first book, *The Psychic Pathway*, which contains information on them. As I said, it's not necessary to use oracles, but they're fun— especially divination decks, my personal favorite, which I will devote a little more discussion to in the next chapter.

# CHAPTER 28

# Oracle Divination Decks

Oracle divination decks such as the tarot are an excellent means of communicating with your guides. A divination deck usually consists of anywhere from 44 to 78 cards, depending on the deck, each one having a specific meaning that conveys a particular message to the questioner. Some divination decks, such as the classic tarot deck, are very sophisticated and complex and focus on growing one's soul, while others are much more basic, such as the old school *Gypsy Witch Fortune Telling Playing Cards* deck, and focus on simple and mundane matters such as, "Is my neighbor a friend?"

To use an oracle deck, all you have to do is shuffle while focusing on a specific question, issue, or even a particular person, and then pull cards at random and lay them out in predetermined patterns designed to address those questions, concerns, or people.

There are literally hundreds of different oracle decks to choose from, including a regular deck of ordinary playing cards. Most decks are centered around the four elements: air, water, fire, and earth, and their corresponding physical, mental, emotional, and spiritual aspects.

Oracle decks have been around for a long time and have a rich history, dating back to the Middle Ages. Some oracles have actually been in existence even longer and are rumored to come from Atlantis. Metaphysicians from times past preserved the spiritual teachings of the masters by creating a set of universally understood symbols and putting them in decks of cards that have endured in various forms to the present time.

The most traditional oracle deck is called a tarot deck and is usually divided into two groups, or arcana: 22 major and 56 minor cards, each representing a communication from your Higher Self and your guides. The major cards represent spiritual laws we all must learn; the minor cards represent the infinite ways in which we'll be asked to learn these laws.

The tarot contains a wealth of guidance and information, but it takes hard work to learn to use it. Each card has specific symbolism and meaning. I've been studying tarot for more than 30 years and feel as though I'm only beginning to fully grasp the most profound meanings of the cards. However, you don't have to master and memorize the meanings to use the deck. Directions are available in myriad published books. Because the Universal Forces of Light want us to tap into our spiritual guidance as efficiently as possible, many intuitives and artists (including me) have been instructed to create modern and accessible versions of the ancient tarot system. Therefore, there are now many oracle decks available that are quite straightforward, including my *Ask Your Guides* deck, which is based on the minor arcana of a traditional tarot deck and is very easy to follow.

No matter what deck you choose to work with, you connect to your guides by asking questions and taking cards from the deck for answers. There are many ways in which an oracle deck can speak to you. The first is a one-card response to a question. You simply pose a question or focus on an issue and pull a single card for insight. For a more in-depth understanding of a problem, you can pick several cards, laying them out in specified patterns.

I've had tremendous success with oracle decks and find that they serve as fantastic conduits. They're also especially useful for transmitting guidance on emotional issues in which you cannot be neutral or unbiased, such as whether or not to continue dating someone you've just met and like but don't necessarily trust, or whether or not to buy a house you love but cannot necessarily afford. They allow you to bypass the subjective part of your brain that wants to hear exactly what you want to hear and give you a more objective perspective. Having said this, I do think it unwise to consult an oracle or try to engage your guides when you're emotionally charged. It's far too easy to misinterpret their signals or, in the case of an oracle, ignore what you receive if you're in a worked-up state of mind. Only when you're open to higher influence will the cards work well.

Again, it's a matter of what you intend. Are you looking for answers, or do you just want to hear what you want to hear? If you're seeking real guidance, the cards will work. If you're just looking for quick fixes or sympathy, they won't.

My friend Kathy became so enamored with using tarot cards that she consulted them daily. Because her biggest issue was her obesity, she consulted the cards for guidance on how to lose weight as quickly as possible more than for any other reason. One day we sat together and laid out the tarot cards. When she asked about her weight, the first card she pulled was the Hanged Man, which suggested the need for her to reverse how she was looking at something. She rolled her eyes when she got the card. "Arggh! I always get this card. I wish I could reverse my weight, but it doesn't work that way. I wish I got something more helpful."

I was surprised because I saw this as a perfectly clear message that she should look inside for the source of her distress instead of focusing on her appearance. I suggested she consider doing that, but she wasn't open. She simply didn't want to hear that message, and no oracle (or friend) would get through.

The beauty of tarot is that by using images instead of words, it speaks directly to our subconscious mind and links directly to our higher consciousness. Tarot cards open a dialogue with the Universe and give you access to greater creativity. The great psychologist Carl Jung once said that if he were locked in prison and allowed only one thing, he'd choose the tarot, for in it lies the wisdom of the Universe.

*The beauty of tarot is that by using images instead of words, it speaks directly to our subconscious mind and links directly to our higher consciousness.*

If you'd like to explore using oracle decks, start by choosing one that appeals to your spirit. You can select one or several, as dialogue with the spirit is an art and not a perfect science. Because I love the cards so much, I have a whole collection and use them all at different times.

Certain decks seem to direct the conversation toward one specific subject; others deal with other subjects. For example, a classic tarot deck such as the Rider-Waite deck may address spiritual issues in depth but be confusing when you ask for direction or guidance on whether or not to take a trip. An angel deck may offer you tremendous soul direction when dealing with difficult emotional issues but leave you less satisfied when asking about a job.

I've created several divination decks myself because of this very distinction. My *Trust Your Vibes* deck is designed to help you make decisions and develop and strengthen your intuitive muscles, while my *Ask Your Guides* oracle deck is designed to enhance and simplify dialogue with your guides. I also have other divination decks, like *The Divine Energy Oracle* and *The Answer Is Simple Oracle*, to help you with your soul purpose and soul lessons, and am planning to create more.

A client named Betsy called me with great excitement to tell me that she used my *Trust Your Vibes* deck to help her write a children's book. Every time she got stuck or became insecure, she pulled a card from the deck, and before she knew it, she found herself encouraged enough to finish it. Then she began to use my *Ask Your Guides* deck to help her get the book published. Before she contacted a potential publisher or agent, she pulled a card on whether or not that person or publisher would be the one to give her book the chance it deserved. To her utter surprise and delight, just by consulting the deck, she landed an agent on her third submission and sold the book within two months of completion. She assured me that without the cards guiding her, she would have most definitely lost courage and dropped the project before it was done. With their help, she was celebrating instead.

I have another client named Marcus who speaks directly to his guides every morning by shuffling and then pulling a single card from his classic tarot deck as he asks his guides to give him the psychic "weather report" for the day. One day he pulled the Tower card, a major arcana card designating upset and destruction. Later that day, he was told the company was being taken over and his job would be eliminated by the end of the month. Ordinarily, this would have sent him spiraling into terrible anxiety, but the early-morning warning prepared him just enough to handle it.

A subsequent pull of the cards yielded the Star, a card indicating that new surprises would emerge from the Universe. Marcus was later contacted by his brother-in-law, who asked him if he was interested in going into business with him running a fast-food Mexican restaurant in Iowa. As the Star card indicated, this came out of nowhere, and yet couldn't have come at a better time. The last I heard, he was going for it, and still consulting with his guides day by day via the cards.

The key to using oracle decks for guidance is to experiment with several decks and see which ones speak to you. Once you choose a deck, work with it for a while. Get familiar with it. Learn how to use it. Consider using a new deck like using a new computer, which allows you to communicate instantly with others around the world. With an oracle deck, you can communicate across the Universe.

People have asked me if they must memorize the meanings of an oracle deck before they can consult it. Many divination experts would say yes, but I say no. I do think you should try to interpret your oracle directly before consulting your guidebook. What does your spirit see when looking at the card? What does your inner voice say? You can work with the guidebook but trust your direct insights as well. And listen for your guides. You can even ask them how to interpret a card if you have no idea or can't fully understand its meaning.

Reading a divination deck is an organic process, and you can experiment with various methods until you find one that suits you. Never use your oracle deck insincerely. Don't laugh at an oracle or make fun of it in any way. If you do, you'll attract low-level entities that, as I've mentioned before, are inclined to give you jumbled, disturbing messages that will only confuse and upset you. Such riffraff is generally harmless, but it's useless psychic interference and not to be invited in by careless consultations. I'm not saying that you can't enjoy using divination decks. Indeed, you should, as they can be a great source of comfort and direction. Just be sincere, that's all.

You can consult a divination deck every day, if you like, but don't repeat the same question in each session. Only if circumstances change can you ask the oracle again on the same subject. For example, I consulted my cards on whether or not to enroll my daughter in a particular school when she was young. However, after asking the question, I was guided to homeschool her instead. Even though the cards said the school in question would be okay for my daughter, this new homeschooling option warranted another look. The new consultation championed the idea of homeschooling and was much more enthusiastic than the first. Based on that feedback, she was homeschooled, and for the first time in her life, she said that she loved learning.

I use my divination decks all the time because they're efficient and fun. But just because they're fun doesn't make their wisdom any less profound or my intention any less sincere. It's exciting and enjoyable to get instant feedback and saves wear and tear on your spirit. But how practical your divination turns out to be depends on you and not the deck. The more receptive you are, the more you can expect it to work for you as a means of communication between you and your guides.

### Did You Know That . . .

All divination decks are relevant, and it's strictly a matter of preference which one speaks to you.

## YOUR TURN

Shuffle your cards thoroughly before using them. This infuses your deck with your personal vibration and attracts your guides. Get a feel for your cards and see if you can sense their presence as you shuffle. Don't allow anyone else to use them. Keep them in a safe place, preferably wrapped in silk or satin, to protect and preserve a clear vibration. Treat the deck respectfully and as a friend. It's a tool that you will come to love if you work with it properly.

When you're ready to consult the deck, focus on your questions and concerns, one at a time, as you shuffle. With a single question in mind, select cards from the deck and then follow the guidebook for how to interpret them. As with all guidance, be sure not to phrase your questions "Should I?" Instead, say, "Show me my options, and all I need to know on this subject." Then engage the oracle for insight and direction.

Use your oracle deck as a springboard to directly connect with your guides and be open to this guidance even if it doesn't make perfect sense the minute it comes through. Give the oracle a chance to play out. Oracles make you aware of what your conscious mind doesn't *yet* know but should.

Now that you've learned to connect with guides through oracles, let's move on and meet your best guide of all, Your Higher Self.

PART VI

# LIVING A
# SPIRIT-GUIDED
# LIFE

## CHAPTER 29

# Your Higher Self:
# The Greatest Guide of All

Of all the guides you have, the most important is your own Higher Self, the voice and frequency of your Divine, fully realized, eternal self, your direct link to your Creator, God. It's the most powerful, concrete, loving, immediate connection you have to all that you desire, all that you are here to learn and to contribute.

The primary task of your angels and other guides is to help strengthen your conscious connection to your Higher Self so that it, rather than your limited, fear-based ego, runs your life. The other guides feel successful when your Higher Self sees through your eyes, interacts with others, makes your decisions, and evaluates your progress. The voice of your Higher Self, as opposed to your other guides, is the most authentic *you* guiding you. When you're connected to your Higher Self, there are no other voices in your head. You're focused solely on how to be a more creative, joyful being. Your ego concerns fall by the wayside while your heart expands.

The way to view your other guides is to consider them as messengers and coaches who assist you in life's matters while leading you to your true self. Your Higher Self, on the other hand, is not a messenger, but the highest expression of you. Your guides are the middlemen; your Higher Self is the direct source of who you really are. Your other guides' job is to connect you to your Higher Self; your Higher Self's job is to connect you to God.

When working with your other guides, you must not turn yourself over and expect them to run your life. When connecting with your Higher Self, it's not only right to turn your power over, but desirable to do so, as it's not an outside source, but the real you.

A client asked me why we need all these other guides if his Higher Self is so powerful. The answer is that you don't. Their only role is assistance, support, companionship, and delight. They're optional, but not essential, helpers in your life's journey.

On the other hand, you do need your Higher Self. Without it, you're lost and consumed with fear and anxiety, as those who are disconnected from or unfamiliar with their Higher Selves will surely attest. Your ego takes over and insecurity and doubt consume you.

The ego thrives on control, so it isolates you from others through stories, projections, and judgments about others and yourself. It will use everything in its power to keep you from feeling vulnerable or asking for guidance. The maneuvers of the ego are so exhausting and futile that they leave you with little energy left to experience and enjoy the wonders of life. You become weak, fatigued, sick, and old very quickly. Being run by your limited, fear-driven ego is guaranteed to ruin your life.

The only antidote for this terminal limitation is to listen to the voice and vibration of your Higher Self and let it lead.

How do you connect with your Higher Self? The first step is to quiet the voice of your ego. You know the voice I mean, the one that rants, blames, defends, judges, justifies, whines, doesn't forgive, never forgets, expects the worst, and trusts no one. Until that voice is muted, you will not hear your Higher Self.

The voice of your Higher Self is even more subtle than that of your other guides, at least in the beginning, when you first connect. Once you do, the signal gets stronger and stronger and becomes hard to ignore. It's like tasting sugar for the first time; it's so sweet, so compelling, and so desirable that you want more.

When you connect to your Higher Self, you immediately know when you're off course. It may signal to you through your body, knocking on your heart, tapping on the back of your brain, and rumbling around in your belly until you pay attention. In these ways, your Higher Self keeps you from feeling good and at peace in your skin when you take a detour. Like a pebble in your shoe or a sliver in your finger, your Higher Self conveys irritation and discomfort when you're less than your authentic, loving, eternal self.

> *When you connect to your Higher Self,*
> *you immediately know when you're off course.*

Unfortunately, so many people are willing to live with this discomfort that they ignore it or go to a great deal of trouble to cover it up by distracting themselves through external preoccupations, including addictions. But the day you decide you're unwilling to ignore these signals, the day you choose to do whatever it takes to get on track, that's the day your connection to your Higher Self kicks into full gear. And when you surrender your ego over to your Higher Self, that's the day your life begins to work.

Another way to connect is to train your subconscious mind to bypass your ego and surrender control to your Higher Self by saying aloud, *Subconscious mind, take me now and always to my Higher Self.* Whenever you feel anxious, upset, insecure, angry, hurt, confused, vengeful, or insignificant, repeat that phrase. To strengthen the connection even more, every morning before opening your eyes say, *Subconscious mind, let my Higher Self, and only my Higher Self, lead me this day.*

My friend Nelson used this strategy as he was ending an acrimonious marriage. Although both he and his wife agreed that it was time to go their separate ways, their egos continued to flare. The most challenging decision was to sell the house and split the money evenly. The day they put the house on the market, they were offered the full asking price in a cash deal with only two stipulations—that they accept the offer in two days and vacate within 30 days. Nelson was ecstatic, ready to move on with his life. He was sure his wife would be, too. Instead, she said no and didn't want to cooperate in any way.

He was furious. It was she who had originally wanted the divorce. Afraid to lose the deal, his ego wanted to go after her full force. He called me and asked me what to do.

I told him to turn the issue over to his Higher Self. "But I have no time," he said. "We have to give the buyer an answer by tomorrow. Turning it over to my Higher Self is a fine philosophy, but my Higher Self can't make my ex-wife sign the deal."

"Turn it over to your Higher Self," I repeated. He remained quiet for a full five minutes. "What does your Higher Self suggest?" I asked.

"It says do nothing," he said.

"That makes sense to me. You can't do anything. Your wife needs to come to terms with this on her own."

"I guess you're right," he conceded. "I could never make her do anything before, so why should it be any different now?"

So he did nothing, as he was advised by his Higher Self. Ten minutes before the deadline, his wife called. All she said was, "I accept the deal," and hung up. The next day the papers were signed, and the house was sold without another angry word. His Higher Self was right.

My client Mary Ellen was beside herself with conflict when she accidentally discovered that her boss and two other employees were stealing funds from the investment company where she worked. She loved her job, but she was the newest employee, the only woman, and not well liked by many of her colleagues. She was afraid to say anything and possibly be attacked for it, but if she kept her mouth shut, she could be implicated as part of the crime.

She called me, upset, worried, indignant, and fearful about what to do.

"What does your Higher Self suggest?"

"I don't know. My Higher Self isn't talking. If I confront my boss, I'll lose my job; I'll be a whistle-blower, and no one else will hire me."

Again, I said, "Quiet your fears and tell me what your Higher Self suggests."

After a long silence, she said, "My Higher Self says to resign in writing and tell my boss and his boss why, without naming names, and trust I will find another job."

A month passed, and the thefts continued to bother her. Finally, Mary Ellen couldn't stand it and she followed her Higher Self's advice and wrote the letter. She left without severance pay or a recommendation. She didn't dare ask for either.

Three months later, her old firm contacted her. They had fired her boss and the two employees and wanted to rehire her—with a raise. No one ever mentioned her resignation or her accusations.

Trusting your Higher Self and bypassing your ego will initially feel like jumping off a cliff blindfolded. Your ego wants you to feel that way so it can stay in control. What you discover, however, if you decide you're willing to jump off that cliff, is that as spirit, you can fly. You become free of your ego's fear and begin to live as your spirit wants you to.

### Did You Know That . . .

Following the guidance of your Higher Self gives you more freedom than you ever imagined was possible, allowing you to live an authentic, loving, fearless life.

## YOUR TURN

The best way to get in touch with your Higher Self is to meditate. It's not difficult to do. You simply stop focusing on the external world for a time and turn inward. Focus on your breathing, inhaling slowly to the count of four, exhaling slowly to the count of four. That's it.

Continue to breathe like this until you achieve a slow rhythm. While breathing, simply repeat the phrases "I am" on the inhalation and "at peace" on the exhalation. If your mind drifts, don't worry. Just continue rhythmically breathing. Simply refocus on your breath. You can add and the phrases "I am" as you inhale and "at peace" as you exhale. That's it. You're meditating.

It's simple to meditate, but it does take discipline and practice. The ego doesn't want to be controlled, so it will fight you. You must be prepared for that and resolve to stick to your meditation practice every day, preferably at the same time. The more you practice on a schedule, the easier it becomes. Your subconscious mind will adjust to the routine and automatically carry out your intention. If you're consistent, in a couple of weeks you'll actually look forward to meditating because it quiets your mind and energizes you. And when your mind is quiet, your Higher Self can emerge.

If you'd like you can listen to music, especially composers such as Bach, Telemann, and Vivaldi. Much of their music has the same number of beats per minute as deep meditation to help you relax your mind.

Adopt some meditative practices with the intention of doing them to relax. By this, I mean things that naturally quiet your mind and divert your attention from the endless chatter, such as going for a walk, folding the laundry, knitting, gardening, cooking, taking a warm bath, painting—anything that gives you a mental break.

By connecting you to your Higher Self, these two practices will help you to recognize and trust that you have a Higher Self that can successfully lead your life, and stop you from automatically giving your power away or blaming others for running (or ruining) your life.

Now that you've met your best guide of all, your Higher Self, let's move on and learn the difference between guidance and only hearing what you want to hear.

# CHAPTER 30

# Good News vs. Guidance

It's imperative when working with your guides to be open to what you receive and not edit their messages to fit your agenda. Needless to say, we seek spiritual guidance to help us attain positive outcomes and happy endings. But the way to get to those positive outcomes and happy endings may be very different from the way you want to get there. The whole point of seeking guidance is to open yourself to new ways of seeing things and to accept new information that can influence your understanding of a situation so that you can then make better decisions. What doesn't work is when you only want your guides or Higher Self to agree with you or support your established way of thinking, even if it's inaccurate.

One of the most challenging aspects of seeking guidance is receiving it even when it's difficult to hear and accept. I had a client who consulted her guides about her marriage by way of an oracle deck and received dire warnings of loss, deceit, and betrayal.

> *One of the most challenging aspects of seeking guidance is receiving it even when it's difficult to hear and accept.*

Upset at the information, she threw the deck away. Her husband, an investment banker and trader was, according to her, "the epitome of dignity" and would never let her down. Besides, there was no chance of an affair. He was home every night, and she knew he was faithful. You can imagine her shock when several months later he was arrested for insider trading and misappropriation of funds, and eventually sentenced to five years in prison.

Mortified and hurt beyond belief that he would bring such shame upon himself and his family, not to mention financial ruin, she said to me, "That stupid deck warned me. I should have never used it," as though the deck was to blame for her husband's fall from grace.

"That's an interesting perspective," I said. "It seems to me your guides tried to warn you through the deck. Why be angry at the warning? Your guides were advising you to take notice and possibly even discuss concerns such as betrayal and deceit with your husband. And you refused to listen. Did you ever suspect any of this in advance?"

"Well, yes," she admitted sheepishly. "He had been acting unusually stressed, flying off the handle a lot, and seeming to shut down—not his normal behavior. That's why I consulted the deck in the first place. I felt something was off and wanted to find out more."

"Well, given your reaction, I'd say you made the classic mistake of shooting the messenger when you threw away the cards and ignored your guides," I said.

"What would you have done?" she asked defensively.

"If it were me, given the situation, I'd confront my husband and say I had bad vibes and ask what he was up to."

"I thought about it, but I was afraid," she admitted. "To tell the truth, I didn't want to know. We were living beyond our means, but I was too comfortable to ask questions. I only wish I had."

"Given that he's now off to jail, I bet your husband wished you had, too."

When asking for guidance, the cardinal rules are: don't ask questions if you don't want to know the answers, and if the advice isn't to your liking, don't shoot the messenger.

Your guides can only give you the truth, at least high-level ones anyway. How you choose to use the information is up to you. If you receive negative information, be honest with yourself before you react. Are you doing anything or is anyone around you doing anything to invite such negativity? Are you in denial about anything or using poor judgment or ignoring something that could come back to haunt you? Are you keeping company with anyone who disturbs or distresses your spirit? If so, pay attention. That's all the guides are suggesting you do.

In all my years of doing readings, I can honestly say I've never truly surprised any client when sharing painful or bad news from their guides. Our awareness is far keener than we admit, and we tend to blot out unpleasant realities. Guides can't and won't, however. If you ask, the guides will answer, but it will be unbiased and not necessarily what you want to hear.

In another case, I had a client who said, "Whatever you do, don't give me any bad news. I can't take it." Agreeing, I didn't tell her that her job was coming to an end (which I saw). Instead, I encouraged her to follow her vibes and begin looking for her dream job as soon as possible. The time was right for succeeding. Ten days later she was laid off and called me, screaming that I should have warned her.

"Given the restrictions you placed on me," I said, "I tried. We spoke of your work at length, and you were advised by your guides to seek a new job. Now you know why." She angrily hung up. Three weeks later, I got a postcard saying she'd just landed a terrific new job and was sorry she'd overreacted.

It's very tempting to discard guidance that doesn't flatter you or complement your perspective, especially when using an oracle. I've had clients shuffle the deck and pull cards for guidance, only to throw what they get aside if it doesn't appeal to them.

One woman, Gina, pulled three cards from her tarot deck while asking a question about opening her own restaurant. The guides warned her against moving too fast and forging unstable partnerships with the wrong people, advice she didn't want to hear. Having made up her mind about the business and partners before asking the oracle, she was visibly annoyed when the guides suggested she change her plans.

She stormed ahead anyway, signing a lease on the first site she found and forming a partnership with a man she hardly knew.

The restaurant flopped after seven months, and she's now suing her partner for leaving her with the debt. She came back to see me, demoralized at her failure, not believing what had happened.

"You were warned," I reminded her. "You just didn't want to hear it."

"I know," she lamented. "I wasn't willing to listen. I just wanted you to tell me I was brilliant and would succeed."

My teacher Charlie always told me never to ask for guidance unless I was truly open to receiving answers. If you ask for guidance but then ignore it, your guides see you as insincere and step away.

---

**Did You Know That . . .**

Being unreceptive to input is perhaps the greatest obstacle to overcome if you want to communicate with your guides.

---

## YOUR TURN

The best way to ensure good rapport with your guides and establish ease and flow in communicating with them is to practice this four-step process:

- **Step #1:** Be open to all guidance, even if it isn't what you want to hear. This means to begin each day with a receptive heart and mind for receiving guidance.

- **Step #2:** Expect guidance. Like everything else you expect in life, the more you expect it, the more you attract it.

- **Step #3:** Trust the guidance you receive. Speak your guidance out loud every chance you get and pay attention to how it feels as you do. (It isn't quite the same if you write it down, but this is another way to create practice accepting guidance.) Even if you're given a warning or receive difficult news, if the guidance is sound, once you express it out loud, you'll feel a sense of relief. It's the healing power of truth.

- **Step #4:** Start acting on your guidance as soon as you receive it. It may feel as though I'm inviting you to jump off a cliff, but I'm not. It's far more frightening and potentially dangerous to ignore your guides and move in the wrong direction than to act on your guidance. This takes practice, so ease into it. Start by acting on your guidance in small ways until you become comfortable trusting it and start seeing positive results. In time you'll be in constant rapport with your guides and live with more ease and flow in your life. Trust me, it happens naturally.

Now that you've learned to be fully available to guidance, let's move on to learning the challenges of living a spirit-guided life.

# CHAPTER 31

# Following Guidance Can Be Challenging

The greatest challenge you'll face when working with your guides is to trust what you sense, especially when nothing in the world seems to confirm what you're receiving. Living an intuitive, six-sensory, guided life takes courage and confidence. The guides will point out the best possible way to fulfill your path and purpose and make day-to-day life easier, but it's still up to you to decide whether to follow their input.

> *Living an intuitive, six-sensory, guided*
> *life takes courage and confidence.*

I had a client named John who was an excellent medium and psychic working a day job in a bakery in New Jersey. He was happily married and a father of two, but extremely unhappy at work. His guides advised him to move to Columbus, Ohio, where his sister lived, and open a professional psychic practice. The thought both thrilled him and scared him to death at the same time.

*What a dream come true!* he thought. *What a fantastic way to serve others! But how will I pay for my insurance? How will I ever buy a house?*

The people around him thought he was crazy and said, "Don't do it," but his wife said, "Let's go for it." So, with no guarantees, he quit, telling his boss he was a psychic and that he had another path to follow. Not only did his boss accept his resignation gracefully, but he also became John's first client. A few short months into his new life, John was offered a chance to be on the radio. He was such a success that he was asked again and again. Soon after, people started contacting him for readings and his career blossomed. By the end of the year, he was fully engaged as a psychic medium. Listening to his guides was challenging because it seemed like such a risk, but when he decided to work with them and trust their advice, it proved to be the best decision he could have ever made.

Another client, Jocelyn, a widow, had excellent guides who spoke to her all the time. They advised her to take a cruise with her girlfriends during the Christmas holiday, even though it would stretch her budget to the limit. Her sons thought she was frivolous and severely criticized her for going, saying she was being very irresponsible. She worried that they were right and set out to cancel her reservation, but her guides screamed, "No!" At the last minute, she went ahead with her plans. To make sure her sons didn't rain on her parade, she even refused to let them take her to the airport.

On the cruise, she met a wonderful man who lived only three miles from her. He was a widower and a recently retired chiropractor, and the two of them hit it off immediately. Their relationship continued after the cruise. Two years later, they married. The best part is that her sons grew to love him. He was a blessing all the way around. She occasionally teases her sons about advising her to stay home. They deny that they ever said that.

### Did You Know That . . .

Regularly calling on guides for help is a way of life—one that is far more blessed, synchronistic, abundant, and joyful than the one you had before.

## YOUR TURN

It can be challenging, even scary, to follow your guides when everything and everyone around you tells you not to. All I can suggest is that you trust what you feel, listen to your heart, and don't ask others for their input. After all, spirit guidance is of the highest level, so there's no need to comparison shop. If you have doubts, outside opinions will only confuse you more. If you do trust your guidance, however, wonderful things will begin to unfold—perhaps not as quickly as you'd like, but they will unfold.

Now that you've learned to be open to all guidance, let's move on to finding "believing eyes."

# CHAPTER 32

# Finding Believing Eyes

When learning to trust your guides, it can be very helpful to engage a receptive friend or two with whom you can comfortably share your guidance. You're looking for support here, not for someone to judge or question the guidance you receive. They should be open-minded, "believing eyes" people—those who understand and encourage you to listen to your guidance, while at the same time know you well enough to identify whatever issues you have that may interfere with clear reception.

I was very fortunate when growing up to have a mother and many siblings with whom I could freely speak about my guides without fear of being censored or laughed at. When I was feeling stressed, insecure, or unclear concerning my guides' input or my ego's fears, my mom or one of my siblings would help clear up my confusion by simply listening as I talked it out.

I was also helped by my teacher Charlie, who didn't verify my guidance as much as he encouraged me to trust what I received, however subtle and vague, and to accept everything that came through my many developing intuitive channels.

I also had, and still have, girlfriends, such as my mentors Lu Ann and Joan, and my daughters, Sonia and Sabrina. We freely talk about our guides as comfortably as we talk about the weather. Being able to share my relationship with my guides is a major factor in strengthening that relationship and connecting to them every day.

Perhaps you already have people with whom you can openly talk about your experiences with your guides. If so, you know how important it is.

But if you're just entering the exciting and wonderful world of guides and don't have anyone to share it with, ask your spirit helpers to bring you someone to fit the bill. One of the quickest ways to identify who's right for you and who isn't is to get some oracle cards, such as my *Ask Your Guides* deck, openly display it, and let your family and friends know that this is your new interest. Those who can offer encouragement and support will do so right away. Those who scoff won't share your interest, so don't try to change their minds, because you won't. Rather, spend your energy seeking out people who don't need convincing.

Connecting with guides is a very subjective experience; rarely do opposing views meet in the middle. Use common sense and careful observation before discussing your experience with others. Don't sabotage the delicate, energetic connection you're forging with your guides by allowing someone to bombard you with negative perceptions.

### Did You Know That . . .

You can engage support by openly talking about your guides, sharing what you feel or receive from them.

## YOUR TURN

I believe that having people with whom you can share your involvement with your guides is so fundamental to your success that I've initiated chat groups through my online courses in which people all over the world can share their guide experiences. They've proven to be of tremendous value in helping people live a more comfortable, six-sensory life.

> *Openly seeking support may seem like a risk, but it will be far outweighed by the rewards you receive from like-minded believers.*

Because I firmly believe that having support and community is essential in comfortably having an angel- and spirit-guided life, I have created the Good Vibe Tribe membership to offer this and more, including all my online courses, weekly written and live lessons from me, and a lively and engaged group of kindred spirits who will soon become dear friends. You can join the Good Vibe Tribe membership on my website at any time at soniachoquette.com. I also launched a podcast with my daughters called *It's All Related* in the spring of 2020.

These are just a few ways to introduce you to "believing eyes" of your own and help you pull back the energetic veil between the third and fourth and higher dimensions. This will help make communication with your guides easy and natural. Openly seeking support may seem like a risk, but it will be far outweighed by the rewards you receive from like-minded believers.

## YOUR TURN

One of the highest ways to honor and appreciate your guides and all Divine helpers is to focus on living with a happy heart and a positive outlook, and leaving your fears in their care. In this way, not only do you accept your Divine blessings, but you also become a guide and blessing to others.

Below is a link to a 40-minute channeled meditation for living with the constant support and companionship of your angels and guides. Listen with headphones anytime you want to connect with your divine crew for a joyous connection.

Visit https://www.hayhouse.com/downloads and enter the Product ID **1381** and Download Code **resources**. You can also visit http://www.soniachoquette.net.

*May God bless you, and your angels protect you. May your runners connect you, your helpers assist you, your healers support you, your teachers enlighten you, your joy guides delight you, the nature spirits balance you, your animals guides recall your soul, and your Higher Self lead you to live a life of peace, grace, creativity, and contribution filled with love and laughter on your personal earthly journey.*

With all my love and support,
Sonia

# EPILOGUE

As I am completing this book I find myself, along with the entire world, in the middle of the coronavirus pandemic in the fall of 2020, an unprecedented global assault on our health that has required everyone to stop their normal lives and quarantine at home for many uncertain weeks and months ahead.

This deadly virus has overwhelmed hospitals with hundreds of thousands of sick and dying people, shuttered businesses, closed schools, virtually ceased all air travel, and stopped the flow of interaction between humans on all but the most essential level. Every nation in the world is simultaneously struggling to arrest the deadly spread of this virus and keep it from causing even more mass devastation than it has already wreaked. The challenge seems insurmountable.

People around the world are feeling scared, trapped, isolated, and alone, some stuck at home with abusers, millions suffering the loss of jobs, income, and deeply needed human connection. If there were ever a time to call on our divine support system for help, it is now.

Thankfully, the angels and guides are "all hands on deck" in answering our calls. More than ever, people are experiencing the reassuring presence of their angels and guides in the most remarkable ways. Many among these are people who belong to my online Good Vibe Tribe membership group for kindred spirits, dedicated to connecting with their intuition and guides, and meeting soul friends and family.

They have shared many photos of white feathers—a classic calling card of angels—suddenly appearing in the most unlikely of places. One on a kitchen counter, one in a shoe, and another on the seat of a chair. All of these are strong affirmations that angels are afoot. Others have shared that angels have actually appeared in person to help them.

One client I spoke with, Elsa, an 86-year-old woman who lives alone in a small town in Switzerland, told me she recently had an unexpected life-saving angel visitation. She recounted through tears that, out of the blue, a young man arrived at her door on a little motorbike and rang her bell. He left a bag of fresh fruits, vegetables, bread, eggs, and coffee, then got on his bike and left without saying a word or leaving a note. His gift relieved her of the need to go into town and get groceries, a necessary task that had been terrifying her for days, as the virus is particularly deadly for older people. She said, "I had been asking my angels for help, but never did I expect for a minute that they would answer in such a literal and generous way. I still cannot believe it!"

I also talked to a nurse who has been working overtime at a New York hospital, battling the virus, along with countless other health-care heroes around the world. She was obligated to stay at a local hotel in between shifts to not risk infecting her family should she herself contract COVID-19. She shared that she awoke one morning at dawn in her room and saw an elegantly dressed older man wearing an ornate mask approaching her bedside. As she nearly screamed from fright, the man stopped short and smiled. He then motioned to his lips as if to both shush and calm her. Realizing it was a spirit guide and not an evil ghost, she sat frozen while he pointed to the pink morning sky outside the window and indicated in a gesture that she would be okay. "He didn't say a word, but I knew he was there to reassure me, which he did," she recounted. "I had been terrified up until then that I would get sick or harm others. Somehow his presence told me that I, and my family, would get through this nightmare in one piece, and my fear left."

CNN television journalist Chris Cuomo contracted a severe case of COVID-19, and, though he was not hospitalized, he became severely ill and was quarantined. Sharing his journey of this illness on CNN one morning, he openly recounted that the night before, while experiencing an intense fever, his father—the late

New York governor Mario Cuomo—who died in 2015, appeared at his bedside and talked with him for a while. While justifying that it was probably a hallucination due to his fever, Chris nevertheless insisted his father was with him the night before. He struggled to make sense of this visitation, but I didn't. The spirit of his father did come to support him through the darkest hours of his illness. He may very well have helped Chris get through what might otherwise have been a terrible turn for the worse.

I sense and see angels everywhere, helping humans get through this global challenge. I also have been told by my teacher guides that this shutdown is a positive turning point for humanity that will ultimately help us reconnect with our hearts and spirits, as we are being cut off from the usual external distractions that keep us from focusing inward. As we do turn inward for help, we are being met with love, reassurance, and assistance by our divine crew at every turn.

I also know that light beings and healing guides are helping our scientists around the world as they frantically search for a vaccine to treat this awful disease. Breakthroughs are being made at lightning speed, and without a doubt, the help of these divine forces will bring quick success.

This global crisis is a spiritual hothouse incubator for awakening our higher consciousness and activating our intuitive centers, if for no other reason than out of necessity and survival. We are collectively waking up in response to this challenge. Our hearts are opening, our unconscious and open racial biases are being confronted and rejected, our connection to one another is becoming undeniably apparent, our need to show respect for the earth is returning, and our awareness of the spirit realm is being felt worldwide. It took unspeakable loss and suffering to bring us to this point, and while the pandemic and following social unrest has been tragic on so many levels, the consequent elevation of global consciousness is something for which I am grateful. We now recognize it is time to wake up, re-evaluate, and heal our disconnected relationships with ourselves, one another, and the living planet. I have confidence that we will overcome this challenge just as we have overcome other crises in the past. This outbreak will eventually end. I'm sure it will already be far more manageable by the time this book is released. But the collective growth and spiritual awakening that comes out of this will not end.

We humans are being profoundly and permanently changed for the better as we find our way forward. As we reconnect with ourselves, open our hearts, reawaken to the need for one another and for our spiritual connections and helpers, we will become a kinder, gentler human race. Not all of us, to be sure, but enough of us to change the future of this planet to a better one than the trajectory we were on before this massive intervention hit us.

Perhaps you, too, have experienced assistance from your guides in this unprecedented time. The more of us who fearlessly and freely recount our divinely guided encounters, the more we part the curtain between this realm and the subtle planes and normalize a connection with our guides for all. If you have an angel or spirit guide story you'd like to share, please consider joining my Good Vibe Tribe membership group. Or you can post it on my social media pages. We all need to share our stories to validate our connection to spirit and open the door for others to do the same.

As I bring this book to a close, I am surrounded by angels, guides, light beings, and our Holy Mother and Father God, eternally loving light of the Universe, just as you are. The human journey is challenging and not meant to be undertaken alone. We have help available at all times. Please join me in taking a breath, opening your heart, smiling, and allowing the infinite flow of unconditional love and support to come flooding in. The love and comfort of your spirit guides is always there for you, and the more you let it in, the softer, kinder, more loving and joyful your life will become. This is the way our health, relationships, and planet will heal.

Ask for divine help every day, for everything, and expect it to show up in the most beautiful and surprising ways. It will. I promise.

All my love and blessings from me and your divine crew,
Sonia

# ACKNOWLEDGMENTS

I'd like to thank my beautiful mother, Sonia Choquette, for parting the veil to the world of spirit and introducing me to the love and support of the heavens. And to my father's spirit for being a steady guide in my highly spirited world. To my daughters, Sonia and Sabrina, for your enduring love, patience, and willingness to understand and eventually join me in this life's work. To my beloved teachers Dr. Tully and Charlie Goodman, for sharing their wisdom and tools with me for establishing the highest level of spirit-guided communication.

To Reid Tracy, my constant publishing earth angel, and the entire staff at Hay House for your dedication and tireless support. To my editors Linda Kahn and Sally Mason-Swaab for helping me shape this book into a presentable manuscript, and to all my clients for lending me your stories. Above all, I'd like to thank God and all blessed bright beings of the Universe for your love, guidance, and hard work on my behalf as you perpetually guide me on my path. I am a grateful and humble servant.

# ABOUT THE AUTHOR

Sonia Choquette is a celebrated worldwide author, spiritual teacher, and intuitive guide who has devoted herself to teaching people to honor their spirit, trust their vibes, and live in the grace and glory of a spirit-guided life. A fourth-generation intuitive guide, beginning her public work with spirit at age 15, Sonia has spent over 45 years traveling the world on her mission to help others lead confident, authentic lives with intuition as their guiding light. She is the author of 27 internationally best-selling books and numerous audio programs on intuitive awakening, personal and creative growth, and spiritual transformation, most notably with the *New York Times* bestseller *The Answer Is Simple.*

Sonia's work has been published in over 40 countries, translated into 37 languages, making her one of the most widely read authors and experts in her field of work. Sonia's legacy is continued by her two daughters, Sonia and Sabrina, both of whom have their own careers in spiritual coaching and guidance and are published authors of the Hay House book *You Are Amazing: A Help-Yourself Guide for Trusting Your Vibes + Reclaiming Your Magic.*

Sonia is an avid traveler, passionate dancer, prolific storyteller, and a natural comedian. She prides herself on her endless pursuit of loving, learning, growing, and living full-out every day. Sonia loves everything about Paris and currently calls it her home.

Website: soniachoquette.net

## Hay House Titles of Related Interest

*YOU CAN HEAL YOUR LIFE, the movie,*
starring Louise Hay & Friends
(available as an online streaming video)
www.hayhouse.com/louise-movie

*THE SHIFT, the movie,*
starring Dr. Wayne W. Dyer
(available as an online streaming video)
www.hayhouse.com/the-shift-movie

\*\*\*

*ATTUNEMENT:*
*Align with Your Source, Become Your Creator Self,*
*and Manifest a Life You Love,*
by Marisa Moris

*EVERYTHING IS HERE TO HELP YOU:*
*A Loving Guide to Your Soul's Evolution,* by Matt Kahn

*LIGHT IS THE NEW BLACK:*
*A Guide to Answering Your Soul's Callings and Working Your Light,*
by Rebecca Campbell

*THE UNIVERSE HAS YOUR BACK:*
*Transform Fear to Faith,* by Gabrielle Bernstein

All of the above are available at your local bookstore,
or may be ordered by contacting Hay House (see next page).

\*\*\*

We hope you enjoyed this Hay House book. If you'd like to receive our online catalog featuring additional information on Hay House books and products, or if you'd like to find out more about the Hay Foundation, please contact:

Hay House, Inc., P.O. Box 5100, Carlsbad, CA 92018-5100
(760) 431-7695 or (800) 654-5126
(760) 431-6948 (fax) or (800) 650-5115 (fax)
www.hayhouse.com® • www.hayfoundation.org

———

*Published in Australia by:* Hay House Australia Pty. Ltd.,
18/36 Ralph St., Alexandria NSW 2015
*Phone:* 612-9669-4299 • *Fax:* 612-9669-4144
www.hayhouse.com.au

*Published in the United Kingdom by:* Hay House UK, Ltd.,
The Sixth Floor, Watson House, 54 Baker Street, London W1U 7BU
*Phone:* +44 (0)20 3927 7290 • *Fax:* +44 (0)20 3927 7291
www.hayhouse.co.uk

*Published in India by:* Hay House Publishers India,
Muskaan Complex, Plot No. 3, B-2, Vasant Kunj, New Delhi 110 070
*Phone:* 91-11-4176-1620 • *Fax:* 91-11-4176-1630
www.hayhouse.co.in

———

## Access New Knowledge.
## Anytime. Anywhere.

Learn and evolve at your own pace
with the world's leading experts.

www.hayhouseU.com